Pelican Books

The Democrati

Geoff Hodgson was educated at the University of Manchester and is now Principal Lecturer in Economics at Newcastle upon Tyne Polytechnic. From 1974 to 1980 he was a lecturer at Manchester Polytechnic, and subsequently he was a visiting professor at Bennington College in the United States. He has published extensively in British and American journals including the *Cambridge Journal of Economics*, *New Left Review*, *Science and Society*, the *Journal of Post Keynesian Economics* and *The Review of Radical Political Economics*. His other books include *Labour at the Crossroads* (1981) and *Capitalism, Value and Exploitation* (1982).

Geoff Hodgson

THE DEMOCRATIC ECONOMY

A New Look at Planning, Markets and Power

Penguin Books

Penguin Books Ltd, Harmondsworth, Middlesex, England
Penguin Books, 40 West 23rd Street, New York, New York 10010, U.S.A.
Penguin Books Australia Ltd, Ringwood, Victoria, Australia
Penguin Books Canada Ltd, 2801 John Street, Markham, Ontario, Canada L3R 1B4
Penguin Books (N.Z.) Ltd, 182–190 Wairau Road, Auckland 10, New Zealand

First published 1984

Made and printed in Great Britain by
Richard Clay (The Chaucer Press) Ltd,
Bungay, Suffolk
Filmset in 9/11 Monophoto Photina by
Northumberland Press Ltd, Gateshead

Contents

Preface

Two political and social movements stand above all others in recent times, in terms of the development of the theory and practice of the democratic economy. They are the Solidarity trade union in Poland in 1980–81, and the Popular Unity government in Chile in 1970–73. To the leaders and members of these movements I wish to dedicate this work. They offer a hope and a warning. The hope is that their attempts to construct a democratic economy may one day be completed. The warning is to beware the iron heel of militarism.

A book may go under the name of a single author, but it is always to some degree a collective enterprise. I would like to thank many colleagues in the academic profession, as well as friends in the Labour Party and elsewhere, for ideas and stimulating discussions over the years. For encouragement, criticism and advice in the immediate production of this work I am very grateful to a number of people who have read drafts of the typescript with enthusiasm, and provided detailed criticisms, when they all had little time to spare. They include Dick Bailey, Barrie Craven, Anthony Easthope, Raul Espejo, Peter Hain, Peter Hodgson, Mike Lloyd, Brian Roper, Brian Snowdon, Jim Tomlinson and Peter Wynarczyk. In most but not quite all cases I have accepted their advice. They cannot be blamed for any errors that may remain. In addition I am grateful to the editorial staff of Penguin Books for their suggestions, and improvements to the text.

Travel has indeed broadened the mind. I have found visits both to the United States and to the Soviet Union stimulating and crucial in developing my own ideas, and in challenging simplistic evaluations of these two very different types of socio-economic system.

An earlier version of Chapter 10 was presented at a conference in September 1981 under the auspices of the Pablo Iglesias Foundation in Madrid. I am grateful to the participants at that conference for their comments, including those from Fernando Claudin, Steven Lukes and Claus Offe.

Special thanks are due to Vinny, for her patience, warmth and support, and to our expected offspring, for timing its entry into the world well after the completion of the typescript.

Newcastle upon Tyne
January 1983

Part One

BASIC ISSUES

One

Introduction

The first, and most truly so called, variety of democracy is that which is based on the principle of equality.

Aristotle, *The Politics*

Well over two thousand years ago, Aristotle and the philosophers of classical Greece saw the connection between political democracy and the distribution of economic power. Recognition of this association survived into the seventeenth century. During the English Revolution, the Diggers and Levellers saw that an extension of democracy would not come about without a challenge to the existing distribution of property and economic power. Seeing the logic of such arguments, the astonished Sir Robert Filmer wrote in his *Patriarcha* (published in 1680) that democracy was 'nothing else than the power of the multitude'. For such a defender of the monarchy that was a sufficient reason for it to be abhorred.

The classical definition of democracy is almost forgotten today. To most people, it means little more than parliamentary or other forms of representative government. The questions of real power, economic as well as political, are largely ignored. As long as there is a chance for every sane adult to have a vote in a general election every few years, then the system is said to be democratic. It does not matter if people have little or no say in matters concerning them at home or at work, or if the distribution of wealth is determined by the luck of inheritance – it is still democracy. According to this narrow and unsatisfactory definition we can live in a democracy yet be subject to the rule of hierarchy and authority for most of our lives.

This does not mean that the value of representative democracy should be ignored. It is real and positive. It may help to preserve civil liberties, for in no country where a parliament has been abolished have such freedoms been maintained. For this and other reasons it is completely mistaken to assert that parliament is a 'façade' or a mere 'bourgeois' formality. Contrary to the propagandists of Soviet-style Communism, freedom and democracy are not purely 'economic' matters. The right of all to work, and to receive education, medical care and a basic income, are important and noble goals. But they, themselves, do not constitute full democracy and freedom. Just as it is unsatisfactory to detach democracy from the distribution of real economic power, it is equally unsatisfactory to remove all consideration of the character of political institutions. Democracy is both a political and an economic matter.

As Sir Robert Filmer understood, substantial democracy means the cession of real political and economic power to 'the multitude'. A democratic economy is one which is run along these lines. It is democratic in its *objectives*, in that these are decided by that multitude. It is democratic in its *regulation*, in that it is supervised not by a hallowed central committee or an anonymous market, but by means of structures that involve maximum popular participation. And it is democratic in its *principle*, in that it is not dominated by inherited wealth, impervious bureaucracy or the power of the mega-corporation.

Democracy is not a purely formal matter. It is not simply about 'being consulted' or about having referendums on every important issue. Many people are uneasy about an extension of democracy in modern society because they imagine it as simply giving everyone a vote on issues where, they fear, prejudice and backwardness are prevalent. Democracy must also involve a change in the structures and relations of economic and political power – an end which is inconceivable unless the majority becomes more educated and socially aware in the process.

We should then beware of simple and formalistic interpretations of democracy in the electoral sphere; but there are no panaceas elsewhere. Lenin, perhaps with tongue in cheek, defined socialism as 'soviets plus electrification'. The democratic economy is not adequately described as 'workers' councils plus public ownership of the means of production', as is the habit of many on the Left. Neither are we in the game of building 'People's Democracies' which are undemocratic and unpopular.

It is the purpose of this book to consider the necessary features of a genuinely democratic economy. It is not a question of conjuring blueprints out of moralistic axioms, in the manner of many utopian thinkers in the past. What we may regard as desirable is not irrelevant to this project: there is a place for a vision of utopia. But all viable utopias have to be grounded on an analysis of what is possible, as well as what is desirable. This book attempts to lay down guidelines for considering what sort of democratic economy is feasible in this century or the next.

The democratic economy must involve economic as well as political pluralism. It must include mechanisms of social planning, auditing, ownership and control as well as attempting to maximize the autonomy of the person and the community. It features popular participation in decision-making, as well as fostering human partnership and cooperation. It is, in short, democratic socialism.

But how rarely do we consider what sort of future is possible and desirable. We rest as comfortably as possible in our existing world. Even the practice of radical political parties and pressure groups, each aiming at some sort of social change, is marked by routine, inertia, and a failure to consider the future. Nowhere is this more obvious than within the socialist movement. Consider the number of meetings held by socialists in the last hundred years, and how rarely the nature of socialism has been discussed. Consider the libraries of socialist theory that have been written in the last few decades. How many books have concerned themselves with the nature of a future socialist society? Very few is an overstatement. There is little else than scattered references to socialism here and there.

Of course, there is a danger of utopian and moralistic dreaming. It is necessary to develop a theory of a future democratic socialist economy which is both analytic and based on historical experience. There is enough theoretical work to assist in this task, and much history to evaluate. A failure to consider the future is no longer excusable.

The New Right

Lack of consideration and discussion of a future alternative society is not merely an awkward gap in the theory and practice of the Left: it is a dangerous omission in current circumstances which, without rectification, will lead to a continuing decline in the popularity of socialist ideas. The breakdown in consensus politics in some Western democracies has led to the rise of a New Right which has no hesitation in attempting to shape society according to its own cherished image. The current battle of ideas is, in part, a battle between visions of the future: a clash of utopias.

The New Right have resurrected many of the ideas and approaches of nineteenth-century liberalism. (In consequence they are sometimes described in the present work as 'classic liberals', referring to the high point of liberalism in the last century rather than to classical antiquity.) They have a narrow view of democracy, and like many of their nineteenth-century predecessors they are concerned that the prerogatives of democracy can be extended too far. Above all, they share a resolute individualism and a commitment to the supreme virtues of private ownership, markets, and *laissez-faire*.

Until recently, these ideas were not taken seriously by either the Left or the Centre of the political spectrum. Economists and political thinkers such as Friedrich Hayek were dismissed as a joke. But with the breakdown of consensus politics the situation has changed. The election of governments in Britain and the United States under the strong influence of New Right ideas has put the joke on the Left.

We are faced with this choice: either the political and economic vision of the New Right is challenged seriously, or it is tacitly allowed to gain force and currency in the modern world. And to challenge seriously such a vision it is necessary to begin to create an alternative.

On the whole, the ideas of the New Right are animated by a predisposition towards market and private enterprise solutions to both political and economic problems. For this and other reasons they have been ignored by the Left. However, their arguments and theories are not devoid of substance. Hayek, for example, has made an important contribution to the theory of knowledge, even if his economic and political solutions are primitive and apparently lacking in compassion. In addition, whatever the merits or demerits of New Right theory, it has to be critically evaluated rather than disregarded. It is a question of priorities. There is always a temptation to devote critical attention to one's closest adversaries; to attempt to win over those who are direct witnesses to our dialogue. The sea of popular opinion is of less immediate concern. But the task of attempting to reach a wider audience should no longer be shirked. The philosophers of the New Right now walk the corridors of power. They are busy dismantling the welfare state and undermining the power and influence of the labour movement. With their strident defence of capitalism they could plunge us into a nuclear war which few would survive.

The task of considering and beginning to build an alternative future cannot be separated from a reasoned critique of New Right ideas. This book is one small contribution. The ideas under consideration are not merely academic – they are matters of urgency.

Theoretical Approaches

It is necessary to develop a theoretical approach that spans both economics and politics. *The Democratic Economy* is a study in 'political economy'. This combined approach is necessary because economics and politics are inseparable in the real world.

However, the idea of 'political economy' is no longer confined to the Left. It is widely recognized, for example, that the performance of modern capitalist economies depends a great deal on their political structures. Many people from Right, Left and Centre alike now argue that there is a relationship between the economic system and the nature and extent of democracy. In particular, the New Right has its own version of 'political economy', in which an attempt is made to extend the orthodox (i.e. neoclassical) economists' analysis of markets into the political arena. The 'economics of politics' has thus emerged. There are two important limitations to this approach. The first is that the political sphere is, by its nature, quite different in structure and function from that of the market. The arguments of the 'economics-of-politics' approach work by analogy: 'competition' for votes is 'like' competition in markets and for profits. But nothing is achieved by this analogy except the reduction of all political phenomena to market forms. The distinctive features of political structures and practices are lost. The 'economics of politics' becomes the dissolution of political analysis into an unsatisfactory economic theory of market behaviour.

The second serious limitation is that the economic theories and methods used reflect and perpetuate the ideological assumptions of classic liberalism. The approach of orthodox economics is subjective and individualistic. Society is conceived merely as the sum of its parts; it is not recognized that the parts can reflect and take upon themselves some of the features of the whole. The individualistic approach of classic liberalism is very unsatisfactory in that it has little conception of society as a *system*, except as a mere aggregate of individual components. Its atomistic method, long discredited amongst political and sociological theorists, survives in economics for one simple reason: individualistic assumptions tend to lead to market-based policy conclusions. The proliferation in Western society of the practice and ideology of private enterprise helps to explain the vitality of this outdated approach.

To understand the interaction of economics and politics, a theory of socio-economic systems as a whole is required. Unfortunately, this has been very slow to develop – in fact there have been only a few major contributions to such a theory in the twentieth century. A second problem is political prejudice. The most outstanding contribution to the theory of socio-economic systems was provided by Karl Marx more than a century ago, but a full discussion and development of his theories has been prevented, largely because it is perceived that these ideas may threaten the *status quo*. On the other hand, the Marxist camp has been marked by dogmatism and fundamentalism, resulting in failure to abandon deficient elements in Marx's thought, or to take account of important positive developments in social science in the twentieth century.

Among both Marxists and non-Marxists, things are far from satisfactory.

There are general and serious problems in the Marxist approach, some of which will be discussed later. Nevertheless Marx remains the most important contributor to the theory of socio-economic systems, and his influence is present throughout this work. However, in strict terms it is far from orthodox Marxism; and the Marxist epithet should not be applied.

The majority of Marxists and socialists have failed to give any consideration to the detailed nature and feasibility of a future socialist society. It is either proclaimed that socialism is inevitable, or simply assumed that it will work. These cavalier attitudes have contributed to a serious crisis faced by the socialist movement in all parts of the world. It is therefore essential to take a critical look at the socialist project itself.

Some people may find the conclusions in this work heretical and alarming, particularly the evaluation of markets and of the political role of the working class. Heretical to the Left they may be: but they are no succour for the Right. A central theme will be a critique of individualism and the attempts to reimpose *laissez-faire*. For reasons that will become clear, this work will tread on corns on the Right, Left and Centre of the conventional political spectrum.

An attempt is made to transcend some of the more sterile debates between Right and Left by giving emphasis to a new dimension: that of democracy. This emphasis is lacking in the orthodox political thought of Left, Right and Centre. Democracy is something which 'everyone is in favour of', but to its extension and development few give a high priority. The systems approach helps to overcome this narrow view. Democracy is envisaged not simply as a set of *political* institutions (such as Parliament) or practices (such as voting) but as a feature of the socio-economic system as a whole. Thus it is not fully established unless it is present in *economic* and other spheres as well. This involves, however, an integrated discussion of other regulatory mechanisms in the system: particularly markets and planning. Hence the subtitle to this work.

It is not possible to deal with all aspects of the democratic economy in one work, and some important topics have had to be excluded. For example, there is some discussion of the effects of the new information technology, but not of the important relationship between certain types of technology (particularly in the nuclear field) and democracy. To some extent this has been dealt with elsewhere. In addition, consideration of the international dimension of economics and politics is confined to the occasional remark. The emphasis is on the development of a theory of socio-economic systems, without detailed discussion of the relationship between such systems, or of their contribution to the global whole. The international aspects will be the subject of a future and more comprehensive study.

The analysis here has been sketched with a broad brush. Much technical detail has been avoided. The state of the art, and the urgencies of our time, force us to postpone the elegant and baroque, and to depict essentials. A single work cannot give all the answers, and this one does not set out to do so. Instead, one of its prime objects is to change the terms of political and economic debate. There is a dialogue between Left and Right which is preoccupied with dogmatic assertions of the virtues of public ownership on the one hand, and of markets and private ownership on the other. What is missing is a serious discussion of the issue of economic democracy: the idea that as well as having the right to choose a government, the people should have the right to decide the priorities and policies within the economy, and have a major say in matters of immediate concern at work and in the community. Economic democracy is an attractive and persuasive idea, but it receives little attention.

By implication, this primary emphasis on the widest possible form of democracy is a critique of much orthodox thinking on the Left. This self-critical theme is developed here, especially in the later chapters. It is not criticism for its own sake, but to the end of providing a powerful and radical alternative to the ideas of the New Right. Without such an alternative the battle is lost.

Two

Is Democracy Really Necessary?

> Show not the *goal*
> But show also the *path*. So closely interwoven
> Are path and goal that each with other
> Ever changes, and other *paths* forthwith
> Another *goal* set up.
>
> Ferdinand Lassalle, *Franz von Sickingen*

What is the value, to human society, of democracy? Is it an end or simply a means to an end? Even if it is of value, is it really necessary? These questions are of vital importance for our time, when in many countries democracy is absent or under threat.

At first sight, it would appear that democracy is at most a means to an end, and possibly a cumbersome and inefficient instrument as well. Evidently, it is not an immediate solution to pressing global problems such as war, hunger, disease and poverty. It is like love and virtue: almost everyone accepts that it is a 'good thing'. But it is not near the top of most people's list of priorities. When we pay lip-service to democracy, is this our assessment of its status?

Such an attitude is very common. It is also found at both ends of the political spectrum. Democracy is often regarded as an expendable luxury, or merely as a means to a set of other, more desirable, ends – a view which is not confined to political extremists. Let us first consider a quotation from V. I. Lenin, as a representative of a prominent tendency on the Left:

> There is absolutely *no* contradiction in principle between Soviet (*that is*, socialist) democracy and the exercise of dictatorial powers by individuals. The difference between proletarian dictatorship and bourgeois dictatorship is that the former strikes at the exploiting minority in the interests of the exploited majority, and that it is exercised – also through individuals – not only by the working and exploited people, but also by organizations which are built in such a way as to rouse those people to history-making activity.[1]

Now for a (not untypical) quotation from the modern New Right. Their position is akin to the classic liberalism of the nineteenth century, and from such a school of thought a more positive attitude to democracy could be derived. Yet the prominent New Right theorist F. A. Hayek has written:

> However strong the general case for democracy, it is not an ultimate or absolute value and must be judged by what it will achieve. It is probably the best method of achieving certain ends, but it is not an end in itself.[2]

Given the remarkable concurrence between these two passages, it is important to disentangle the basic similarities and differences in the theories which lie behind them. For advocates of a broad democracy, based on universal adult suffrage and the freedoms of speech and political organization, both quotations should be disturbing.

Lenin, of course, described himself as a Marxist. Marxists have the objective of replacing capitalism by socialism in which there is collective ownership of the means of production and in which the working class is controlling and dominant. Notably, however, Marx and Engels identified the latter objective with democracy itself. They wrote, in the *Communist Manifesto*, 'the first step in the revolution by the working class is to raise the proletariat to the position of ruling class, to win the battle of democracy.'[3] However, there is a significantly different attitude to democracy in the Bolshevik tradition, in which Lenin was the most important leader. Means and ends are not in the same relation. Lenin regarded the Bolshevik or Communist Party as the guardian of 'the interests of the exploited majority'; as such, it could use dictatorial methods. As Fernando Claudin has put it:

> Lenin's theory made the party the custodian of Marxist theory, depositary and guarantee of the historic interests of the proletariat into which its task was to instil a socialist consciousness. The party was not subject to any democratic judgement that the masses might pass on it, but set its own course. It was ideologically prepared, therefore, should the masses fail to reach the level of consciousness required by 'historic necessity', to accept a position of authority, of guardianship over them. In a word, should the free expression of 'proletarian democracy' run counter to what the party considered to be the interests of the revolution, the party was ideologically predisposed to substitute for that free expression.[4]

Both Lenin and Trotsky, his ally, generally favoured democratic forms of organization, but regarded them as items of luxury, and subordinate, at least in the short term, to other ends. The conditions of civil war under which such choices were made in 1918–21 in Russia were very hard, and it would be wrong to judge the regime without recognition of this fact. The attitude to democracy of Lenin and Trotsky was more favourable than Stalin's; nevertheless, the seeds of bureaucratic dictatorship are there, in the writings of the Leninist and Trotskyist tradition. Perhaps its most poignant expression is in the Trotskyist view that the Soviet Union remains a 'workers' state' (albeit 'degenerated'). Collectivization of the means of production is identified with a state of 'proletarian' character:

> Classes are characterized by their position in the social system of economy, and primarily by their relation to the means of production. In civilized societies, property relations are validated by laws. The nationalization of the land, the means of industrial production, transport and exchange, together with the monopoly of foreign trade, constitute the basis of the Soviet social structure. Through these relations, established by the proletarian revolution, the nature of the Soviet Union as a proletarian state is for us basically defined.[5]

A great number of socialists and Marxists, including those hostile to Trotskyism, would agree with the above statement. In this book, however, its identification of the end of working-class power with collective ownership is questioned.[6] The upshot of such an approach is to regard democracy, to some degree or other, as a desirable 'extra', but not as an immediate end in itself. The establishment of collective ownership and planning is said to relate to 'the economy'; it is thus 'more fundamental', and takes priority over the development of democratic institutions. It is easy to see how this relates to the over-used base/superstructure metaphor in Marxism.[7] Nationalization of the economy is a restructuring of the all-important 'base'. The widening of democracy is merely the addition of, albeit desirable, 'superstructural' trimmings.

Let us compare the position of the New Right.[8] As we have seen, F. A. Hayek does not regard democracy as an end in itself: the primary goal is to maximize 'freedom' or 'liberty', words used almost interchangeably and in a nineteenth-century sense. Following Jeremy Bentham and like thinkers, liberty is defined as 'the condition of men in which coercion of some by others is reduced as much as possible' (Hayek). This condition exists in a system which is based on 'free' contracts between individuals. According to the New Right, this is a market system. In contrast, a planned economy is seen as being based on command and other forms of coercion: it is by definition 'unfree'.

It appears that the aim of the New Right is an unrestricted, free-market capitalism. Democracy, though desirable, is not an end in itself. The basic conflict of principle is between collectivism and centralized planning on the one hand, and market relations and private ownership of the means of production on the other: the former is the antithesis, the latter the haven of liberty. Thus once again the 'economic base' is seen to define the essential character of society, and the system is favoured or disfavoured on that basis, democracy being a secondary or 'superstructural' element, largely irrelevant as a criterion of evaluation. Hence there is a striking similarity in the approach of (say) Lenin and Trotsky on the Left, and Friedman and Hayek on the Right, despite their very different political conclusions.

It should be made clear, however, that neither the New Right nor the Leninist Left detaches politics from economics entirely. In the writings of Lenin, Stalin and Trotsky (but not in the works of Marx[9]) a distinction is made between 'bourgeois' and 'proletarian' democracy. Accordingly, a 'qualitatively different' type of democracy is associated with capitalism and with socialism. In New Right writings the connection between economics and politics is made in a different way. In particular it is asserted that collectivist planning and socialism are by their nature infertile ground for a healthy democracy, which is more likely to be associated with capitalism.[10] The strong and weak points in these positions will be discussed later.

It is not being argued here that the 'extremes' of the New Right and the Leninist Left are similar or identical, nor am I supporting the old liberal adage that the political continuum is circular rather than in a straight line. First, there are important differences (often ignored by the Left) between the New Right ideology and fascism. The New Right holds that fascist regimes are very similar to Communist ones, and is much closer to the liberals of the nineteenth century. In contrast, there is a strong corporatist element in much twentieth-century 'liberal' thinking. Second, it is highly dubious that politics can be represented either as a circle or as a straight line, since both require only one dimension to define a single position. Third, democracy is often treated as a secondary issue – an additional extra – both in the 'extreme' and in the 'moderate' regions of political thinking.

One of the most graphic and explicit quotations from a politician of any shade can be taken from the work of a prominent 'moderate' (and so-called 'wet') Conservative Member of Parliament and former member of the Thatcher Cabinet, Sir Ian Gilmour. He wrote:

> Conservatives do not worship democracy. For them, majority rule is a device ... democracy is a means to an end and not an end in itself ... And if it is leading to an end that is undesirable or is inconsistent with itself, then there is a theoretical case for ending it.[11]

Gilmour goes on to suggest that military action is justified against a democratically elected Left government bent on radical change – a view supported by others less honest and explicit than this man of 'moderate' views.

Even more widespread among Left, Right, and Centre alike is the idea that democracy is a secondary matter, a possible means and not an end in itself. The opposite is contended here: that such means and ends cannot be separated. Two of the aims of this book are to demonstrate that democracy, in a sense, is an end as well as a means, and to reject a hermetic division between economics and politics: it is thus not possible to consider which economic 'base' is desirable in separation from the attached political structures.

Marketplace Democracy

The New Right often depreciates the value of democratic institutions by suggesting, along with many other economists, that the market itself is a viable (or even superior) institution through which the individual can 'vote' and influence the direction of the economy. This notion, of alleged 'consumer sovereignty', is at the heart of the defence of economic systems in which the market is the dominant means of allocating resources and attaching a value to goods and services. It has been explained, very clearly by Enoch Powell:

> The free enterprise economy is the true counterpart of democracy: it is the only system which gives everyone a say. Everyone who goes into a shop and chooses one article rather than another is casting a vote in the economic ballot box: with thousands or millions of others that choice is signalled to production and investment and helps to mould the world just a tiny fraction nearer to people's desire. In this great and continuous general election of the free economy nobody, not even the poorest, is disenfranchised: we are all voting all the time.[12]

A wide range of economists, from Paul Samuelson to Milton Friedman, would accept the validity of this account. It is the standard hymn of praise to the market mechanism, and one reason why Enoch Powell, on his own admission, prays to God in gratitude for the gift of capitalism. Serious evaluations and critiques of the notion of consumer sovereignty are less widespread, although oblique references to it are made in much of the literature. An important and well-known line of criticism has been developed by J. K. Galbraith. He shows that modern capitalism, dominated as it is by a few large companies in each industry, does not conform to the model of 'perfect competition' in the economics textbooks.[13] The evidence indicates that, rather than responding automatically to pre-existing individual demand, large firms play a major part in actually creating and manipulating consumer wants. Furthermore, given the complexity of most products, the consumer is rarely in a position to make a completely informed choice and thus indicate to the manufacturer a meaningful preference for Product A rather than Product B. The thrust of the Galbraith-type criticism of the notion of consumer sovereignty is to argue that reality does not conform to the model of perfect or near-perfect competition with complete information that is necessary for the notion to hold substance.

It could be asked, more fundamentally, if the idea of consumer sovereignty would be valid even if the economy were not dominated by a small number of large companies, and consumers were more aware and informed of the choices provided for them by a large number of competing firms. The belief in consumer sovereignty depends on the one-sided view that the consumer is the active element in the economic process, with wants and needs that are independent of the behaviour of the firm, and that the producers are largely passive. In fact the economy is not a one-way-street leading to the consumer; the process is interactive. Consumers are bombarded with products, and involved in social experiences at work and in the community, as well as the marketplace, which continually form and re-form their wants, and prompt their demand for certain products. Firms are not enslaved by the laws of the market, even without mass advertising; through pricing policy and product design consumer demand can be buffeted, altered, and, to some extent, manipulated. The mechanical models of consumer demand in the textbooks pay far too little attention to the volatility of tastes and preferences and the direct influence of the firm on demand itself.

Another criticism of the notion of consumer sovereignty is that it involves injustice. 'Votes' in the marketplace are not allocated on an equal basis to each adult: those with higher incomes are able to have more influence, by choosing and buying things of greater total monetary value. Everyone votes in the 'economic ballot box' but some have far more votes than others – a contradiction of a fundamental principle of democracy. Friedman takes this criticism head-on. He argues that voting in the political ballot box is inferior to the (effectively unequal) voting in the 'economic ballot box', for in the former voters do not have to consider their own pockets, nor are they constrained by overall budgetary considerations: they can vote for a political party which promises the moon. In a democratic political system, the argument runs, political parties compete against each other to offer more than the next, and the system becomes overloaded with promises which it cannot fulfil. In contrast, in the marketplace, the consumer spends, and has influence, in proportion to what is earned. Unequal incomes, and 'votes', in the marketplace arise from different 'contributions' through work, etc. As Friedman puts it: 'In the economic market ... each person gets what he pays for. There is a dollar-for-dollar relationship. Therefore, you have an incentive proportionate to the cost to examine what you are getting.'[14]

There are several major criticisms to be made of this counter-argument. First, in practice not all incomes are proportionate to what is 'contributed' through work or otherwise. Take inherited wealth as an example. In modern society a great deal of personal wealth is not 'earned' by the individual concerned but inherited through family and other connections. Although some economists may argue that a 'sacrifice' is involved if the person uses that wealth, through investment, etc., to generate an income, no sacrifice is involved in coming by the wealth in the first place. Is wealth, and derived income, acquired through one's own labour, equivalent to wealth, and derived income, acquired through inheritance? It would seem that it is not. Yet the advocate of the virtues of marketplace democracy treats them as the same. In the end, it is very similar to the old argument that certain (usually male) persons through their family connections have the right to noble status and to rule over others. It is ironic that such essentially feudal arguments still emanate from, among other places, the United States of America, with its strong republican and democratic traditions.

Second, the counter-argument assumes that all incomes, from work or from property, are somehow in proportion to the recipient's 'contribution' to the economy and society. The orthodox theory is that incomes from labour or capital are in proportion to their respective 'marginal productivity'. Yet it has been shown that there are enormous logical difficulties in this argument. For example, capital cannot be valued independently of the distribution of income between wages and profits, and these are meant to be determined as a *result* of the theory.[15] The orthodox theory is a device to compare two quite different types of income: income from work, and income from ownership of the means of production. In assuming that the latter is as justifiable as the former, the theory is assuming what it has to prove.

Perhaps one of the strongest arguments against the theory of consumer sovereignty is the widespread existence of uncertainty and ignorance in any complex society. The consumer is involved in a number of transactions each day. Many purchased items are complex and potentially variable in quality. It is not possible to compare prices and quality for each type of product: it would take far too much time. Neither is it possible to know the technology of each commodity and assess its potential uses, life, and performance. We are compelled to make decisions to purchase in a climate of ignorance and uncertainty. We have to guess: to take risks. In these circumstances it is rash to assume that we can make a 'rational' choice. It should be pointed out, however, that ignorance and uncertainty exist also in a planned society, albeit perhaps to a lesser extent. Thus it does not follow that all markets can, or should, be completely abolished. But the existence of ignorance and uncertainty in a market system shows that individual decisions cannot always or generally be meaningful or rational. If we cannot always make a rational choice between A and B, then our choice of A does not signal rational information to the producer. The consumer is not acting as sovereign.

This problem of uncertainty (particularly about the future) and inadequate information has not been universally recognized. There is a strange parallel between the simplistic solutions of a completely *laissez-faire* system on the one hand, and a completely planned economy on the other: both give insufficient attention to the problem of uncertainty and ignorance. We shall return to this important theme later.

Our brief discussion of alleged 'democracy' in the marketplace has opened a Pandora's Box of both ideological and scientific controversy. It would be naive to assume that the issues will be resolved here for all time. In the context of this book, however, the key questions concern the relationship between economic structures and political institutions. While the argument for consumer sovereignty is weak, the market has to be evaluated in terms of the system as a whole.

Planning for Need

To give a political evaluation of the market means looking at the alternatives. For socialists, the alternative to the corrupting power of the market is the institution of planning, to allocate and generate resources according to human need. It is relatively easy to make an attractive case for planning in these terms. Under the capitalist market, millions of people are in need of proper housing, yet building workers are unemployed. Hospitals are full, yet labour and resources to build and develop new ones lie idle. The education system stagnates and fails to provide a full basic education, yet trained teachers cannot find jobs. The list of failures within the unplanned capitalist economy is apparently endless.

These arguments for planning are important and should not be belittled. At the same time, the serious practical difficulties should not be ignored.

The most fundamental problem in a system of 'planning for human need' is how, and by whom, are the needs to be determined? To ignore this question is to weaken the case for planning: to expose it to a potentially fatal counter-attack. In some cases 'needs' are obvious: people living in damp and overcrowded accommodation need dry and spacious dwellings, cancer patients need expert medical attention, the illiterate need basic education, and so on. But beyond that point the issue becomes more complex: what type of housing – high rise or low density? what type of medical care – preventive, curative, or holistic? what type of education – school-based, community-based, part-time or full-time? Even with basic needs there are problems for even the most enlightened planner, or planning committee, in determining the best allocation of resources. With secondary needs the problems are compounded. How many motor cars are to be produced? What is the role of public transport? Does *every* family need a video recorder or a washing machine? The slogan 'planning for human need' does not provide an answer to these problems. Human need, itself, is not always obvious or unambiguous. It is a problematic concept.

Supporters of the capitalist economic system detect these gaps in the case for planning. Only the market, they claim, can be truly sensitive to human need. Market forces rush in where planners fear to tread. Despite the limitations of the market mechanism, some of which are discussed above, there is some force in the argument for market relations in certain spheres, where planning, itself, is insensitive to needs. This issue should be explored in much more detail, and to some extent this is attempted below.

Some awareness of the inherent problems is shown by those socialists who advocate democratic structures within the planning system, such as workers' councils, consumer councils, regional councils, etc. Planning is much more likely to be successful, and sensitive to human need, if its agents are elected by the people and have direct links with the workplace and the community. Further measures, such as the linking of the salary of the planning official to the average working wage, and mandatory reselection or recall of all officials, are suggested. In all this there is an implicit recognition of some of the problems, which have received a certain amount of discussion in socialist literature.[16] One of the most important is the potential growth of bureaucracy within, and adjacent to, the planning apparatus.

Another problem is the potential conflict of planning objectives between the limbs of any partially or wholly decentralized planning system. This has received less attention, probably because it has been obscured by the mythology that 'when the workers are in power' their real and perceived interests will be everywhere identical and uniform. But, even under socialism, would there not be some resistance, say, by workers in a coal-mining area to heavy investment in wave generators of electricity in the north of Scotland? Workers' interests are not always and everywhere the same. Any realistic planning system must recognize a continuous conflict of objectives, and embody the means of compromise and resolution. Planning, as well, is a problematic concept.[17]

A Place for Democracy

A conclusion from this brief examination of the market and of planning is that neither is necessarily responsive to human needs, and neither is a straightforward means of expression of popular power. Thus we cannot evaluate an economic system in terms solely of planning, or of markets. To determine the extent of freedom or democracy we have to consider the 'superstructure' of political institutions in conjunction with the 'base' of economic forms.

Democracy is not simply a means to an end, or an attractive appendage; it is part of the end itself. It is part of the system, and the system has to be considered as a whole. The case for the market as a maximizer of human freedom has been vastly overstated by the New Right. The necessary role of democratic political institutions within an economic system of collective ownership and planning has not been accepted by many on the Left.

The close relationship between democratic structures and various types of economic system raises the question of their compatibilities. Democracy itself has varied forms. While a simplistic distinction between 'bourgeois' and 'proletarian' democracy has to be rejected, it must be recognized that there is a world of difference between on the one hand the Tsarist Duma and the eighteenth-century British Parliament, and on the other the models of a participatory democracy which have been put forward in recent times.[18] Thus we have to consider which form of democracy is desirable and appropriate in relation to the economic system involved. In this book a case is made for a wide participatory democracy in which pluralist party organization is retained,[19] combined with an economic system of a socialist nature, but containing diverse centres of economic and political power. It is argued that only under such a system will genuine popular participation in power be generated and maintained on the widest possible basis.

The planning *versus* markets debate is largely inadequate because it is conducted without consideration of the integral political structures.

It is intended in this book to introduce the dimension of democracy into the debate, and to move us off the overworked soil ploughed repeatedly by the Leninists and the New Right. First, however, it is necessary to look at these doctrines in more detail.

Three

Capitalism and Freedom

Licence they mean when they cry Liberty.

John Milton, *Sonnet XII*

Economics used to be regarded as a social science that was value-free. Its aim was to explain or predict, not to tie itself to morality. The predominant concerns were to develop positive (rather than normative) theories of markets, inflation, and the like. Judgements of fact and value were kept in separate compartments. Policy recommendations were by-products of a supposedly innocent 'positive economics'.

The recent rise of the New Right has changed all that. The myth of a value-free economics depended on a political consensus as to economic objectives. The postwar era was marked by a widespread commitment to full employment and economic growth. Orthodox economists took such shared objectives for granted and discussed the technical means of their achievement. In response to the rise of the monetarist school, in the late 1960s and early 1970s, mainstream economists concentrated on the underlying technicalities. What was neglected was the fact that the rise of monetarism was just one aspect of a forceful challenge to the postwar, Keynesian consensus. Common values and objectives were being challenged. It was not simply a debate over the technical causes of inflation. The New Right was asserting a conception of what sort of economic system was desirable.

The very preoccupation with inflation as an issue is itself an acceptance of certain political priorities. Hence monetarist theory was in part a façade for those who were most concerned about the effects of inflation on the cherished market system. It should be made clear, however, that this was not a dishonest stratagem. The leaders of the New Right had always made their political position clear. Friedrich A. Hayek did so in his famous book *The Road to Serfdom*, published in 1944, and Milton Friedman in his *Capitalism and Freedom*, published in 1962. It should have been noticed a great deal earlier that in economics technical and moral issues can never be completely separated.

With the formation of the government of Margaret Thatcher in Britain in 1979, and the election of President Ronald Reagan in America in 1980, this point was made even more clearly. At the time of writing the economic records of both these governments have been records of failure. Unemployment has escalated. Output and investment have slumped. Productivity has shown no marked improvement. Bankruptcies are at record levels. Only on the question of inflation has there been a small success. Why, then, is there no change of policy? To answer this question fully it has to be realized that these governments do not pursue only 'economic' objectives: they are wedded to a new moral vision of a market society.

In their view the extent of capitalist and market relations is the measure of freedom. Cuts in public expenditure do not, therefore, have to be justified in terms of any contribution to the growth of the economy. Attacks on trade union rights and the welfare state are part of a moral crusade. If there is massive unemployment and sustained economic recession, 'Thatcherism' and 'Reagonomics' have not necessarily failed in their own terms. One of their central objectives is to maximize 'freedom', according to the New Right definition. Thus if market relations have been extended, and public enterprise privatized, then success is claimed whatever the 'economic' repercussions.

The New Right have succeeded in replacing the Keynesian objective of full employment with the quest for 'freedom' through an extension of private ownership and the market system. This pursuit of 'freedom' is seen as a much higher and more worthy objective than that of mainstream economists in the past. The old Keynesian consensus was committed, in the view of the New Right, merely to the 'artificial' creation of full employment through 'inflationary' public expenditure. The pursuit of 'freedom' seems a more noble ideal.

Most economists used to believe (many still do) that their science was purely technical in character – a search for the right instruments and adjustments to achieve well defined and widely accepted goals. There is some doubt if this was ever a valid description of the subject. But now it is plain for all to see that there are wide disagreements on the objectives of economic policy. The spanners from the economists' tool kit are banging on the dissonant drums of varied political ideology.

Thus 'positive economics' is dead. It has been killed by the New Right. It is unmourned by the Left. No politician or economist can afford to ignore this fact. To challenge the politicized economics of the New Right the Left must respond with its own radical political economy. A scientific analysis of present conditions should not be divorced from an image of a just and free society. For many economists of the past, including Adam Smith, David Ricardo, Karl Marx, and John Maynard Keynes, such a divorce was never made absolute. Economic theory cannot survive and prosper in a moral vacuum. The history of social science informs us that theory is rarely, if ever, detached from ideology.

This does not mean that we abandon all claim to science. On the contrary, it means placing science in a human and social context. Alongside 'pure' theory we have to evaluate political and social objectives. It is in this spirit that the capitalist system is discussed and appraised in this chapter.

What is Capitalism?

Freedom is to be discussed here not in complete abstraction but in relation to a real social phenomenon, i.e. the capitalist system. It is necessary, first of all, to define this real object and to describe its principal features.

The best short definition of the capitalist system is 'generalized commodity production'. One must, however, be precise about the elements of this term. First, a commodity is a good or service which is brought to the market for sale or hire. It can be either bartered for another commodity or exchanged for money. The latter, of course, is most often the case. Second, the word 'generalized' is included for two important reasons. It refers to the fact that under capitalism most goods and services are commodities, i.e. they are traded on the market at some stage; and in particular it refers to the special feature of capitalism that labour-power (i.e. the capacity to work) is also a commodity. Under capitalism, people work, after a 'free' and voluntary contract with their employer, for a wage or salary. This was not the case under preceding systems of production, such as slavery in ancient Greece or Rome, or feudalism in medieval England. Strictly speaking, neither slaves nor serfs received wages, and their labour-power was not traded regularly and voluntarily by themselves on the market.

For labour-power to be hired on the market its owners must be deprived of an alternative source of livelihood, and they cannot have ownership or direct access to the means of production. It follows, therefore – from the statement that labour-power is hired as a commodity – that workers are separated from ownership or control of the means of production. The means of production (i.e. factories, machines, land, etc.) are privately owned by the capitalist class. 'Generalized commodity production' implies a class-divided society where workers are separated from the means of production, which is concentrated in the hands of a capitalist class.

It should be stressed that the above is not a moral evaluation of capitalism but a definition of it with which both its supporters and its critics could agree. Clarity on this point is important, as there is much confusion as to the precise meaning of the word. Our definition highlights the significance of markets, commodities, private ownership of the means of production, and class relations.

Coercion and Freedom

As noted in the previous chapter, advocates of the classic liberal view, particularly Friedman and Hayek today, define liberty and freedom in terms of the absence of coercion. The capitalist market, it is argued, minimizes coercion by providing 'freedom of choice'. As Friedman has put it:

> So long as effective freedom of exchange is maintained, the central feature of the market organization of economic activity is that it prevents one person from interfering with another in respect of most of his activities. The consumer is protected from coercion by the seller because of the presence of other sellers with whom he can deal. The seller is protected from coercion by the consumer because of other consumers to whom he can sell. The employee is protected from coercion by the employer because of other employers for whom he can work, and so on. And the market does this impersonally and without centralized authority.[1]

The precursors of this defence of markets in terms of freedom are a number of political and economic theorists all noted for their individualistic and *laissez-faire* ideas. In criticizing this school of thought it would be hazardous, and probably incorrect, to deny any substance to their ideas and to reconstruct from scratch an entirely different notion of freedom, although the liberal version of it is inadequate. The argument here is that the utilization of the concept by the New Right is extremely narrow and blinkered. Even in its own terms the argument that capitalism is the provider of freedom is unconvincing. Having demonstrated this we shall go on to suggest some broader insights.

We shall start by discussing freedom from the point of view of the individual. Freedom, it is asserted, is the absence of coercion. Markets are not coercive because the individual is provided with a voluntary choice. But does the existence of a voluntary choice imply the complete absence of coercion? We shall see that it does not.

In any case, what is a 'voluntary' choice? Let us consider a couple of examples. A highway robber brandishes a gun and demands of a traveller:

'Your money or your life!' Few would suggest that the traveller is acting voluntarily if he (or she) agrees to part with his money rather than his life, even if the reply to the robber was in terms of voluntary consent: 'Yes, I will let you have the money.' Similarly, a 'confession' in a police cell is not necessarily voluntary if the accused signs a statement under the threat of violence or harassment.

The classic liberal could counter, first, that both these actions are against the law, which is supposed to safeguard the property of the individual and protect the person against violence. However, such laws put limitations on the 'freedom' of action of the robber and the violent policeman. If similar coercion can be found in the marketplace, then that would also seem a justification for the intervention of the law. Second, the classic liberal would point out that both these agreements under duress gave the victim little or no choice: money or death; confession or violence. In contrast, in the marketplace, there are a number of competing parties which offer choice to both buyer and seller. However, this does not abolish coercion, just as the traveller would still be coerced if faced with the choice of being robbed of his wallet by one robber or his overcoat by another. In certain circumstances the existence of choice can reduce coercion, but it need not abolish it altogether, even if we are faced with the 'choice' of a million robbers all with different things to demand in exchange for our life.

In classic liberal thinking the market system is often an Arcadia in which individuals are more or less equal in terms of wealth and power. The employed worker is envisaged as having a strong chance of rising prosperity, or of becoming self-employed. This picture has never corresponded to the reality of the capitalist system. Generally, market transactions take place between people or corporate bodies disparate in terms of wealth and power. The costs and benefits of each transaction are not, therefore, symmetrical between agents in a contract. This inequality is no accident. It is generated by capitalism itself.

One of the most important cases of inequality and asymmetrical bargaining is between employer and employee. Devotee of capitalism as he was, Adam Smith always had an eye on reality, and he realized that workers were at a number of disadvantages in their determination of a wage contract with an employer. He noted the asymmetries of existing legislation against trade unions: 'We have no acts of parliament against combining to lower the price of work; but many against combining to raise it.' In addition, there were many asymmetries which would survive the repeal of the Combination Acts. For example, in the case of a strike over wages, Smith observed that:

> the masters can hold out much longer. A landlord, a farmer, a master manufacturer, or merchant, though they did not employ a single workman, could generally live a year or two upon the stocks which they have already acquired. Many workmen could not subsist a week, few could subsist a month, and scarcely any a year without employment. In the long-run the workman may be as necessary to his master as his master is to him; but the necessity is not so immediate.[2]

Thus, Smith concludes, there is an asymmetric bargain between employer and worker, which acts to keep down the general level of wages. The position of the worker is not dissimilar to that of the traveller vis-à-vis the robber: capitalism presents the choice 'Your labour or your life' when the alternative to work is starvation. Thus, as C. B. Macpherson and others have pointed out, coercion is not necessarily absent in the hiring of labour-power.[3] A worker faced with the choice of poverty, social degradation and starvation on the one hand, and going to work on the other, is not entering an entirely 'free' contract. A society which is not rid of the threat of starvation or poverty is not displaying the quintessence of liberty when people 'choose' to enter employment to escape these ills. If people choose to work to escape death then they are not free. Poverty and starvation are coercive.

Today, in some capitalist countries, starvation and poverty have been marginalized. However, there is still considerable validity to the arguments of C. B. Macpherson and Adam Smith. Even if unemployed workers receive some form of dole payment, and do not starve to death, there is still considerable asymmetry in power and wealth between employer and employee. Even when strong trade unions have pushed up wages, the employers remain stronger, and the necessities they face are 'not so immediate'. There is much fat to lose in a business before the livelihood of the businessman is threatened. In addition we must note the counteracting influence of the large firm. There has been growing trade unionism but there has also been the growing power of the monopolies and multinationals. The relation between employer and employee remains very unequal.

Important work on the relationship between freedom and equality has been carried out by Hillel Steiner.[4] Starting from the classic liberal definition of freedom, he challenges the idea that it can be maximized in a simple way. According to the classic liberal criterion, a dictator enjoys considerable freedom, albeit at the expense of others. The dictator, as coercer, is 'free'. His subjects, being coerced, are not. Coercion is not the minimization of freedom, but its maldistribution, in favour of the coercer and against the coerced. The classic liberal plea for liberty and freedom is meaningful only if it means a more equal distribution of liberty amongst all members of society.

Steiner goes on to consider the issue of inherited wealth in these terms. In a capitalist society, the owners of the means of production have always managed to pass on the bulk of their gains to their descendants. Most personal wealth is obtained by inheritance. Yet its concentration in the hands of a small minority goes against the classic liberal ideal of equal liberty. The unequal distribution of inherited wealth imposes a pattern of choice upon succeeding generations that is largely beyond their control. Neither those fortunate enough to inherit, nor the unfortunate majority, choose their fate. Each generation is 'coerced' by the pattern of inheritance that it acquires from the past, and to which it did not consent. We enter no voluntary contract with preceding generations. The only way to overcome this problem is to remove the right of inheritance of large amounts, and to distribute wealth more equally. Taken literally, the classic liberal assumptions lead inexorably to equality and some form of socialism.

Classic liberals and New Right ideologists are blind to the inherited or other inequalities present in most 'voluntary' contracts. They stress only 'freedom of choice', in a current and limited sense, and the absence of more blatant forms of coercion in a 'free' market system. They rush headlong to the conclusion that it is within capitalism that freedom and liberty are maximized, ignoring the fact that in capitalist countries there is a very unequal distribution of wealth, even when house ownership and pension funds are taken into account.[5]

Under capitalism the overwhelming majority of the population have little choice other than to live by hiring out their labour-power, while a small minority can exist on the income from property. This involves a highly unequal distribution of liberty.

To some extent Hayek and others have recognized the existence of asymmetrical power and wealth. They argue, however, that it is a consequence of state intervention in the economy. Left alone, the capitalist system would create greater equality. This argument is totally unconvincing. It has to be admitted, of course, that governments have promoted mergers and helped to create large industrial conglomerates (such as the merger-wave promoted by the Labour government of 1964–70 in Britain). But on the basis of economic theory and historical experience it seems ridiculous to assume that there are not strong forces within capitalism preserving inequality, and creating larger and larger firms. Despite inheritance taxes, vast inequalities of wealth persist. Big firms continuously gobble up the small. The concentration of wealth and capital in the hands of the few is an outcome of the capitalist system, with or without the assistance of the state.

Authority and Subjugation

The economic advantage of employer over employee is not simply a matter of inequality in wealth, income, or power: it is reinforced within the sphere of production. In a famous passage, Marx has described, with characteristic wit, the difference between the apparent freedom in exchange and the lack of freedom in production. The marketplace is 'a very Eden of the innate rights of man'. It is this aspect of the system which provides classic liberals with grounds for their views, for they claim that it is based on consent and 'free' exchange between 'equals'. On the conclusion of an employment contract, however, there is a change in the 'equal' relationship between the two participants in exchange:

> He who was previously the money-owner now strides out in front as a capitalist; the possessor of labour-power follows as his worker. The one smirks self-importantly and is intent on business; the other is timid and holds back, like someone who has brought his own hide to market and now has nothing else to expect but – a tanning.[6]

Marx thus emphasizes the contrast between apparent freedom and legal equality (i.e. formal equality under the law) in the marketplace, and authority over the worker in the factory. It is important to realize that an employment contract is very different from a normal contract for the sale of goods or services. In the case of an employment contract the actual pattern of work is not laid down in advance: a range of possible tasks could be specified[7] or, as in most cases, specified imperfectly.[8] Meanwhile the worker agrees to submit to the authority of an employer, so that management can exercise its discretion as to the precise directions given at work when the occasion is pressing. In return, the worker receives a wage or salary. A sales contract is quite different, in that it does not involve an explicit authority relationship, and the characteristics of the goods or services to be exchanged are specified in advance.

When the authoritarian nature of the employment contract, and of employment itself, is pointed out to devotees of the New Right, they reply that entry into such a contract is entirely voluntary. However, as has been indicated above, seemingly voluntary contracts may be subject to inequality, and greater pressure on one side than on the other. A poor worker with a family to feed may have little alternative but to accept an employment contract, whereas the employer may have the pick of many thousand unemployed.

In addition, the New Right do not notice an important contradiction in this position. They see real authoritarianism under the guise of socialism only, not within the capitalist firm. As Charles Lindblom has pointed out:

> In developed market systems, most gainfully employed people in fact spend their working hours in an authority system – typically an organized business enterprise. The consequent threat to freedom is all the more obvious in large corporations: an organization in which few men command thousands of others in the standardized patterns of bureaucracy does not nourish freedom. Libertarians [the American term for the classic liberal] reply that employees accepting managerial authority are still free because they voluntarily accept that authority and are free to terminate it. Then whether authority permits men to be free depends on whether they choose to enter the authority system? If so, the liberal argument that men are free in exchange and unfree in authority systems is destroyed; it all depends.[9]

Thus, according to the logic of the New Right, an inhabitant of an Eastern Bloc country is 'free' if that person consents to be there. If freedom is marked by consent, then the consent of a population to any form of dictatorship means that they are free.

However, it is not satisfactory to regard mere consent as the *sine qua non* of freedom: there are other factors to be taken into consideration. The value of the consent has to be assessed in terms of the pressures and other circumstances acting upon the person. Thus, to return to our example of the employment contract, freedom is not marked simply by the consent to work for an employer. Although that consent is meaningful and real, it has to be considered alongside the economic and social pressures which are pushing that person into work.

The Creation of Consent

The New Right argument that under capitalism people are free is based on an over-simplified notion of voluntary consent. We need only to study history and anthropology to warn us against such over-simplifications. Anthropology provides evidence of varied forms of social ritual, hierarchy, authority and dominance. There are examples of consent to practices which would be regarded as exploitative and absurd by Western standards. History is full of instances of the apparent consent of slaves to slavery, tribes conniving in their dominance by others, serfs in their thousands seemingly paying voluntary homage to a monarch, and Hindu untouchables seeing righteousness in their own subjugation and exploitation. Acquiescence and consent, even when the system appears to us coercive and unfree, is the norm rather than the exception.

True enough, no society is a seamless whole. There is contradiction, conflict and dissent. But these rarely express themselves in terms of overt lack of consent to authority for prolonged periods of time. Revolt and protest, though rich in historical consequences, and never beyond the horizon, are infrequent compared with long periods of stability and inertia in all forms of society.

It is necessary, therefore, briefly to examine the processes through which consent is generated and sustained within social systems, in spite of the impossibility of doing full justice to the topic here.

It is wrong to regard consent as being formed purely through the action of a misleading and dominant ideology, as in much crude Marxist writing. Consent does not result simply from pouring ideas into people's heads. It is more important to place emphasis on other factors, particularly the role of institutions and of routinized social practice. Institutions act to legitimate the social order. They implicitly mark out what is legitimate and acceptable, thus containing dissent and revolt. Existing social practice defines what is apparently feasible and meaningful. Dull routine is more conservative than the media, the church and the education system acting together.[10]

In a sophisticated passage in *Capital*, Marx discusses the way in which resistance to the discipline of wage-labour in Britain was suppressed in the early period of capitalist development. He emphasizes tradition, habit and routine:

> It is not enough that ... masses of men who have nothing to sell but their labour-power ... are compelled to sell themselves voluntarily. The advance of capitalist production develops a working class which by education, tradition and habit looks upon the requirements of that mode of production as self-evident natural laws. The organization of the capitalist process of production, once it is fully developed, breaks down all resistance ... The silent compulsion of economic relations sets the seal on the domination of the capitalist over the worker. Direct extra-economic force is still of course used, but only in exceptional cases.[11]

In a recent work on the concept of power, Steven Lukes effectively criticizes over-simplistic notions of domination and consent. He proposes a 'three-dimensional' concept of power, in which there is recognition of the role of social institutions and practices in obtaining consent. The very agenda of issues regarded as relevant for consideration or choice can be determined by the conscious manipulation of others. Lukes writes:

> To put the matter sharply, *A* may exercise power over *B* by getting him to do what he does not want to do, but he also exercises power over him by influencing, shaping or determining his very wants. Indeed, is it not the supreme exercise of

power to get another or others to have desires you want them to have – that is, to secure their compliance by controlling their thoughts and desires? One does not have to go to the lengths of talking about *Brave New World*, or the world of B. F. Skinner, to see this: thought control takes many less total and more mundane forms, through the control of information, through the mass media, and through the process of socialization.[12]

A more lengthy argument, putting more emphasis on the role of habit and routine, is provided by John Westergaard and Henrietta Resler:

> In any society, the pattern of people's lives and their living conditions take the forms which they do, not so much because somebody somewhere makes a series of decisions to that effect; but in a large part because certain social mechanisms, principles, assumptions – call them what one will – are taken for granted ... In a capitalist society the social mechanisms and assumptions which are generally taken for granted in this way are those, in the first instance, of private property and the market ... It is taken for granted, 'in the way things work', that profit should be the normal yardstick for investment in most areas of activity; that the living standards of the propertyless majority should be set primarily by the terms on which they sell or once sold their labour ... To put the point in general terms, there is power inherent in anonymous social mechanisms and assumptions – in 'social institutions' – not just in individuals or groups ... Power is to be found more in uneventful routine than in conscious and active exercise of will.[13]

The purpose of this section is not to demonstrate that the existence or non-existence of consent is irrelevant; rather it is to put consent in the context of the institutions and practices which wear down dissent, and confer power upon those with wealth and privilege. An employee of a capitalist firm is in many senses more free than a slave, but consent to managerial authority does not mean that the worker is enjoying the quintessence of liberty.

The Social Character of Individual Choice

These arguments on the nature of coercion and power lead us to consider the idea and basis of individual choice. The supremacy of individual choice is, of course, a cherished tenet of the New Right. If we were to take some economics textbooks seriously, it would appear that the individual's preferences are, for practical purposes, innate. They are taken as given. Little attention is paid to the social and other forces which create and mould such preferences. However, not all orthodox economists conform to this pattern. Alfred Marshall, one of the most perceptive and level-headed of neoclassicists, wrote:

> it is man's wants in the earliest stages of his development that give rise to his activities, yet afterwards each new step upwards is to be regarded as the development of new activities giving rise to new wants, rather than of new wants giving rise to new activities.[14]

Thus Marshall rejected the notion that wants and preferences are innate: in his view they can be created through experience and action. Neither is the assertion that human beings exist in a social environment inconsistent with the subjectivism and individualism of much economic theory. This is true even of the Austrian School. Thus a staunch defender of methodological individualism such as Ludwig von Mises can agree and emphasize that the 'isolated asocial man is a fictitious construction'.[15] Individual choice is social in a much deeper sense.[16]

From the moment we are born we experience the world through others. We mimic. We acquire a language. We begin to assimilate a shared symbolic order. We become socialized in the strongest sense of that term. Our sense of identity and being depends on social interaction. Our goals and desires are forced into the mould of our social culture. Even our 'biological' desire for food is dependent upon this. (Muslims and Jews do not eat pork; the English are sticklers for tea.) Another 'innate' desire, for sex, has been shown to be dependent on social culture, to the extent that in some societies certain forms of incest or adultery are taboo, but not in others. Thus we do not exist simply alongside and *with* others: our being, purposes and action are created socially *through* others.

Thus the knowledge that the individual may have of the choices that are available is generated socially and passed through a set of socially acquired cognitive filters. We perceive much of the world through language and symbols that have no meaning in an individual sense: they are purely social. The values and purposes which give meaning to our desires and intended actions are *necessarily* formulated in such a social language. A good number of our concepts and beliefs must be acquired through public language and experience with others in society. The same is largely true of knowledge.

The existence of mass advertising under modern capitalism merely makes the social character of wants more obvious, and more under the manipulation of the large firm. Instead of wants and preferences emerging fairly slowly through an informal and formal network of activities and communication, the whole process becomes more articulate and subject to the mass media. Furthermore, the social basis of culture and choice is widened through the development of the world market. The important point to realize, however, is that choice and preference do not simply become social through the existence of mass media advertising: they are social as a consequence of the social character of individuality itself.

Thus it is quite wrong to assume with Friedman that 'the central feature of the market organization of economic activity is that it prevents one person from interfering with another in respect of most of his activities'. We are continuously being buffeted through social interaction and communication. The Austrian School of economists are wrong when they write of knowledge as if it were a substance which is poured from one individual receptacle to another. Knowledge is screened and understood through a social language. The conception of the individual in the writings of the New Right is fundamentally flawed.

However, the fact that the individual is enmeshed within society does not justify a Stalinist 'the party knows best' approach. Any passionate Bolshevism which claims to know all the true interests of the working class before they are aware of them themselves is not acceptable. And for similar reasons a paternalistic, social democratic reformism, which assumes that things are best left to the government and the planners, must be rejected. The fact that individuals are fundamentally social does not imply a dissolution of individuality itself, nor the absolute supremacy of a party, government or state.

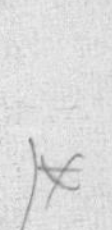

Furthermore, markets are not adept either at developing the individual or at improving the nature of social communication and interaction. Markets do not promote an educative dialogue within society. They promote the power of money, not of ideas. Real individuality cannot develop simply on the basis of a cash transaction: it requires social interaction on a number of bases and levels.

It is here that democracy can have a crucial function. The existence of public discussion, rivalry, criticism and debate play an important educative role in enriching our perceptions and widening the horizons of choice. It is not being suggested that the existing limited democracy in Western countries is that forceful or radical. But if we compare capitalist countries where democracy is absent with those where it exists, albeit in a limited parliamentary form, the benefits in terms of education and cultural development are evident. If this argument is correct, then there is a strong case for a more deep and extensive form of (participatory) democracy covering many aspects of social life.

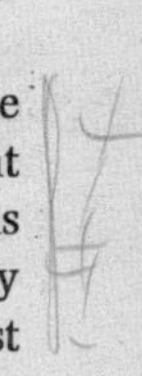

To summarize, therefore, the capitalist system encourages the enlargement of 'freedom' and minimizes 'coercion' only if these concepts are applied in a blinkered and inconsistent manner. There is much real coercion, of a subtle and multi-dimensional kind, within capitalism. The classic liberal escape route, to exclaim that if people 'consent' to the stringencies of the system their freedom is preserved and all is well, gets nowhere. It can be used in support of any social system where apparent consent is widespread, and it ignores the process of legitimization and socialization through which consent is generated or managed. At this crucial point in the argument democracy comes into its own. Democratic institutions play the important role of providing a forum for debate and controversy, in which more enlightened choices, in all spheres, can be made. The greater the extent of democracy, bringing participation in the community, industry, and local government as well as national politics, the wider the compass for the progressive development of ideas and conceptions, as well as for the dissemination of knowledge. Choice is a social as well as an individual act, depending on acquired priorities and conceptions of the world. The apparatus for choice does not reside within the individual alone, neither is the individual inside the marketplace free of preconceptions and other elements of socialization. Orthodox economists and New Right thinkers may accept this fact, but they then proceed to ignore it. The various social processes which cultivate preferences have to be examined. Institutions of a democratic and participatory nature are of vital importance in this regard.

Four

Markets Versus Democracy

NICOLE SALINGER: Are you saying that, in fact, no one really likes the market except the economists?
JOHN KENNETH GALBRAITH: Precisely. The market is an admirable vision which appeals greatly to economists with a secure income and tenure. But every person in real life seeks, above all, to get some control of his own income ... Control – emancipation from the tyranny of the market – comes with control of one's price or wage.

J. K. Galbraith and N. Salinger,
Almost Everyone's Guide to Economics

It is often presumed that people will turn to the radical ideas of the Left in periods of political or economic crisis. However, this is not always the case. The conservative mind can blame the crisis on the structural reforms of the economy that accompanied the preceding period of expansion. Thus planning and state regulation of the economy can be regarded as the cause of the slump, rather than the dominant system of private enterprise. The anarchy of the market is then tolerated as a necessary evil – or, by those with a more secure income, as a positive virtue. Scapegoats can be found elsewhere, as Margaret Thatcher has demonstrated with expertise.

Consequently, a period of crisis does not necessarily challenge our basic assumptions – it may merely reinforce our prejudices. In a conservative culture, the welfare state and even democracy itself are easy to blame. Crises can cause political reaction as much as revolution. In such circumstances the New Right has emerged.

This reaction is not confined to a single country. In 1975 the Trilateral Commission in the United States produced its *Report on the Governability of Democracies*. It declared: 'Quite apart from the substantive policy issues confronting democratic governments, many specific problems have arisen which seem to be an intrinsic part of the functioning of democracy itself.'[1] The Trilateral Commission went on to give the verdict that the main problem was an 'excess of democracy'. In France, similar ideas have found support from, among others, the editor of *Le Figaro*, a journal with half a million readers. In Britain the ideas of the New Right now dominate the Conservative Party and have found significant support elsewhere. Many prominent writers insist on the 'need to recognize limitations to the rights of government'.[2] The case for a more 'limited democracy' is argued in more depth by Samuel Brittan (a prominent financial journalist and former government adviser). He puts in a nutshell one of the prime arguments of the New Right for a straitjacketed democracy:

> Excessive expectations are generated by the democratic aspects of the system ... The basic trouble is *the lack of a budget constraint among voters*. This means that errors are biased in a particular direction. In their own private lives, people know that more of one thing means less of something else, on a given income and capital ... In the absence of such knowledge in the political sphere, electorates tend to expect too much from government action at too little cost ... The main point to stress is that democracy, viewed as a process of political competition, itself imparts a systematic upward bias to expectations and compounds the other influences at work ... Most issues are too complex to be decided by a competitive vote-seeking process. Although Parliament may vote on such issues and ministers may introduce legislation, their actions are purely formal, as the real decisions will have to be made elsewhere.[3]

It was the economist and social democratic theoretician Joseph Schumpeter who first clearly articulated the view of democracy as a 'competitive vote-seeking process'. He sees it as a sort of political market-place in which small, competing elites try to obtain as many votes as possible from the inert multitude. The striking feature of this theory is that it combines an elitist view of democracy with the analogy of the market. Brittan quotes with approval the conclusion that Schumpeter derived from his theory: 'the effective range of political decision should not be extended too far'.[4]

The Achilles' heel of democracy, the New Right would have us believe, is the tendency of elected governments to extend public expenditure in response to pressure from the (self-interested) voters. In contrast, there is no such pressure to raise taxes. Thus public spending outstrips taxation, leading to budget deficits and inflation. Milton Friedman is not alone in putting forward this argument:[5] it has been accepted and repeated by many academics and politicians elsewhere. A large body of economic theory has been transformed into an instrument of New Right theology. 'Welfare' economics has become a misnomer: many of its exponents are concerned with cutting public expenditure, minimizing democracy, and dismantling the welfare state. A leading theorist such as Charles Rowley can write:

A democratic society, therefore, will make excessive use of deficit finance once the Keynesian paradigm has been accepted and has induced a revision in the fiscal 'constitution'. For those who view the advance of the public sector as eroding the liberty of the individual, Keynesian demand management policies are seen to be malignant and to require immediate surgical treatment.[6]

A further development of the New Right argument has come from William A. Niskanen.[7] His thesis, which is meant to apply to the democratic countries of the West, is that a 'rational' bureau will always act not to benefit society or carry out the real wishes of their governors, but to maximize its budget. In such a way both the power and chances of survival of the bureau are enhanced. Thus, it would seem, the 'welfare state' is an impossible construction. It ends up as an ant-hill of bureaucracies, each acting in their own selfish interest, while the poor and needy go to the wall. Niskanen's 'solution' is to return to the nineteenth century: no sizeable welfare state, a tiny public sector, and *laissez-faire*. Of democracy he writes: 'Democracy is an instrument, not an ideal ... A government that serves only the interests of the majority is neither achievable, desirable, nor stable.'[8]

These New Right ideas are in many ways a continuation of the classic liberalism of more than a century ago. In this tradition society is viewed as the sum total of its individual members, who are largely autonomous, and each the best judge of his or her own interests. At the same time it is assumed that this self-interest will be egotistically and energetically pursued, given sufficient incentive. Like many of their intellectual forefathers, the New Right pushes away any commitment to a more equal distribution of wealth.[9] In many respects, New Right ideas are old liberalism with little change.

Yet there is an important difference. The liberals of the early nineteenth century wished to reform and extend democracy. The New Right says that democracy is 'out of control' and has to be put in a straitjacket. Classic liberalism has survived for most of two centuries, but now it is notably less keen on democracy. Many of the old liberals were not that enthusiastic about universal suffrage or a wide democratization of society, but they did at the time work for more democracy, not less.

There has been no fundamental change in political philosophy or final goal. What has happened is that the world has changed. In the early 1800s the foes of liberalism were the old absolutist states in Europe and the remnants of absolutism elsewhere. In Britain absolutism had been shattered but not completely destroyed by the revolutions of the 1640s and 1688. For most of the eighteenth and early nineteenth centuries British society was subject to bouts of political repression and denials of civil rights. In this elitist and undemocratic society the liberals cried out for reform. Their aim was to reduce the arbitrary powers of the state, to lessen the intervention of government in most spheres of socio-economic life, and to place the remaining trimmed-down state machine under the guardianship of a small elected elite. This small element of democracy was seen as a kind of safety measure: a check on corruption, repression and excess. Apart from the more radical wing of the liberal movement there was little enthusiasm for a more extended and powerful form of democracy. Most matters would be left to the market.

Today, the New Right faces a very different situation. Instead of the semi-absolutist state we have the welfare state. According to the New Right, the guardians of liberty have overstepped the mark. The powers of the state have been allowed to expand to the extent that it now interferes in all spheres of social and economic life. The New Right exclaims that the bandwagon of public spending has been pushed on by democratic pressure and has run over our liberty. They argue that political excess has got to come under the control of discipline in a new constitutional framework. In the name of freedom the New Right desires to hand many of the nominal powers of elected governments back to a reconstituted elite. This elite, now under strict constitutional controls and protected from many of the pressures of democracy, will become our new guardians. History has appeared to turn full circle. The progressives of yesteryear have become the reactionaries of our day.

The Alleged Failings of Democracy

Much of the recent New Right critique of democracy stems from the work of Schumpeter and its development by Anthony Downs.[10] Downs adopted Schumpeter's view of democracy as a competitive struggle between parties or elites for the people's vote. He explicitly assumes that both politicians and voters are egotistical and self-seeking. Politicians aim to hang on to power and maximize their votes. The voters are the egotistical 'utility maximizers' of the textbooks of neoclassical economics. In fact, Downs's work was one of the first attempts to apply the framework of neoclassical economics to the political sphere. The analogy with economic competition in the marketplace, with the 'profit maximizing' firm and the 'rational' and maximizing 'economic man', was used to the full. The voter was akin to the consumer; the party like the firm. Once reality had been forced into these little boxes no end was in sight. Even politics could be explained in 'economic' terms, along with marriage, divorce, crime and suicide.[11] The 'economics of politics' was born: 'The age of chivalry is gone. That of sophisters, economists and calculators has succeeded.'[12]

There are a number of fundamental assumptions of the 'economics of politics' approach which are worth emphasizing. First, it presupposes the rational and maximizing, egotistical individual. Second, it assumes that the individual behaves (politically) after an assessment of the costs and benefits of the actions involved. Third, there is a separation between voters and representatives, where the vast majority elect a small minority elite to make legislative and budgetary decisions. Thus the 'economics of politics' involves a particular view of the individual, a particular theory of social and individual behaviour, and a particular conception of democracy. It is not a 'general theory' at all. It makes assumptions about people and society which are not far removed from the writings of Jeremy Bentham and others in the classic liberal tradition.

Yet, after some time it became hailed as a 'breakthrough'. Much of the work of this genre has been carried on by the 'Virginia School', centred at the Virginia Polytechnic Institute in the United States. Two leading members of this school are James Buchanan and Gordon Tullock.[13] They have both developed and extended the Downs model, reaching the conclusion that the power and scope of democracy should be limited: 'even under the most favourable conditions the operation of the democratic process may generate budgetary excesses. Democracy may become its own Leviathan unless constitutional limits are imposed and enforced.'[14]

Buchanan uses examples of voting 'paradoxes' to support such arguments. A number of projects may each separately be put to the vote, and a majority of voters may see an advantage in each project. Buchanan shows, however, that it is possible that everyone might be worse off as a result of all projects being adopted. The projects that are to their disadvantage have much greater demerits than the merits of those that they support.[15] Such 'paradoxes of voting' are familiar in the literature. Some time ago Kenneth Arrow showed that individuals with consistent preferences may express them, through some majority voting rule, in incoherent social choices.[16] But this does not mean that such an outcome is likely. Amartya Sen demonstrated that coherent voting was possible if the choices were restricted within broad and realistic limits, such as those pertaining to a society with some shared values and beliefs.[17] Buchanan uses an intellectual curiosum as a major argument to limit democracy, failing to determine how realistic or applicable that curiosum may be.

In its place Buchanan and others propose an extended market mechanism presided over by a constitutional oligarchy. But this alternative is not clearly examined or evaluated. Its own problems and limitations are not put alongside the existing system or other possible systems for comparison. Is it not reasonable to assume that a combination of oligarchical government and market allocation would produce just as many, if not more, paradoxes and anomalies? The existing system is far from perfect, but is it to be improved by a reduction in democracy? This has not been demonstrated. Some of the paradoxes and anomalies of the market will be examined below.

Not only does the 'economics of politics' literature point to an unsavoury political outcome, it is also based on very dubious assumptions. As we have seen, there is a repeated insistence that governments which are subject to democratic pressure will outspend their budgets. As Jim Tomlinson[18] and other critics have pointed out, the facts are otherwise. Even after the 'Keynesian Revolution' there was no dramatic change in the pattern of public spending. In fact, in Britain until the mid 1970s governments had a current account surplus. This is not the same thing as the Public Sector Borrowing Requirement, which has frequently been positive as a result of the inclusion of public investment in its accounts. Nevertheless, there is still no evidence that the pattern of public finance altered as a response to democratic pressure on the lines suggested by the New Right. In fact, in 1969 and 1970 there was a negative Public Sector Borrowing Requirement. The rising deficits of the 1970s did not come about as the result of the adoption of Keynesian principles: there has not been a secular trend of increasing deficits, or a gradually increasing PSBR, since the war. Thus we cannot blame the adoption of a Keynesian 'fiscal constitution'. To find the roots of the fiscal crisis of the 1970s we have to look elsewhere. The New Right version of recent history does not square up with the facts.

It is also dubious to regard the existence of national debt as a consequence of democracy. In the late 1970s and early 1980s undemocratic countries such as Argentina, Brazil and Nigeria have piled up enormous public debts. Clearly, this has not resulted from domestic democratic pressure, but from the economic weakness of those countries in a time of world instability and recession. It is always possible that debt is an 'easy solution' to political pressure from interest groups in a democracy, but the fact that huge debts have been amassed in undemocratic countries indicates that there are many other significant factors at work.

The New Right insists that there is a lack of a voters' 'budget constraint'. However, contrary to popular belief, the state alone is not responsible for the supply of money in the economy. Money includes credit, as well as cash and coin, and much of this credit is created by private banks. The 'budget constraint' upon banks is in practice quite flexible. The state attempts to impose limits on the capacity of the private banks to issue credit, but these limits are never entirely rigid or incapable of circumvention. In Britain, the expansion of credit money in the private banking sector is by far the largest element in relieving the national 'budget constraint' in terms of the aggregate money supply. According to Nicholas Kaldor, bank lending to private firms accounted for as much as 83 per cent of the increase in the money supply in the 1966–1979 period.[19] In contrast, the public sector was directly responsible for no more than 5 per cent of the increase. Notably, the New Right tends to ignore the fact that 'budget constraints' are flexible, to some degree, for private money-creating institutions. Their vision is blinkered. Only the state, they argue, is free of control on its spending.

In contrast, there are democratic bodies that do face budget constraints. A local town council operating under strict cash limits would not be able to escalate its expenditure. A democratically run workers' cooperative would face a similar (and sometimes more stringent) budget constraint to a privately-owned firm. Deficits are not endemic to democracy. The 'lack of a budget constraint' argument against democracy has relevance at the level of a nation only, not to other democratic institutions.

We now return to the basic assumptions behind the 'economics of politics' treatment of democracy and voting behaviour. As we have seen, the arguments are based on the assumption that people vote in an egotistical and self-centred way. The individual knows best and acts rationally in his or her own interests. It is not difficult to see how such a theory will turn into a critique of representative democracy and a defence of the market system. The existence of democratic government implies an aggregation of views which is bound to do violence to individual preferences. If the individual is always right then it clearly follows that the government will rarely be right, save in exceptional circumstances, such as when we all agree. The system of representative democracy implies that other people are going to make decisions on our behalf. If everyone is self-seeking, then the politicians are bound to look after themselves. The critique of democracy follows from the initial assumption about the individual.

Likewise, this initial assumption leads inexorably to a defence of the market system. If the individual is rational and knows best, then the individual should be left to get on, without coercion or constraint. According to the prejudices of the New Right, the market system is the best means of ensuring this state of affairs – which is a romantic and unrealistic view. However it remains clear that with the prevailing ideology, individualistic assumptions are going to lead to market-based prescriptions.

The individualistic assumptions involve not only a dubious view of the individual, even in the existing capitalist society, but also an unrealistic view of the democratic process itself. It has been observed by many critics that the attempt to explain voting behaviour in terms of the subjective calculation of individual 'costs' and 'benefits' falls foul of the facts. Most people know that their individual vote, on its own, will make little difference. So why do people vote? In an extensive critique of the 'economics of politics' approach, Brian M. Barry makes the following point: 'It may well be that both the costs and ... benefits of voting are so low that it is simply not worth being "rational" about it. Thus habit, self-expression, duty and other things have plenty of room to make themselves felt.'[20]

It is preferable to view society as a whole, rather than as the sum of its parts. A holistic approach would examine cultural and other reasons for voting, and the social mechanisms which generate attitudes and expectations on behalf of the voter and the elected representative. It would attempt to explain individual behaviour in terms of the social system, not the social system in terms of individual behaviour.

It should be recognized, nevertheless, that the 'economics of politics' approach is not without its insights. It has produced an effective critique of the notion that once elected the representatives will be guided by their principles and can be left to get on with the job. It has identified and rebutted the mistaken view that ideas and persuasion are the supreme forces in political life. The attitude of Keynes has been criticized in these terms. Donald Moggridge has described it as follows:

> Keynes always believed that 'a little clear thinking' or 'more lucidity' could solve almost any problem ... reform was achieved by the discussion of intelligent people; public opinion must be wisely guided; the government of Britain must be in the hands of an intelligent aristocracy using the methods of persuasion.[21]

The limitations of Keynes's approach to politics have been noted by the New Right.[22] Some of their criticisms apply also to other policy-makers and politicians, typically the paternalistic reformers of social democratic persuasion, past and present. Unfortunately, the New Right argument is based on unacceptable premises. The social democrats tend to believe that all politicians (of their viewpoint at least) are strongly altruistic. This is rather naive. But it is equally naive and mistaken to assume that all politicians (or parties) are totally self-seeking, and that expressed ideas and ideologies are nothing but cynical instruments for the vote-seeking politician. It is wrong to replace an assumption of individual altruism by one of individual egoism. Both standpoints are dogmatic and far too simplistic.

A more adequate approach would give due weight to the role of class and vested interests in politics, but it would also recognize that institutions and social forces play a very important part. Quite often in politics it is not what is said that is crucial: it is the institutions and persons that propound a theory, and the social forces involved, that determine whether it is accepted or even considered for action. For example, Keynesian ideas did not take hold simply because of the brilliance of the arguments in the *General Theory*, but because they were reinforced in 1940 by the circumstances of war, when a coalition of Labour, Liberal and moderate Conservative politicians forced a change of direction.[23] Ideas do not become effective on their own. Institutions and social movements are critical in political change and development. Organized extra-parliamentary forces, such as the trade unions and the women's and peace movements, can have a significant effect not only upon the behaviour of politicians but also upon the formation of public opinion. In short, politics is the outcome of the social relations, social institutions and social forces through which ideas and ideologies are refracted and transmitted. The approach of the New Right underestimates both the social and the ideological elements involved in the political process and postulates a system of egotistical maximization, in which self-interest is all that matters.

However, if we agree with the New Right that it is naive to leave politics to the politicians, what then should be done? The New Right medicine is less democracy and more markets. In contrast, it is argued here that we need more democracy, not less. (And, as will be argued below, less markets, not more.) Many of the problems in Western democracies result from the fact that elected representatives are not in touch with the wishes and needs of the voters. A radical and viable solution to this problem is to increase the degree of political accountability, to increase popular participation in decision-making, and to begin to break down the barriers between the rulers and the ruled. The radical response to the genuine deficiencies of the modern political system is to transform society into a broad, participatory democracy. The objective is not simply to bring power to ordinary people, but also to involve them in key decisions so that they can learn and develop through their successes and their mistakes. The result may be that the budget is not balanced.

But at least in that process people can discuss and appreciate with more intimacy the validity (or otherwise) of that policy, and be more educated as to the beneficial (or other) consequences of its implementation.

Markets and Planning

If the New Right has its way, many of the decisions taken in our 'excessive' democracy will be delegated to the marketplace rather than being put to the democratic vote. But the market too has problems and anomalies.

For example, in the absence of outside restraint, a firm may pollute the environment by dumping its waste in rivers, or by despoiling the atmosphere. Without controls and discrimination in favour of public transport, individual car users may create excessive congestion, noise and exhaust fumes. Factors such as pollution and congestion are known as *social costs*. These costs do not appear as an item on the profit-and-loss account of the firm, nor do they affect the budget of the car user: they fall upon those that suffer the pollution or congestion.

These non-pecuniary social costs mean that a firm may be able to make a financial gain while producing a net social loss. The firm may be in the black, but if the expenses of bearing or removing the resulting pollution of the environment were deducted from their profit they would probably be in the red. Similarly, it may be 'rational' for individuals to use a motor car when they compare the expense of running it with the corresponding public transport fares; but if the costs of pollution and traffic congestion created by that car are taken into account, the picture changes. The market promotes criteria of individual 'rationality' without necessarily paying heed to the good of society as a whole.

The existence of social costs resulting from acts of production or consumption, known as 'externalities', is widely recognized by economists, and an extensive body of literature is concerned with the development of policies to deal with them, including the well known solutions of a 'pollution tax' and subsidies to public transport. Until recently it was widely accepted that such policies would be necessary to deal with externalities and other such types of 'market failure'. But now the balance of opinion among orthodox economists has changed. Instead of public intervention, the New Right proposes actually to extend the market mechanism through an ingenious new system of 'property rights'.[24] Under this system a number of people will own, for example, the air we breathe and the environment generally. Thus the firm or the car user would have to come to an agreement with the owners of the atmosphere, or be sued for pollution.

However, there is no clear agreement among New Right theorists as to how these property rights are to be distributed on a just or egalitarian basis. Who would decide? It is also difficult to envisage how the system would work. We would need an army of lawyers to deal with those we sue, and those that sue us, and the legal and transaction costs would be enormous. The 'property rights' proposal is a desperate attempt to construct a market solution to problems best resolved on a social and non-individualistic basis. It is political prejudice writ large as economic theory.

The market system is also deficient in respect of inequality of income. E. K. Hunt and Howard Sherman have constructed a striking example to illustrate this point. They hypothesize an island economy in which there are a thousand children who are periodically struck by an outbreak of a potentially fatal disease which does not affect adults. Without preventive medicine the chances are that 72 per cent of the children will die during an epidemic. An antidote is available which reduces the chances of death to 8 per cent if each child receives one dose. If it receives two, the chances are reduced still further, and four will bring them down to 4 per cent. Ideally, of course, the children should each be given a number of doses, but there are only a thousand on the island. If they were distributed equally by some rationing system, then each child would receive one dose and about eighty children would die.

> On the other hand, suppose the relative distribution of income and wealth that exists in the United States today. According to this income distribution, the islanders leave the allocation problem to the private-enterprise, free market system, with the following results: the 250 children who have the wealthiest parents will each take four doses of the antidote; of these 250 ... about 10 will die; of the remaining 750 children ... about 540 will die. Using a nonmarket allocative mechanism, the islanders were able to save 920 children while 80 died. Given the unequal distribution of income and wealth that exists in the private enterprise market allocation, they saved 450 children while 550 died.[25]

This hypothetical example represents the real situation faced by people in a large number of countries with unequal distributions of income and wealth, and where medicine is (or may become) available only to those that have the money to pay for it. Consider the table on page 44.[26]

The market system prevails in most countries. In all of them there is vast inequality in income. In contrast, basic needs such as food or housing are more evenly distributed. Such a system can be judged unresponsive to many human needs. In some cases, rationing or administration might be the answer. Alternatively, income might be distributed more equally – a course supported by some members of the New Right as well as

Country	Year	Share of Total Income of:	
		Richest 20%	Poorest 20%
Brazil	1970	62%	3%
India	1964	52%	5%
France	1962	54%	2%
United Kingdom	1968	39%	6%
West Germany	1970	46%	6%
United States	1970	39%	7%

traditionally by the Left. But, however desirable, it is unlikely that this policy can be carried out without massive state intervention and overall planning. Furthermore, radical redistributive policies are likely to meet political resistance from the favoured few. Without radical action with popular support, inequality on its present scale will remain. Also it is unlikely that it will be reduced substantially without taming the market.

Another problem arises in a market-dominated economy. As Keynes pointed out in *The General Theory of Employment, Interest and Money*, the market system is unstable and prone to cumulative breakdown. The level of economic activity is largely dependent on the level of investment by private firms, which is in turn dependent on expectations of the state of the economy in the future. Given that the future is inherently uncertain, such expectations can be little more than inspired guesses which are likely to become more pessimistic if the economy enters a period of downturn, when capitalists will reduce their investment and the output of the economy will fall. The downturn becomes cumulative: the system enters a slump. The result is mass unemployment. This Keynesian argument has not been refuted, by theory or evidence, in the decades since the *General Theory* was published.[27] It provides a powerful justification for state intervention to smooth out recessions and maintain the level of effective demand. The market is unable to do this alone.

Following Keynes and others, the problems of risk and uncertainty should be emphasized. When they are introduced into the theoretical model of the market system, the picture of marginal adjustments towards a stable equilibrium, as found in neoclassical theory, is inapplicable. A more adequate model is provided by game theory.[28] This can be illustrated by a well-known simple example, known as 'the prisoners' dilemma'. A prosecutor has locked up two prisoners in different cells. They cannot communicate with one another. Each has the choice of confessing or not confessing to a specific crime. The prosecutor informs them individually that if they both confess, each will go to jail for five years. If neither confesses, they will both get a one-year sentence (for other crimes).

But if one confesses and the other does not, the talkative one will go to prison for only six months while the other is sentenced to ten years (for the crime and for obstructing the course of justice). What is the best and 'rational' strategy for each prisoner?

If a prisoner does not confess he knows that the worst possible outcome for himself will be ten years in jail (in the event that the other prisoner caves in). If the prisoner does confess, the worst possible outcome will be a five-year sentence (in the event that the other prisoner confesses as well). However, the prisoner does not know if the other will confess or not. Thus if he is cautious in the face of this uncertainty he will confess, and expect at worst a five-year sentence, and at best a six-month sentence if the other prisoner does not confess. But both prisoners are in the same situation, with the same alternatives, and they are likely to reason in a similar way. Facing this uncertainty, not knowing what the other has decided to do, both will probably confess and go to prison for five years. This appears to be the outcome of decisions which are individually 'rational'. In contrast, if both had kept silent, each would have got a one-year sentence. If they had been able to cooperate in the calculation of their chances, each would have been better off.

The example shows that the sum total of individually 'rational' actions is not necessarily optimal or rational for society as a whole. Self-interested behaviour may be collectively self-defeating. This undermines the idea of a benevolent 'invisible hand' in the market system, in which the sum total of individual and selfish actions leads to a socially desirable outcome. In exactly the same way as the prisoners' dilemma, the market system can produce a result which goes against the wishes of the majority. The New Right claim that the same can be said of democratic voting procedures. However, there is an important difference: democracy involves some conscious overall regulation, and the possibility that mistakes will be debated and understood, leading to a guided change in direction; the market permits no overall guidance other than that of a shaky, erratic and untrustworthy invisible hand.

The theoretical basis for the unlikely idea of a firm and steady invisible hand is found in neoclassical general equilibrium theory, which has now reached a cul-de-sac. On the admission of Frank Hahn, a leading expect in the area, its underlying assumptions are profoundly unrealistic. The theoretical models do not include money, oligopoly, or situations where there is an asymmetry of information between agents.[29] It is notable that some of the defects are recognized and criticized by 'Austrian' economists on the New Right.[30]

Radical criticisms of general equilibrium theory go even further. It proceeds as if the system were the sum of atomistic parts, rather than a whole. The alternative (holistic) approach is found, for example, in cybernetics. Norbert Weiner, the founder of this science, has written:

> There is a belief ... that free competition is itself a homeostatic process: that in a free market the individual selfishness of the bargainers, each seeking to sell as high and buy as low as possible, will result in the end in a stable dynamics of prices, and will redound to the greatest common good. This is associated with the very comforting view that the individual entrepreneur, in seeking to forward his own interest, is in some manner a public benefactor and has thus earned the great rewards with which society has showered him. Unfortunately, the evidence, such as it is, is against this simple-minded theory. The market is a game ... thus strictly subject to the general theory of games, developed by von Neumann and Morgenstern ... The individual players are compelled by their own cupidity to form coalitions; but these coalitions do not generally establish themselves in any single, determinate way, and usually terminate in a welter of betrayal, turncoatism, and deception, which is only too true a picture of the higher business life, or the closely related lives of politics, diplomacy and war. There is no homeostasis whatever. We are involved in the business cycles of boom and failure, in the successions of dictatorship and revolution, in the wars which everyone loses, which are so real a feature of modern times.[31]

Concluding Remarks

A general case has been made here that the market is a limited and imperfect instrument. However, it is important to qualify this statement. Although a case for economic planning has been implied, it is important to compare the limitations of the market system with the limitations of a planned economy. The faults of the market are not enough to condemn it on its own. The problems of a planned economy are raised below in Chapters 7, 10 and 11. As far as the market goes, problems of, for example, overall coordination, effective demand and uncertainty may be ameliorated by the introduction of overall planning. It will be argued that, in any case, the complete removal of markets is impossible in the foreseeable future. The extent to which planning can ameliorate market deficiencies, and the degree of central or other planning that is possible and desirable, are complex and open questions. What is argued here is that democratic planning should dominate markets, not *vice versa*.

Five

The Leninist Rebuttal

In place of the representative bodies created by general popular elections, Lenin and Trotsky have laid down the soviets as the only true representation of the labouring masses. But with the repression of political life in the land as a whole, life in the soviets must also become more and more crippled. Without general elections, without unrestricted freedom of press and assembly, without a free struggle of opinion, life dies out in every public institution, becomes a mere semblance of life, in which only the bureaucracy remains as the active element. Public life gradually falls asleep, a few dozen party leaders of inexhaustible energy and boundless experience direct and rule. Among them, in reality only a dozen outstanding heads do the leading and an elite of the working class is invited from time to time to meetings where they are to applaud the speeches of the leaders, and to approve proposed resolutions unanimously . . .

Rosa Luxemburg, *The Russian Revolution* (1918)

Lenin's disgust with many socialist leaders in Europe for supporting the First World War effort led him to criticize their attachment to the institutions of parliamentary democracy. From this time he strongly insisted on a distinction between 'bourgeois' (i.e. representative or parliamentary) democracy, and 'proletarian' democracy (i.e. soviets, workers' councils, or similar bodies, with delegates subject to direct recall, and based on the workplace and its environs). He made the case for 'proletarian democracy' in his classic work *The State and Revolution.*

In later writings, such as *The Proletarian Revolution and the Renegade Kautsky* and *'Left Wing' Communism – An Infantile Disorder*, Lenin clarified his position further, criticizing not only the 'parliamentarian' wing of the socialist movement but also the 'ultra-Left' which opposed all involvement in parliamentary elections, which Communists should contest, he believed, for tactical and propaganda reasons. Upon the foundation of the Russian-dominated Communist International (Comintern) in 1919, Lenin's ideas were of the highest influence. His positions were elaborated and codified in Comintern documents. The Communist (or Third) International, centrally organized on lines of strict discipline and with an insurrectionary policy, superseded the 'bankrupt' Second (Socialist) International, with its parliamentarism and compliance with imperialism.

From 1917 Trotsky was a close ally and collaborator of Lenin. In fact the Bolshevik Revolution of October 1917 was often referred to as the 'revolution of Lenin and Trotsky', both in Russia and the West. After Lenin's death in 1924, however, Stalin rose to power, and Trotsky was eventually exiled. Up to his assassination in 1940, Trotsky claimed, with considerable justification, that he, in contrast to Stalin, was acting within the Leninist tradition. He maintained that the first four congresses of the Communist International had left 'an invaluable programmatic heritage' including topics such as the 'relation between democracy and proletarian dictatorship' and the 'relation to parliamentarism'.[1] In evaluating Leninism from 1917 to the beginning of Lenin's final, fatal illness in early 1923, we also judge a major and essential part of the Trotskyist heritage.

One of the most concise and clear expressions of the Leninist and Trotskyist position on parliamentary democracy is in the 'Theses on the Communist Parties and Parliamentarism', drafted by Bukharin, and accepted by the majority at the second congress of the Communist International in August 1920. Similar arguments and statements can be found in plenty elsewhere in the writings of Lenin and Trotsky. The preamble to the theses, written by Trotsky himself, asserted:

> At present, parliament, for communists, can in no way become the arena for the struggle for reforms, for the amelioration of the position of the working class ... The centre of gravity of political life has at present been removed finally and completely beyond the bounds of parliament ... it is the historical task of the working class to wrest this apparatus from the hands of the ruling class, to smash it, to destroy it, and to replace it with new proletarian organs of power. At the same time, however, the revolutionary general staff of the class has a strong interest in having its scouts in the parliamentary institutions of the bourgeoisie to make this task of destruction easier.[2]

Thus Communists and Leninists stand for election and, if successful, enter parliament only to destroy it. The first six theses are here quoted in full:

> 1. Parliamentarism as a state system has become a 'democratic' form of the rule of the bourgeoisie, which at a certain stage of development requires the fiction of popular representation which outwardly appears to be an organization of a 'popular will' that stands outside the classes, but in essence is a machine for oppression and subjugation in the hands of ruling capital.
> 2. Parliament is a definite form of *state* order; therefore it cannot at all be the form of a communist society, which knows neither classes nor class struggle nor any state power.

3. Nor can parliamentarism be a form of proletarian state administration in the period of transition from the dictatorship of the bourgeoisie to the dictatorship of the proletariat. In the moment of sharpened class struggle, in the civil war, the proletariat must inevitably build up its state organization as a *fighting organization*, into which the representatives of the previous ruling classes are not permitted. In this stage any fiction of the 'popular will' is directly harmful to the working class. The proletariat does not need any parliamentary sharing of power, it is harmful to it. The form of the proletarian dictatorship is the soviet republic.
4. The bourgeois parliaments, one of the most important apparatuses of the bourgeois state machine, cannot as such in the long run be taken over, just as the proletariat cannot win the bourgeois state. The task of the proletariat consists in breaking up the bourgeois state machine, destroying it, and with it the parliamentary institutions, be they republican or a constitutional monarchy.
5. It is no different with the local government institutions of the bourgeoisie, which it is theoretically incorrect to counterpose to the state organs. In reality they are similar apparatuses of the state machine of the bourgeoisie, which must be destroyed by the revolutionary proletariat and replaced by local soviets of workers' deputies.
6. Consequently communism denies parliamentarism as a form of the society of the future. It denies it as a form of the class dictatorship of the proletariat. It denies the possibility of taking over parliament in the long run; it sets itself the aim of destroying parliamentarism. Therefore there can only be a question of utilizing the bourgeois state institutions for the purpose of their destruction. The question can be posed in this, and only in this, way.'[3]

The insurrectionary nature of this strategy is clarified in subsequent theses, which also insist that Communist Parties must participate in parliament and elections simply to use them as rostra for propaganda, and to facilitate their destruction:

9. The most important method of struggle against the bourgeoisie, i.e. against its state power, is above all mass action. Mass actions are organized and led by the revolutionary mass organizations (trade unions, parties, soviets) of the proletariat under the general leadership of a unified, disciplined, centralized Communist Party . . .
10. The mass struggle is a whole system of developing actions sharpening in their form and logically leading to the insurrection against the capitalist state. In this mass struggle, which develops into civil war, the leading party of the proletariat must as a rule consolidate all its legal positions by making them into auxiliary bases of its revolutionary activity and subordinating these positions to the plan of the main campaign, the campaign of the mass struggle.
11. The rostrum of the bourgeois parliament is such an auxiliary base. The argument that parliament is a bourgeois state institution cannot at all be used against participation in the parliamentary struggle. The Communist Party does not enter into these institutions in order to carry out organic work there, but in

order to help the masses from inside parliament to break up the state machine and parliament itself through action ...
12. This activity in parliament, which consists mainly in revolutionary agitation from the parliamentary rostrum ... should be totally and completely subordinated to the aims and tasks of the mass struggle outside parliament ...
14. Election campaigns should not be carried out in the spirit of the hunt for the maximum number of parliamentary seats, but in the spirit of the revolutionary mobilization of the masses for the slogans of the proletarian revolution.[4]

It is important to point out that modern Communist Parties, even when they misleadingly claim adherence to 'Leninism', have explicitly contradicted the above positions in their programmatic statements. As early as the 1930s the Communist Parties had moved closer to the old ideas of pre-First-World-War Social Democracy than to the canons of Leninism.[5] The explicit acceptance of parliamentary authority, and the abandonment of a strategy to 'smash' parliaments and the state machine and to create the 'dictatorship of the proletariat', was much publicized in the 'Eurocommunist' turn of the 1970s.[6] But all these moves were prefigured in the 'Popular Front' strategy of the 1930s. Orthodox Communism has abandoned Leninism and is now indistinguishable from the 'Social Democracy' which it vilified from 1914 to the early 1930s, and whose 'bankruptcy' was one of the main reasons for the split in the international socialist movement and the formation of the Communist International. In contrast, the Trotskyist movement remains within the Leninist tradition, and has never disclaimed the positions of the first four congresses of the Communist International.

'Bourgeois' and 'Proletarian' Democracy

As we have seen, the Leninist rebuttal of parliament depends on an alleged distinction between 'bourgeois' (or capitalist) and 'proletarian' (or socialist) democracy. It is assumed that every socio-economic system has a single, dominant, ruling class, and each system is associated with a distinct type of democracy, its class character thus defined. However, this sharp division between 'proletarian' and 'bourgeois' democracy, and their one-to-one relationship with certain types of economic system, is misleading, historically inaccurate, and politically unsatisfactory.

First, let us consider so-called 'bourgeois' democracy, i.e. parliamentary democracy. This does not exist in all capitalist countries, and furthermore parliaments have existed in quite different social systems – in feudal medieval England and absolutist Tsarist Russia, as well as in modern

Western capitalism. There is no distinct feature of parliamentary democracy which links it with capitalism *per se*. It is a form (or set of forms) of government, not a system of productive or property relations. There are good historical reasons why the rise of modern parliamentary democracy has been connected with the expansion and triumph of capitalism, but it would be wrong to see their association as inevitable. As Barrington Moore has remarked in an influential book on this subject, 'Though a great deal of the impetus [towards parliamentary democracy] has come from trading and manufacturing classes in the cities, that is far from the whole story.'[7]

To make the same point with reference to the future, consider a possible parliamentary democracy within a socialist society. Does the mere existence of a parliament mean that the power and wealth of the capitalist class is restored, and class divisions appear anew? Of course not. As long as a wide participatory democracy is in existence, with full democratic rights and freedoms, and all military threats to the socialist regime are removed or neutralized, there is no reason to assume that the existence of a parliament would lead to an increase in the power of the capitalists (unless, of course, the regime had the support of a minority of the population only, in which case, according to Marx and further arguments in this book, it would not be a socialist regime). It would be wrong to tar all parliaments with the capitalist brush.

Neither Lenin nor Trotsky gave an adequate reason why parliaments should be abolished in all countries, in the process of building socialism. It is likely that their attitude was coloured by the grossly inadequate and largely corrupt nature of most assemblies before the Second World War. In a survey of the development of parliamentary democracy, Göran Therborn has shown the limitations of this view. If full political democracy is defined to exclude all racial, sexual, or class disqualifications, then its emergence is very recent: it was instituted in Britain in 1928 (when women, for the first time, had the vote on the same basis as men), in Germany in 1919 (later to be abolished by the Nazis and reintroduced in West Germany after the Second World War), in France and Italy in 1946, and in the United States as late as the 1960s (when blacks in the South were effectively allowed to vote).[8] On the whole, full parliamentary democracy, on the basis of an equal and non-exclusive adult suffrage, is a post-Second-World-War phenomenon which Lenin and Trotsky did not live to see; it is possible that their view would have been revised if they had witnessed the structural changes which have occurred in the West since 1940. In any case, the vast difference between, say, parliamentary democracy under the Kaiser in Germany before 1918, and parliamentary democracy in Western Europe after the Second World War, should not be belittled or ignored.

In addition it is important to emphasize that the working class played a very important role in the reform and development of 'bourgeois' democracy. Working-class agitation for parliamentary reform was brutally dealt with in the Peterloo Massacre in Manchester in 1819, it played an important part in the campaign for the Reform Bill of 1832, it was the backbone of Chartism in the 1830s and 1840s, and it re-emerged in the struggles for reform in the 1860s. Later, working-class women played a very important role in the Suffragette movement.[9] Conversely, the capitalist class has not been always the greatest friend of parliamentary democracy: examples of big-business support for dictatorships abound, from funding the Nazis in the 1930s to helping overthrow the elected government of Salvador Allende in Chile in 1973.[10] A great number of parliamentary reforms have been supported by the working class, and the most influential sectors of capitalism have often acted in intentional opposition to democracy.

Let us now scrutinize the concept of 'proletarian democracy'. Lenin and Trotsky repeatedly made the claim that it was far superior to the 'façade' of bourgeois democracy. In so far as it involves an extension of democracy to the workplace and to the planning institutions it is a very positive step. Indeed the limitations of a system which is confined to the election of parliamentary representatives every four or five years should be stressed rather than ignored. The introduction of democracy into the workplace and into control of the economic system is very important, and the issue is often belittled or ignored by parliamentarists. But is this reform in opposition to parliamentary democracy, or is it rather an important supplement to it? According to Lenin and Trotsky it is, most emphatically, the former: in their view parliament must be abolished in favour of workers' councils or soviets.

In response, it is necessary to point out the limitations of a non-parliamentary system. First, and most obviously, elections on a soviet or workers' council basis will, deliberately, exclude those of independent income not living or working in the area. Although we may have no sympathy with capitalists, it has to be recognized that the denial of their right to vote is a retreat from the principle of universal adult suffrage, a positive rallying cry for over 150 years whose value or significance it would be wrong to underestimate. In practical terms, granting the vote to capitalists would make little difference, as they constitute less than five per cent of the adult population in most advanced capitalist countries. Moreover under a soviet system it would be difficult to operate universal suffrage on a satisfactory basis, with rights to a secret ballot etc., and its lack, even if there is workers' control at the point of production, would be an important rallying point for a broad range of opponents to the socialist regime. The best way of keeping universal suffrage would be to retain a parliament.

Second, if democratic institutions are organized solely in relation to the workplace, it will be the workers that will dominate discussion and voting. Even if the unemployed, the self-employed, and the housebound (usually women) in the local community are fully enfranchised and given the right to attend meetings, it would be difficult for them to balance the employed workers on a *per capita* basis: they would be discriminated against, not by decree, but by unintended sociological and cultural mechanisms of exclusion. The non-employed would be acting on less familiar ground. This is an argument not against workers' councils, but in favour of additional and sovereign democratic institutions in no immediate relation to the workplace, organized on the basis of universal suffrage: namely a system of national and regional parliaments and local councils. To all these, Leninism is hostile.

Third, experience with the soviets in Russia in the 1917–20 period shows that they can be subject to manipulation and abuse by a small minority, especially when politics is dominated by a single party. Rosa Luxemburg perceived this at a very early stage. Of course, parliaments too can be corrupt, and this cannot be avoided without a wide cultural commitment to democracy. However, as C. B. Macpherson[11] and others have pointed out, one important means of combating both apathy and corruption is to retain an electoral system with competing political parties. There are similar reasons for retaining a national parliament, free elections, and universal suffrage. Parliament, far from being the antithesis of workers' councils or soviets, would help them breathe a full democratic life.

Fourth, the institutional weight of parliament should not be underestimated. Parliament has a capacity to mould opinion and to promote or resist social change. It forms part of the process of legitimation.[12] In normal circumstances under capitalism this acts to preserve private ownership of the means of production and inequality of wealth and power; the democratic system gives the stamp of approval to the *status quo*. If, however, a government is elected that is committed to a new socialist order, it is radical ideas that become legitimated.

The institutional weight of parliament derives from the hundreds of years of history and struggle in which it has played an important role. Working-class movements, such as Chartism, have looked to it for change and campaigned for its reform. It appears to people as the legitimate arena for resolving conflict and making fundamental decisions. Thus any movement for radical change has to win a majority in parliament in order to achieve support in the country as a whole. This does not mean that a parliamentary majority is *sufficient* to bring about radical change: also indispensable are extra-parliamentary activities, such as demonstrations and campaigns, and localized institutions of popular power. Leninists present a false antithesis between activity inside and outside parliament, belittling the former. What is in fact required is both.

Parliament retains its legitimating role even in periods of political stability. Social democratic and Left ideas become more acceptable when parties of those colours gain office. In Britain since the Second World War there have been three mildly radical Labour governments. In office, each has maintained most of its electoral support: defeat has been due to the nature of the electoral system rather than to a major collapse of allegiance. Similarly, each time the Conservative Party has come to power, conservative ideas have found a new lease of life, and the Labour Party has lost a sizeable portion of its electoral support.[13] The mere existence of a government with some degree of radical commitment helps to legitimate support for radical policies, and to undermine the dominant conservative culture. The legitimation process is capable of being used to much greater effect by a more radical and socialist government in the future.

Fifth, the abolition of parliament by a socialist government would help to strengthen its opposition. The dissolution of parliament, with its history and traditions, would provide a very effective rallying-cry for anti-socialist forces: reactionary interests would mobilize a large section of the population, and claim the stamp of legitimacy for their anti-socialist actions. The rebuttal of parliament would push the democratic and liberal elements in the population towards the Right, and might provoke a militarist reaction. The gaining of a parliamentary majority does not ensure, of course, that a military coup against a socialist government will not happen; but there is no doubt that such a coup would be assisted by the destruction of parliament.

For these and other reasons it is necessary for a socialist movement to (1) gain a majority in parliament and form a socialist government through the ballot box, (2) keep parliament as a legislative institution and as an agency of legitimation, and (3) retain power as a socialist government only if the government is re-elected through the legitimate process. If a socialist government fails to win elections it should not attempt to hold on to power.

Social democratic and reformist parties have concentrated on trying to bring about change through legislation in parliament alone. Leninists have rejected reformism and proposed insurrection. Neither strategy has worked in any advanced capitalist country. Both should be rejected. What is required is an alternative based on a combination of extra-parliamentary and parliamentary action, recognizing the sovereignty of parliament and accepting the intrinsic value of democracy.

Smashing the State

In the Leninist view there are two types of state machine, 'bourgeois' and 'proletarian', which are mutually antagonistic. Parliaments are the democratic organs of the former, soviets of the latter. One has to be replaced by the other. However, once it is accepted that there is no Chinese Wall between 'bourgeois' and 'proletarian' democracy the Leninist idea of 'smashing' the entire 'bourgeois state' becomes unacceptable. There is bound to be a conflict between different types of institution, but not necessarily an irreconcilable contradiction. If parliament is necessary to legitimate and assist mass democratic institutions such as workers' councils, an element of mutual reinforcement must exist. Far more important become struggles for domination towards progressive ends within the organizations themselves, *combined* with extra-parliamentary action and efforts to create a wider democracy with additional grassroots institutions of power.

Leninism tends to play down conflicts and contradictions within the state machine and to urge a simplistic 'all-or-nothing' view. In reality, things are much more complex. (This is to be discussed further in Appendix B.) The state comprises many different levels, with potential or actual conflict within each, and its different agencies carry out diverse and sometimes discordant functions. In contrast to the idea that the entire 'bourgeois state' should be destroyed, certain elements and agencies within it can be used by socialists as part of a general strategy of radical change.

It should be emphasized that this alternative strategy is not secretive or conspiratorial. The use of elements of the state apparatus for radical and socialist ends is most likely to be effective when it is backed up by extra-parliamentary action. Such outside pressure can often be much more powerful than a thousand arguments in a top committee. But representation on that committee can give a popular movement vital assistance at critical times.

It may be necessary to dismantle some potentially repressive agencies, such as the police or the army, if they threaten a democratic movement for radical change. In most advanced capitalist countries there has been a disturbing growth of 'counter-insurgency' training, with files kept on members of the peace and socialist movements, all of which could be directed against the Left if its policies gained majority support. Such a threat should be pre-empted by a major restructuring of the police and armed forces, to place them under democratic surveillance and control.[14]

Even in the case of the police and the army, however, the language of 'smashing the state' is not appropriate. It implies a direct physical confrontation. A more viable strategy would be to campaign for powerful watch committees to oversee these bodies, and to push for legislation through parliament and local government institutions. The next stage would be to ensure that the police were accountable to the community, the army were accountable to the population as a whole, and they both served the interests of the majority of the people. Once again this would involve exploiting contradictions, or differences of view, within the police and army, rather than holding a Leninist posture of full confrontation.

The rather simplistic attitude to the state within Leninist theory is conditioned, in part, by the circumstances in Russia up to and during the Revolution. The soviets emerged in Russia in a clamour for constitutional reform, and with the initial impetus of Tsarist legitimation. However, the Tsarist state was a brittle autocracy which could neither accommodate nor defuse this movement for democratic change. As mass struggle intensified, popular organs of power were thrown up and quickly forced into confrontation with the state. Even the Tsarist Duma (or parliament), which had very limited powers, was occasionally propelled to challenge the autocracy. The soviets of 1905, after a period of pressuring for reform of the existing state, were rapidly forced into insurrection. In an autocracy, such immediate conflict between democratic institutions and the repressive state is likely to occur in times of crisis. In Russia the liberal-minded intelligentsia and middle class were faced with the alternatives of mass insurrection on the one hand, and continued support for the autocracy on the other. Few other choices were viable. The 'middle ground' therefore was broken up and society became politically polarized into 'dual power': a period of coexistence between soviets and – until its overthrow – what remained of the old state. This concept of dual power is very important in Leninist and Trotskyist strategy. What is not realized, however, is that its emergence in Russia in 1917 was a result of unique circumstances: it is no accident that these circumstances have not been repeated, and indeed they are never likely to be.

It is useful to compare Leninist theory with Leninist practice on the question of state bureaucracy. According to Lenin, the bureaucracy, like the entire capitalist state, should be dismantled or smashed. After the Bolshevik Revolution of 1917, however, he and his followers faced an acute shortage of skilled and trained personnel to staff the administrative apparatus of the state and were forced, reluctantly, to offer jobs to former Tsarist officials. It could be argued that such a problem would not arise in a revolution in an advanced capitalist country: with a working class with a much higher level of general education the workers themselves would be able to staff the administration. However, this ignores the fact that structures and processes have become much more complex under advanced capitalism, and higher levels of education do not mean, necessarily, that there are sufficient workers immediately able to carry out administrative and other tasks. Furthermore, the state bureaucracy has grown to such a size that it, itself, employs many thousands of workers, who are unionized, and not part of the administrative elite. In these circumstances talk of radical reform of the state apparatus is relevant, but arguments for the dismantling of the entire bureaucracy are misconceived. The language of Leninism is inappropriate.

In his classic work *The State and Revolution*, Lenin claimed that his ideas on the state flowed directly from Marx. However, Marx's words are not precise or unambiguous, although he does seem to come close to Lenin in a letter written on 12 April 1871 to his friend Ludwig Kugelmann at the time of the Paris Commune:

> If you look up the last chapter of my *Eighteenth Brumaire*, you will find that I declare that the next attempt of the French Revolution will be no longer, as before, to transfer the bureaucratic-military machine from one hand to another, but to *smash* it, and this is the precondition for every real people's revolution on the Continent.[15]

This famous passage can be used by Leninists and Trotskyists to claim a Marxian pedigree for their ideas. However, first, it is an isolated and quite exceptional statement, written at a time when Marx was clearly full of enthusiasm for the Paris Communards. Second, it can be interpreted as a specific reference to the type of state machine that existed in France and other parts of the Continent at the time, and there is no suggestion that it applied to all possible types of state under capitalism, even those with an extended bureaucracy and a standing army.

Leninists often quote another passage from Marx and Engels: 'One thing especially was proved by the Commune, viz., that "the working class cannot simply lay hold of the ready-made state machinery, and wield it for its own purposes".'[16] Yet here it depends very much on exactly what is meant by words like 'simply' and 'lay hold of'. It is easy to conceive of an interpretation of the passage that would be acceptable to the most reformist and gradualist Fabian social democrat. In the same year that Marx and Engels wrote it, a year after the Paris Commune and the letter to Kugelmann, Marx spoke in the following terms:

> The workers will have to seize political power one day in order to construct the new organization of labour; they will have to overthrow the old politics which bolster up the old institutions, unless they want to share the fate of the early Christians, who lost their chance of heaven on earth because they rejected and neglected such action. We do not claim, however, that the road leading to this goal is the same everywhere. We know that heed must be paid to the institutions, customs and traditions of the various countries, and we do not deny that there are countries, such as America and England, and if I was familiar with its institutions, I might include Holland, where the workers may attain their goal by peaceful means. That being the case, we must recognize that in most continental countries the lever of the revolution will have to be force; a resort to force will be necessary one day in order to set up the rule of labour.[17]

Remarkably, there is no actual inconsistency between these three statements from Marx (in one case, Marx and Engels). It is unfortunate, however, that Marx was not more clear as to why he considered a peaceful socialist transformation possible in Britain and America. Lenin thought that it was because of the absence of 'a militarist clique' and, 'to a considerable degree', a bureaucracy.[18] This was hardly true in 1872. Britain was a developed imperialist power, with both a strong 'military clique' and an expanding bureaucracy. America had just emerged from its Civil War, which not only left a large standing army but also aided centralizing forces in the state machine. Lenin's interpretation quite simply does not stand up to the facts. As a result, both the validity and the alleged universality of the Leninist principle of breaking up the entire state machine, and its origin in the words of Marx, are thrown into doubt. There is no unambiguous statement in the works either of Marx or of Engels which points to the need to destroy parliamentary institutions, 'bourgeois' or not.

Incidentally, the word 'commune', as in 'Paris Commune', derives not from the communist ideas of the insurgents of 1871, but from the established French, Italian and Spanish word for municipality. It was therefore an elected city council – albeit one forced into revolutionary actions – that Marx was supporting, in apparent contradiction to the thesis of the Second Congress of the Communist International which calls for the destruction of all existing local government institutions under capitalism, and their replacement by soviets. The Paris Commune was not based on the workplaces of the city, and it was not a soviet. Leninists and Trotskyists do not seem to be aware of this inconsistency in their support for the 1871 Commune and the position on municipal councils adopted by the Second Comintern Congress.

The 'Dictatorship of the Proletariat'

Pages and pages have been written in interpretation and debate of the phrase 'the dictatorship of the proletariat'. Had Marx not written in a letter to Joseph Weydemeyer in 1852 that 'the class struggle necessarily leads to the dictatorship of the proletariat'[19] much of this ink would have been spared. It has been suggested that Marx meant 'dictatorship' to be understood in the classical, i.e. Ancient Roman, sense of a brief period of dominance by a single group, not necessarily to the exclusion of all others.[20] In any case, it is very unfortunate that he used such a phrase (which in fact appears only about half a dozen times in his entire works and recorded speeches) without defining its precise meaning.

Whatever Marx may have meant by the 'dictatorship of the proletariat', Lenin gave the words a new twist. In a furious polemic with Karl Kautsky in 1918 he wrote: 'Dictatorship is rule based upon force and unrestricted by any laws. The revolutionary dictatorship of the proletariat is rule won and maintained by the use of violence by the proletariat against the bourgeoisie, rule that is unrestricted by any laws.'[21] Marx (who advocated universal suffrage and a democratic and peaceful transition to socialism when possible) is here interpreted by Lenin as opposed to the principle of the rule of law. For Lenin, proletarian might is right. The outcome of such a doctrine is to undermine rights and freedoms won and preserved in law in capitalist democracies, many of them through energetic political struggles by the working class itself.

Trotsky denied repeatedly that Stalin's excesses as a dictator had any root in Lenin's ideas. And, indeed, it is important to point out that in order to consolidate his power Stalin had to get rid of all of Lenin's colleagues on the Central Committee, and to purge thousands of others from the Party. Nevertheless, Lenin did believe that the dictatorship of the proletariat was compatible with the 'exercise of dictatorial powers by individuals', and that this dictatorship was to be 'unrestricted by any laws'. Without a framework of law, without checks and balances, without democracy, it is easier for a tyrant such as Stalin to rise to power. Within Leninism, despite its 'good intentions', the seeds of Stalinism are nurtured.

Supporters hasten to explain, backing their argument with plentiful quotations, that by 'dictatorship' Lenin and Trotsky really meant 'democracy': 'The dictatorship of the proletariat, the period of transition to communism, will for the first time create democracy for the people, for the majority, along with the necessary suppression of the exploiters, of the minority.'[22] However, the historical experience of Stalin's rule, which was responsible for the deaths of millions of workers and peasants in the 1930s, has extinguished all popular belief in the 'democracy' of 'proletarian dictatorship'. In addition, to assert that 'the dictatorship of the proletariat' really means democracy for the majority flies in the face of the accepted meaning of the word. The phraseology of Marxism–Leninism has become a liability for the socialist movement. For this and many other reasons the advocacy of *any* form of dictatorship should be dropped.

A rejection of the term 'dictatorship of the proletariat' by no means implies that an elected socialist government has no right to defend itself from the use of force by an internal minority or an external power. But we do not need the term 'dictatorship' to stress the point. Everyone is aware that even democratic regimes have employed force to resist the rebellion of a minority or a foreign invasion of their home soil. The same principle would apply to a socialist democracy.

On the question of democracy, Leninism is not without its strong points. In *The State and Revolution* we find a passionate argument for an extension of popular power, for the abolition of hierarchy and elitism, and for the construction of a full participatory democracy in which ordinary people have much more say in running their own lives. Trotsky provided an eloquent critique of Stalin's dictatorship and a continuing appeal for workers' control of the process of production, in both the Soviet Union and the West. However, somewhere along the line it all goes dreadfully wrong. Just as we cannot blame Christ for the tortures and executions of the Spanish Inquisition, neither Marx nor Engels nor Lenin nor Trotsky can be blamed for Stalin's purges or Pol Pot's brutal holocaust in Kampuchea in the 1970s. But some of the words and phrases of 'Marxism–Leninism' can provide a rationalization for tyranny, or an excuse for the abolition of democracy. A Christ who preached non-violence cannot be quoted in support of the racking, burning or mutilation of human beings; but a Lenin who wrote of unrestricted force, or personal dictatorship, and of the undesirability of 'bourgeois democracy', is liable to quotation by tyrants, torturers and executioners against his better will. The three most horrific and murderous regimes to emerge in this century are Stalin's Russia, Hitler's Germany, and Pol Pot's Kampuchea. In each case, a million or more people were liquidated. Two out of the three were 'Marxist–Leninist' in name.

Leninism with a Human Face?

But words, of course, are not all. Many modern Leninists would say that conditions in 1917–21 were quite different from those obtaining in capitalist democracies today, and that the statements of Lenin and the Comintern of that time should not be taken out of context and applied to present circumstances. Many contemporary Leninists or Trotskyists would claim to be 'undogmatic' and suggest that the writings of their mentors should not be applied word for word. (At the same time, however, they fail to distinguish between the tenets which are still applicable, in their view, and those which are not. Furthermore, I have heard few modern Trotskyists reject the programmatic statements of the Second Congress of the Communist International, or disown Lenin's polemic with Kautsky.) In some quarters, an image of a humane, undogmatic and democratic Leninism still survives.

It is impossible to evaluate a political creed which is 'undogmatic' to the point of vagueness. If it is a simple matter of hero worship of Lenin or Trotsky, little more can be said. In most cases, however, something else is involved, namely an idea of what is possible and desirable under socialism. In this vision, socialism concentrates ownership of the means of production in the hands of the state. Planning is carried out, avowedly on the basis of satisfying human need, by a central authority, under the control of a hierarchy of soviet-type organizations. It is hoped that the state will 'wither away', but in the meantime there is a concentration of ownership and planning in its hands.

Leninists with a human face argue that in the Eastern Bloc countries today there is a travesty of the democratic socialism envisaged by Marx and Lenin. It is necessary to infuse these systems with democracy: to reconstitute civil liberties, to open up debate and dialogue, and to ensure genuine democratic workers' control of production and planning. The 'good intentions' behind this argument are beyond doubt. But one important possibility is neglected. Could there be a causal connection between the centralization of ownership and planning on the one hand, and the absence of democracy on the other? Could the stillbirth of genuine socialist democracy be a result, in part, of concentrating the weight of economic power in the hands of the state? Unfortunately, these questions have been posed most often by critics, rather than supporters, of any form of socialism. This is hardly a satisfactory state of affairs. To preserve an intellectual vitality the Left should come to terms with eloquent statements such as these:

> It is widely believed that politics and economics are separate and largely unconnected; that individual freedom is a political problem and material welfare an economic problem; and that any kind of political arrangements can be combined with any kind of economic arrangements. The chief contemporary manifestation of this idea is the advocacy of 'democratic socialism' by many who condemn out of hand the restrictions on individual freedom imposed by 'totalitarian socialism' in Russia, and who are persuaded that it is possible for a country to adopt the essential features of Russian economic arrangements and yet to ensure individual freedom through political arrangements ... such a view is a delusion ... there is an intimate connection between economics and politics ... only certain combinations of political and economic arrangements are possible.[23]

I know of few superior or more forceful statements of the integrated approach that has come to be known as political economy. Its author was Milton Friedman. Much of Friedman's economics is defective, and his political standpoint is a naive and untenable individualism. However, in his contention that there is an 'intimate connection' between economic systems and political structures he is absolutely right. Unfortunately, and characteristically, he then jumps to the conclusion that the best way of preserving freedom is in a capitalist market economy:

> The fundamental threat to freedom is power to coerce, be it in the hands of a monarch, a dictator, an oligarchy, or a momentary majority. The preservation of freedom requires the elimination of such concentration of power to the fullest possible extent and the dispersal and distribution of whatever power cannot be eliminated – a system of checks and balances. By removing the organization of economic activity from the control of political authority, the market eliminates this source of coercive power. It enables economic strength to be a check to political power rather than a reinforcement.[24]

The terms of this conclusion cannot be accepted. Market systems are notorious for concentrations of monopoly and bureaucratic power, and they did not prevent the rise of fascism in Italy and Germany in the inter-war period and in Latin America today. It is important, however, not to throw out the baby with the bathwater. There is a *prima facie* case for supposing a connection between the political totalitarianism of the Soviet Union under Stalin and the concentration of economic power in the hands of the state. For instance, the supporters of the Solidarity trade union movement in Poland in 1980–81 were fans neither of Friedman nor of Stalin, yet they accepted the view that economic ownership should be decentralized in certain industries, with cooperatives, municipal enterprise, and a limited market mechanism, as well as nationalized industry and central planning. This proposal was motivated, in part, by a desire to create the conditions for the development of democracy in that country.

Surely it is in the spirit of Marxism, and not against it, to suggest such a relationship between political and economic structures?

The Leninist sidesteps the issue by resorting to a type of theoretical reductionism. A connection is asserted between economics and politics, but in the following manner. Socialism is identified with nationalization of the means of production, which by definition is a proletarian dictatorship, which by definition is a socialist democracy ('in the interests of the majority'). On the other hand, capitalism is identified with private ownership of the means of production, the 'dictatorship of the bourgeoisie' and 'capitalist democracy'. There are one-to-one relationships between forms of property within the economy, the configuration of power between sociological classes, and the nature of the political system. In effect, the 'political' and 'sociological' factors can be collapsed into the economic: just determine the type of economic system and all the rest follows. Alternatively, and less frequently, the 'economic' and 'political' factors are collapsed into the 'sociological'.[25] Leninism does not embrace an adequate notion of the relationship between the 'economic', the 'sociological' and the 'political'. All three are reduced to one, and there is little appreciation that a social system cannot be properly evaluated by isolating one factor, such as the presence of private ownership or nationalized property: it has to be diagnosed as a whole, seeing each of its parts (markets, political institutions, elites, etc.) in relationship with each other.

In this holistic-systems approach Marx is both a help and a hindrance. It was Marx who perceived that the social system had to be analysed as a whole, who developed a unified social science, and promoted the key concept of a 'mode of production'.[26] However, to some extent his view of history was determinist; he saw the victory of the proletariat as an 'inevitable' result of thousands of years of advancing class struggle. Consequently, he was extremely vague as to the nature of a future socialist system: it was reduced, descriptively, to the ascendancy of the proletariat and the abolition of private ownership of the means of production. This combination of determinism with a type of class-reductionism enables Marx to dismiss all discussion of the precise nature of socialism as 'utopian'. As to the nature of the public ownership involved, the role of cooperatives, the existence or non-existence of a market, and the structure of political institutions, he is unclear. If Leninism contains some of the seeds of Stalinism, so too can some of the seeds of Leninism be found in the Marxism of Marx.

In conclusion, both the analysis and the strategy of Leninism are defective. The condemnation of parliamentary democracy as 'bourgeois' and largely a 'façade' does not stand up to critical scrutiny. There is no

Chinese Wall between different forms of democracy. As well as helping to build democratic institutions outside parliament, a socialist movement cannot afford to ignore parliament itself, and the will of the electorate must be respected. Lenin had an over-simplified view of the state, ignoring its inner contradictions, and he argued that it should be 'smashed'. Such a strategy cannot work, as experience after 1917 indicates. It is more fruitful to treat the state as a set of institutions in potential conflict with each other. These conflicts can be exploited by either Left or Right.

Many Leninists wish to dissociate themselves from some of Lenin's more extreme statements, or to regard them as inapplicable to current circumstances. This manoeuvre cannot save the movement's soul. In their enthusiasm for centralized planning, the Leninists overlook the consequences of such a dangerous concentration of economic power. Without economic and political pluralism the 'dictatorship of the proletariat' is very likely to evolve into a true dictatorship of a party, a group, or a single individual. Ironically, Lenin foresaw such a possibility, but he did not condemn it outright. A seed of totalitarianism is found in Lenin's recommendation in *The State and Revolution* that the socialist economy should be organized as 'a *single* country-wide state "syndicate"'. This in turn reflects the words of Marx and Engels in the *Manifesto of the Communist Party*, looking forward to the day when 'production has been concentrated in the hands of a vast association of the whole nation'. Neither Marxists nor Leninists can justifiably wash their hands of their twentieth-century legacy.

Part Two

GENERAL THEORY

Six

Capitalism and Markets

If human life is to be regarded as a commodity, we are forced to admit slavery.

Eugène Buret, *De la misère des classes laborieuses en Angleterre et en France* (1840)

On grounds both of efficiency and of human freedom we are told by the New Right that the market is a superior mechanism of economic allocation. There is a plethora of words and voices urging the extension of the market to every sphere of human life. It would seem that everything is to be, or should be, privatized, from health services to refuse collection. Competition and market forces will then rule.

But is it practical or even logical to extend market relations to all fields of activity in a capitalist country? Is a hundred-per-cent market system possible? If it is not, then there are limits to New Right thinking, and in a sense to capitalism itself. In particular, if the state is necessary for capitalist development, the thrust of New Right doctrine is arrested. It is the aim of this chapter to examine these questions, and to develop a holistic-systems approach at the same time.

Despite some important criticisms of the work of Marx that will be raised later, his analysis of economic systems, especially in *Capital*, remains invaluable. No other economist has developed such an illuminating account of the nature of the capitalist system and its internal relations.

Labour-Power

Labour is the human creative force within production. The term labour-power refers to the capacity, or potential, for work. Every fit and able human being possesses labour-power in some quality or form. By definition, capitalism is a system in which labour-power is a commodity. In other words, it is a characteristic of the capitalist system that labour-power is hired by a worker to an employer. For the majority of the population, such an arrangement provides their main source of income.

A striking and ineradicable feature of the capitalist system is that labour-power is not itself produced under capitalist conditions. By the production of labour-power we mean the production of fit and suitably trained persons. Now this takes place as we are reared as children and later educated and trained. The maintenance of fit and able persons is also considered part of the production of labour-power. Thus we also include household services, such as the provision of food and rest, and medical care. At first sight it would seem that all this is integrated into the capitalist system, and thus labour-power is a product of capitalism just like any other commodity. In what sense can it be asserted that labour-power is not produced under capitalist conditions?

It is necessary to be precise about terms. Strictly speaking, production under capitalist conditions involves production within a capitalist firm. Such a firm has two essential features. First, a product is owned by the firm during its production and up to the point where it is sold on the market (for profit). Second, the workers are under the authority of the capitalists and their managers.[1] It is the first feature that concerns us here.

The institutions in which labour-power is produced do not own the labour-power. A family does not own its children, a school does not own its pupils, and a hospital does not own its patients. Neither do these institutions sell the persons concerned: this would mean that they were deprived of their rights as 'free' citizens. Such a system would no longer be capitalism: it would be a form of slavery.

Labour-power is, of course, hired out to an employer. But it is not sold. Its ownership always remains with the worker – which is not the case with slaves or with the commodities produced by a capitalist firm. A family may send its children down the mines or into the mills to work under the most punitive and degrading conditions, but these children are not owned by their parents or masters: they are not slaves. Although this point is of little consolation to the children involved, and does not involve a judgement of their being better or worse off than slaves, the technical distinction is of importance.

The household or family may depend on the capitalist system for its income, for many articles of consumption, and for vital services. But the family itself is not run on capitalist lines. The majority of households do not employ servants: most of the work is not done through an employment relationship. Even where there are servants, the object is not to emulate the capitalist firm: the household is not in business to produce commodities to be sold for profit. Any goods and services are generally consumed directly. The market does not intervene.

The modern family is moulded and dominated by capitalist society but it is not, in its innermost essence, capitalist. Once again, this does not imply that the family is either a desirable or an undesirable institution: any such normative conclusion should be based on an analysis of its present structure and role.[2] It should be pointed out that the family often is an authoritarian and sexist institution, but it remains to be seen if it is necessarily so.

Ironically, many of the politicians of the New Right appeal to the principles of 'family budgeting' in their attempts to run (or ruin) the national economy. It would be very interesting to see the whole economy run on family lines. This would involve production for (some notion of) need, and not for profit. It would involve the abandonment of the market as the internal mechanism for the distribution of goods and services. It would be no inconsistency for the New Right to argue, instead, that the family should be run on capitalist lines, including, perhaps, the trading of sex for money. It is significant that the ideas of the New Right are never brought to their logical conclusion.

Whether educational institutions are private or state-funded, their students are not sold on the market. Private schools or colleges may aim to make a profit, but, even if they are run on capitalist lines, they trade educational services, not people.

Another important aspect of education or training is carried on within the workplace, either formally through an apprenticeship, or informally through 'learning by doing'. Although this takes place within the capitalist firm, the firm does not end up owning the trained worker; if it did it would be a system of slavery.

The fact that the employer does not own labour-power creates problems for the system as a whole. From the point of view of the capitalist there are obvious advantages in having trained, rather than untrained, personnel. However, if an individual firm undertakes to train its workers – possibly at considerable expense – there is no guarantee that they will remain in its employment. This constitutes a disincentive for the individual company to train its personnel, despite the fact that such a course would be advantageous for the capitalist system as a whole.

Thus we may conclude that the production of labour-power is not, and cannot by definition be, carried out under capitalist conditions. This does not mean that the worker is not dominated by capitalist social relations. It does mean, however, that the market system cannot encompass all spheres of human life without degenerating into slavery, for to produce labour-power for profit is to produce slaves.

All this has important consequences for the dynamics of the capitalist system. Because people are not produced for sale or profit, the birth rate does not readily adjust to conditions on the labour market: an increase in the level of wages does not necessarily give rise to more babies. In contrast, if the price of a commodity like bread is relatively high (due to excess demand), bakeries will be encouraged to increase their production. Bread is sold by its producers; babies are not. Hence the market is not the principal means by which the supply of people and potential labour-power is adjusted. Even if wages fall and less people are inclined to work, the market cannot get rid of the 'surplus' unless, in Malthusian manner, it starves them to death. In reality, of course, the supply of labour will not readily fall off when wages fall, other than by possible part-time working and reductions of overtime. The possibility of a 'perverse' relationship between the supply of labour and its price, contrary to the laws of supply and demand, is recognized in orthodox economic theory. What is not recognized, however, is the possibility of a permanent mismatch between the size of the labour force and the actual demand for labour-power. This mismatch can take the form of an acute and enduring shortage of labour. We are more familiar with the alternative form of this mismatch: a surplus of labour and mass unemployment.

In one of his early books, Marx recognized that the market system does not automatically ensure that the supply and demand of labour are matched, owing to basic differences in their regulation. Thus permanent unemployment is possible under capitalism. Marx wrote:

> When political economy maintains that supply and demand always balance each other, it immediately forgets its own assertion that the supply of *people* (the theory of population) always exceeds the demand and that therefore the disproportion between supply and demand finds its most striking expression in what is the essential goal of production – the existence of man.[3]

The Capitalist Firm

We have demonstrated that the market mechanism, although it dominates the capitalist system, is not ubiquitous. This is true even for the heartland of production: the capitalist firm. Some time ago the economist R. H. Coase set out to answer a simple but important question: why should production be organized under the umbrella of the firm?[4] Why, for example, do not workers sell and buy raw materials and half-completed products at every stage of production amongst themselves? In other words, why does the market mechanism not appear within the firm itself? Coase notes that the firm is defined by its absence. Instead of the allocation of resources being decided by the market, there is coordinated *planning* under the direction of the management.

This striking feature of the capitalist system was noticed, of course, by Marx, long before Coase. Marx observed that a division of labour was present within every factory, 'but the workers do not bring about this division by exchanging their individual products'.[5] Marx did not attempt to explain this fact; Coase, however, points out that it would be cumbersome to organize production on the basis of repetitive contracts between individual workers, and that the 'transactions costs' would be excessive. But while his answer is valid, it is not complete. He highlights the cost of 'using the price mechanism' and of 'discovering what the relevant prices are'. But these costs emerge because of widespread uncertainty and imperfect knowledge within the uncoordinated market system. If a factory was organized on the basis of an internal market there would be chaos resulting from the fact that no-one would know the overall pattern of work and disposition of resources. The costs (in terms of time and resources) of obtaining limited information would be imposed on every individual.

Quite simply it is not practical to run a business on such a market basis, and it is rarely, if ever, attempted. The firm is a domain of planning (albeit not socialist planning) in a capitalist world and a testimony to the limits of market relations. As in the production of labour-power, markets cannot, on either practical or logical grounds, penetrate every institution that exists within capitalism. The market may dominate the system, but it does not completely penetrate the family or the firm.

Almost every introductory textbook on economics propounds a false dichotomy. Economic systems are organized on the basis either of 'planning' or 'command', or of a 'free market'. The author will then on the one hand overwhelm the reader with the defects of the former and the virtues of thc latter and adopt an 'extremist' position in favour of the market; or on the other exude 'moderation' and common sense and plump for a 'mixed economy' at the centre of the spectrum. Many socialists endorse this dichotomy, and prefer the 'extreme' solution of planning and centralized control. Our discussion of the firm shows that the dichotomy itself is specious and invalid. A capitalist system is of necessity a combination of market and non-market forms of regulation, including, within the firm, deliberate planning. The 'extreme' solution of complete market regulation is not possible; neither (it will be argued below) is the 'extreme' solution of completely centralized planning. But the 'mixed economy' as it is generally understood is not the answer either: in practical terms it means little else than support for the *status quo*. A mixture? Yes – but in very different proportions from the present one.

Under capitalism, production has been concentrated in fewer and fewer firms. The giant company grows apace, assumes multinational connections, and begins to dominate the entire world economy. The ideologists of 'perfect competition' have not succeeded in resisting this process. Anti-monopoly legislation in most advanced capitalist countries has had little effect in slowing down the rapid concentration of capital. In Britain, the largest fifty firms were responsible for 15 per cent of manufacturing net output in 1935, 25 per cent in 1958, and 32 per cent in 1968; the comparable figures for employment were 15 per cent, 21 per cent, and 29 per cent.[6] In the United States in 1955 the largest five hundred firms accounted for 40 per cent of all assets of the manufacturing and mining sectors; in 1970 they accounted for 70 per cent.[7] In the European Economic Community the largest 50 manufacturing companies accounted for 15 per cent of output in 1965, 20 per cent in 1970 and 25 per cent in 1976.[8] Similar patterns can be discerned in all advanced capitalist countries.[9] The result is that world capitalism is being increasingly dominated by large and multinational firms, each with its own empire of planning and non-market coordination. Between firms market competition is as real and fierce as ever,[10] but within them the market gives way to other forms of command and control.

In short, therefore, the very existence of the capitalist firm means the exclusion of market mechanisms from the direct organization of production. Production is *planned* by management, albeit under the pressure of market forces. The expansion of monopolies and multinationals increases the power of management and widens its planning domain. The role of the market and competition (especially international competition) is combined with a wider and more complex planning system within the workplace and the firm. Capitalism is inseparable from planning which – as history has shown – tends to grow with the expansion of a firm. The planning *versus* markets dichotomy, at least in its simple textbook form, is invalid.

Information, Markets and Grants

The economic models of the textbooks are based on a world of few commodities (usually two), in which each commodity is homogeneous and capable of complete description, and in which information is readily and easily available. In macroeconomics we are in a world of heroic aggregates: 'capital' and 'labour'. The mathematical analyses that follow are sufficient in volume or complexity to divert our attention from the essential lack of realism of the initial assumptions.

In fact, of course, the world is not like that. A great deal of the problems arising from basic activities such as production and consumption concern difficulties in assessing, interpreting and acquiring information. We do not know where to buy the cheapest shoes, or the quality and durability of the shoes that we decide to purchase. The manager of a firm is not only unsure that the product will sell, but whether supplies of raw materials will be delivered on time, or where to find a suitable replacement for an old machine that has broken down.

Knowledge and information are important in any economic system. With the complexity of technology and production in modern capitalism, however, their role is much more significant.[11] In the early 1960s it was estimated that about 29 per cent of the Gross National Product in the United States was devoted to the production and processing of information and knowledge.[12] Today the proportion is estimated to be much greater. Indeed, information technology appears to be one of the few dynamic industries in the current world recession.

Information is not gathered or provided without the expenditure of time and resources. Attempts have been made by economists to include knowledge in their theoretical models without the assumption that its processing or provision has zero cost. One approach is to treat information as a sort of commodity, with a price just like any other. However, this solution is far from satisfactory because it is in the nature of such an 'information commodity' that it is not known before it is purchased. In this it differs fundamentally from normal commodities.

Realizing that real-world knowledge cannot be modelled in a neo-classical general equilibrium framework, Hayek adopts a more sophisticated approach.[13] As in other writings of the so-called 'Austrian School', the economy is conceived as a *process* involving learning and the acquisition of knowledge. The Austrian School argue (convincingly) that it is impossible to centralize all knowledge in an institution such as a single planning authority. The 'Austrians' then go on to argue (unconvincingly) that *all* central planning leads to disaster and that the market system is the best mechanism for processing and transmitting knowledge. As so often in the Austrian School, an important theoretical insight is turned to the ends of a strident and unwarranted pro-market ideology.

The 'Austrian' argument is based on the assertion that the price mechanism is a sophisticated processor and transmitter of information. On reflection, however, it is clear that it is adept at communicating certain types of information only. For example, the prices on the stock exchange tell us a great deal about what the dealers expect of the future, but much less about the level of productivity on the shopfloor of the firms concerned. If the price of potatoes has risen, this does not immediately tell us why. Are they in short supply? Have they come under increased demand? Has the price of substitutes risen? Have potatoes improved in quality? The price mechanism is a complex coordinator but it is a very crude and limited transmitter of information.

The market is moreover inefficient as a distributor of knowledge. We have noted that knowledge and information have become increasingly important in the modern capitalist system. Can they be traded through the market? They can, but there are serious problems. The nature and content of information cannot be known to the potential purchaser before it is sold: thus it is impossible to make a 'rational' choice. If we knew what we were going to get, there would be no need to purchase.

Another remarkable feature of this sector of the economy is that what is supplied to the consumer is still available to the producer. The information we buy remains equally the property of the seller: the knowledge or understanding we receive is not lost by the educator. Information and knowledge are very unusual in that they are not readily and literally *exchanged* (for money, etc.) when purchased. They do not fit into the image of a 'normal' commodity which changes hands from seller to buyer as money passes in the opposite direction. Information and knowledge are strange commodities, unsuited to the traditional world of market trading.

The Austrian School are right to point out that sufficient knowledge cannot be pooled, processed and acted upon to plan an economy on a completely centralized basis. But that is no argument against the centralization of some knowledge. It is impossible for one person or institution to know everything, but it helps to know where certain types of knowledge can be obtained. It is essential for certain information to be centralized. Consider the telephone system. A single body is necessary to allocate telephone numbers and to publish them in the form of a directory. This body may be public or private. It sells its telephone directories or distributes them free of charge. Both capitalist and non-capitalist forms of organization are possible. The point, however, is that there is no place for market competition in the gathering and distribution of such information. There is no point in having more than one firm providing this particular service. It is what is known as a 'natural monopoly'.

It is naive to assume that the modern economy can be planned efficiently on a completely centralized basis: it is much too complex for this, and the volume of information required is far too great. Furthermore, no-one can know the importance or relevance of any particular piece of information unless it is considered with the whole. The centralization of information is not always efficient. However, it is at least as naive to assume that the market is a good transmitter: it is in fact a crude and unreliable instrument. In addition, on the grounds of efficiency much vital information *has* to be centralized and monopolized by a number of single institutions. A competitive market is ill suited to such a task.

While accepting many of the arguments of the Austrian School as to the importance of information and knowledge, we are led to quite different conclusions. As the economic system becomes more and more complex and dependent on the efficient transmission of information, the market system becomes of less and less use for the purpose. We enter a world where much information has to be readily available from central institutions, where a large proportion of the population are occupied in its processing and distribution, and where market trading of much of the economic output does not occur in the normal manner. The market ceases to be appropriate for much activity. It becomes an anomaly.

Even where the market remains, the reproduction of the system depends upon institutions and devices which reduce uncertainty. Trade unions may be anathema to many businessmen, but at least they provide a framework through which collective wage contracts can be concluded. Chaos and greater uncertainty would result if each negotiation was done on an individual basis. Other uncertainty-reducing devices include fixed agreements with suppliers, insurance, and administered prices. Money, rather than corn or steel, is used as a unit of account because it is a generally more reliable means of dealing with an uncertain future. The market survives with the assistance of inbuilt rigidities. Although these ostensibly restrict the 'free' forces of supply and demand, they have a vital role in providing economic agents with relatively reliable and unchanging information. A completely 'free' market system would be burdened with an exacerbated problem of insufficient knowledge. Institutional arrangements and internal rigidities such as these have the necessary role of reducing uncertainty and providing information which is less likely to change through time. For these reasons it is doubtful if a completely fluid and unrestricted market could ever function.

In most societies, much information is provided free. We do not need to pay to find out the time of the train to London or to consult many public records. Free information is important in any complex social system, and cannot be dispensed with, despite the fact that its provision is rarely without cost.

Free information is a form of grant. A general theory of grants has been developed by Kenneth Boulding.[14] He notes that goods and services are often transferred free from one person or institution to another. Examples are payments to charity, student grants, inherited wealth, state pensions, and unemployment benefits. These 'grants' are significant within the family, where many services are performed without the expectation of direct reward. In contrast, the market system is based on exchange, i.e. a two-way transfer of commodities (one of them often being money). It has been estimated that between a fifth and a half of the United States economy is run on a system of grants rather than exchanges.

Boulding argues that there are two types of grant. There is the 'gift', arising out of 'love'; and the 'tribute', arising out of 'fear'. An example of the tribute is the payment of taxes to maintain a large army or police force to keep law and order. An example of the gift is the resources and attention devoted to the rearing of a child within the family. In both these cases, although through different mechanisms, the effect is to provide integration and cohesion within society. Force and repression produce social cohesion through fear. The care of a child produces the expectation that each generation will care for the next. It is suggested that the exchange system tends to encourage social disintegration, whereas the grants system fosters social bonding and cohesion. Boulding thus implies that a pure market system is unlikely to survive, and that a formal or informal network of non-market social relations is required, in any conceivable socio-economic system, to provide cohesion. No society can function on the basis of egotism and exchange alone.

In the past, social integration has been assisted by such features as kinship, tradition and routine. With the development of capitalism in Western Europe, remaining elements of the old feudal and absolutist societies were important in providing networks and social bonds. They may appear in retrospect as anachronistic, but they had an important integrating function.

As Joseph Schumpeter pointed out in *Capitalism, Socialism and Democracy*, a capitalist system which progressively erodes these old bonds of tradition and loyalty will create discord, a breakdown in solidarity, and a division of society into antagonistic cultures and groups. This is one reason why the United States, which lacks a feudal past, is less unified in a cultural and sociological sense, and has failed to create a common identity for the working class.

However, in the history of capitalism one integrating factor stands above all others in importance: it is the state. Through either 'love' or 'fear' there has always been an important grants element in its activities. But its significance is more than that, as we shall see.

The Necessary Role of the State

We are frequently invited, both in economic theory and everyday life, to imagine a system of capitalism in which independent firms work free from state interference, relating to each other through voluntary contracts in the marketplace. This is presented as a picture of *laissez-faire* capitalism in Britain in the nineteenth century, or as an attainable ideal, or both. But both presentations are false. Complete *laissez-faire* has never existed: it is a mistaken conception, and a practical and theoretical impossibility. In this section it will be argued that the state and capitalism are inseparable: capitalism requires the economic intervention of the state.

It is obvious, of course, that in terms of state intervention Victorian capitalism is very different from that of today, and the state did, in fact, play a much smaller economic role a hundred years ago. This may even justify the description of the nineteenth century as the period of *laissez-faire*, for if the label is not appropriate for that period it is appropriate for no other. But it would be a mistake to suggest that, for example, government expenditure was insignificant during the nineteenth century. For the whole period in Britain it averaged about ten per cent of Gross National Product.[15] In other countries industrialization came later, so a contemporary comparison is not relevant. But if we take, for example, the United States and Germany from 1870 to 1913, the state intervened in the economy on a significant scale.

For the purpose of our argument it is not important to enter into the controversy amongst economic historians as to whether nineteenth-century Britain should be described as a period of *laissez-faire*. This debate often hinges on the definition of the term, or on the statistics of government intervention that are chosen. It will be sufficient to note that no economic historian denies that the state did play a significant role in the last century, even if a much smaller one than within capitalism since 1945.

The important point to realize is that *laissez-faire* is, in all actual and conceivable economic circumstances, a creation of the state itself. This remains true even if the state later retreats somewhat (as it did in Britain). It has been argued, most forcefully, by Karl Polanyi that *laissez-faire* in Britain was the product of deliberate state action. For the classic liberals the significance of this is difficult to realize. For them, *laissez-faire* is the natural order of things. It is this naturalistic conception that Karl Polanyi vigorously and convincingly denies:

> The road to the free market was opened and kept open by an enormous increase in continuous, centrally organized and controlled interventionism. To make Adam Smith's 'simple and natural liberty' compatible with the needs of a human society was a most complicated affair. Witness the complexity of the provisions of the innumerable enclosure laws; the amount of bureaucratic control involved in the administration of the New Poor Laws ... or the increase in governmental administration entailed in the meritorious task of municipal reform. And yet all these strongholds of governmental interference were erected with a view to the organizing of some simple freedom – such as that of land, labor, or municipal administration ... [The] introduction of free markets, far from doing away with the need for control, regulation, and intervention, enormously increased their range. Administrators had to be constantly on the watch to ensure the free working of the system. Thus even those who wished most ardently to free the state from all unnecessary duties, and whose whole philosophy demanded the restriction of state activities, could not but entrust the self-same state with new powers, organs, and instruments required for the establishment of *laissez-faire*.[16]

A market economy requires the establishment of defined individual rights to private property and a system of contract law. It requires a legal machinery to enact these laws. It needs a continuous process of legislation to minimize anomalies and keep the system up to date with a continuously changing social and economic reality. Such legislative intervention would be necessary even if the market system paid no heed to the poor and weak, who could be crushed in the 'free' bargaining process with the rich and powerful. Thus *in addition* some market systems put limits on, for example, child labour or the length of the adult working day. Even without these 'interferences' the state would have to intervene. *Laissez-faire* requires an active and interventionist state. That is the paradox.

A similar point was made by Antonio Gramsci in the *Prison Notebooks*. Long before the rise of the modern New Right he identifies one of the fundamental errors in such an approach:

> The ideas of the Free Trade movement are based on a theoretical error whose practical origin is not hard to identify; they are based on a distinction between political society and civil society, which is made into and presented as an organic one, whereas in fact it is merely methodological. Thus it is asserted that economic activity belongs to civil society, and that the State must not intervene to regulate it. But since in actual reality civil society and State are one and the same, it must be made clear that *laissez-faire* too is a form of State 'regulation', introduced and maintained by legislative and coercive means. It is a deliberate policy, conscious of its own ends, and not the spontaneous, automatic expression of economic facts.[17]

For an illustration of the positive contribution of the state to the development of the 'free market', consider the financial sector. In Britain prior to 1844 there was virtually a free market in finance, with very little state regulation or control of the banks. This anarchic monetary system greatly exacerbated economic instability. There were booms in which more and more enterprises were floated on credit. Eventually, confidence failed, credit was withdrawn, and there ensued commercial crisis and economic slump. The Bank Charter Act of 1844 began to put restrictions on credit and aimed to concentrate the right of issue of paper money in the Bank of England. As the monetary and financial system developed in the nineteenth and twentieth centuries, so grew the centralized control and state regulation of the banks. In a monetary economy this process is unavoidable. The state has to be the ultimate guarantor of business confidence. No private firm can fulfil this role. Money is a social, not a private bond. It is a commodity which dominates all other commodities. Its creation and regulation have to be entrusted to the institution which dominates all others: the state. This institution, above all others, can act most effectively as lender of last resort.[18]

At the international level, few New Right philosophers would deny an essential role to the state: the defence of the nation cannot simply be left to the market. Here 'as an exception' the state must take over. It has been pointed out, however, that such intervention is not exceptional in the economy as a whole. Furthermore, the role of military force in actually creating and protecting a 'free' market should be recognized. Economically, no nation is an island: it must trade with others. In most cases the development of an internal market is tied up with the development of trading relations with other countries. Britain's position as a *laissez-faire* industrial nation was developed by imposing trading relations upon other countries with the use of military force. The traditional frameworks for production and distribution were broken up and replaced by the market, under the sovereignty of the British Empire, within which 'free trade' was maintained by state-organized physical force. As Stephen Hymer put it: 'In the last analysis, markets come out of the barrel of a gun, and to establish an integrated world economy on capitalist lines requires the international mobilization of political power.'[19]

In the twentieth century the United States moved to a position of dominance, although without a formal empire. However physical force was still used to maintain the 'free' market: in Africa, South America, Asia, and elsewhere.[20] Strikingly, it is the two countries which have in the past assumed such a position of dominance, i.e. Britain and the United States, which are the most firmly wedded to the idea of *laissez-faire*. Other capitalist countries, which have more often and energetically had to use state regulation and protection to safeguard their economies, have always accepted a considerable role for the state. This applies, for example, to West Germany, France, and Japan.[21] Furthermore, the advocacy of *laissez-faire* in Britain and the United States is in contradiction to the enormous state expenditures on the military in those countries. These have the effect of distorting the so-called 'natural' market system towards certain types of military-related technology, in the field of electronics and nuclear power, for example.

New Right theorists are so ardent in their championship of the removal of state powers from many spheres of economic and social activity, and of the introduction of competition and markets, that one wonders why they hesitate at a certain point and accept a limited role for the state. Both Hayek and Friedman support the existence of a central state to carry out legal and military functions. At that point markets go no further, and the state remains necessary to protect the nation and deal with crime. Unlike Hayek, Friedman accepts that the state should maintain a monopoly in the production and regulation of money. However, some members of the New Right go much further and bring competition and markets into areas traditionally under the authority of the state. If 'more competition' is the panacea for all economic and social ills, then why not have competition in every sphere? Thus Milton Friedman's son, David, has followed his father's footsteps to their logical conclusion and argued with eloquence for private armies and police forces. Describing himself as an 'anarcho-capitalist', David Friedman asserts that it is best to have a choice of rival courts of law and law-enforcement agencies.[22] Competition thus magically ensures that justice will triumph in the long run. Another New Right theorist, Murray Rothbard, rejects arguments for a publicly funded police force and promotes the idea of private provision.[23] Markets and private property are to go where capitalism has not been before.

However, such extensive 'freedom to choose' is too much for some admirers of the market. Samuel Brittan realizes that such competition in the field of law and order would degenerate into civil strife not unlike that in Renaissance Italy, with warring private armies.[24] One is also reminded of the Lebanon in recent years, with several hundred private armies, unending civil war, and massacres of the civilian population. The majority of the New Right have the sense to realize that 'freedom to choose' between rival police and army units can lead to brutal chaos. But if such 'freedom' is to be limited in one place, why should it not be limited elsewhere?

The State and Capitalist Development

It has just been argued that state intervention is necessary for capitalism to emerge, as well as being a theoretical and practical condition for its very existence and survival. In this section we briefly focus on the role of the state in the industrial development of the advanced capitalist countries.

The establishment of the factory system in Britain, at the end of the eighteenth century and during the first few decades of the nineteenth, coincided with the rise of the theories of *laissez-faire* and free trade, promulgated by Adam Smith and David Ricardo, amongst others. Yet, even before the mid-century triumph of free trade with the repeal of the Corn Laws in 1846, Parliament had seen fit to interfere in the running of the privately owned factories spawned by the Industrial Revolution. Minimal legislation in 1802 and 1819 restricted child labour, albeit to little effect until factory inspection was introduced in 1833. The 1844 Factory Act, amongst other things, restricted the working day for women to twelve hours. Another Act followed in 1847, but it was not until 1850 that, for the first time, a restriction was put on the working day for adult males to supplement preceding legislation for women and children. The 1850 Act came into force in 1853 and reduced the working week to a maximum of sixty hours in cotton and some other industries. Other factories came under the Act in 1860, 1861 and 1863.

Why did these reforms take place, at a time when the trade union movement was weak, and against the resistance of many of the factory owners? Historians have pointed out that some of the landed interests in Parliament supported the reforms in opposition to the manufacturers. Marxists point to the working-class agitation that accompanied the legislation to shorten the working day. Both observations are valid, and there is no doubt that class struggle was very important in helping to force the legislation through Parliament. But this is not a *sufficient* explanation. If class struggle was the only force for change, then why did the legislation, until 1850, concentrate entirely on restrictions on the working day for women and children? At the time, the working-class movement was dominated by adult males; the demands of the Chartists, for example, included adult suffrage for men, not women. And why was the most extensive and significant legislation passed in 1850, shortly after the catastrophic defeat of the Chartist movement and when working-class morale and organization was at a low ebb? A picture of legislation resulting solely from working-class pressure against entirely reluctant employers does not correspond to the facts.

That a large section of the capitalist class was against the restriction of the working day is beyond dispute. It appears, however, that the legislation was initially pushed through by working-class pressure with support from a section of the landed aristocracy, the factory inspectorate, and – most strikingly – a minority of the manufacturing capitalists themselves. After 1850 this handful of capitalists swelled in numbers and accelerated the extension of restrictions into the 1860s. This partial 'conversion' of the capitalist class to the cause was discussed by Marx in *Capital*. After the reduction of the working day, Marx noted, manufacturing firms enjoyed a new lease of life:

> Their wonderful development from 1853 to 1860, hand-in-hand with the physical and moral regeneration of the factory workers, was visible to the weakest eyes. The very manufacturers from whom the legal limitation and regulation of the working day had been wrung step by step in the course of a civil war lasting half a century now pointed boastfully to the contrast with the areas of exploitation which were still 'free'. The Pharisees of 'political economy' now proclaimed that their newly won insight into the necessity for a legally regulated working day was a characteristic achievement of their 'science'.[25]

As a result of the restriction of the working day, employees were less exhausted and more capable of acquiring and using skills. Consequently, industry prospered. A growing number of manufacturers then recognized that the limitation of the working day was in their own interests, as well. However, further reductions were difficult of achievement by individual capitalists: they feared that they would lose a share of the market to their competitors if they, alone, restricted the working day. The market system is not favourable to such a solution, and the state had to step in:

> We therefore find, for example, that at the beginning of 1863 twenty-six firms owning extensive potteries in Staffordshire, including Josiah Wedgwood and Sons, presented a petition for 'some legislative enactment'. Combination with other capitalists, they said, did not allow them to limit the hours worked by children voluntarily, etc. 'Much as we deplore the evils before mentioned, it would not be possible to prevent them by any scheme of agreement between the manufacturers ... Taking all these points into consideration, we have come to the conviction that some legislative enactment is wanted.'[26]

In Blackburn in 1873, for slightly different reasons, some mill owners actually 'turned to the factory workers, urged them to mount a serious agitation for the 9-hour system, and promised them monetary contributions for the purpose!'[27]

Thus, in the heyday of *laissez-faire*, it was realized that the market, left to itself, would not provide an optimal solution: instead it would produce an exhausted and debilitated workforce, incapable of developing its skills. The development of capitalism required the intervention of the state. As Polanyi has pointed out, this growing state intervention was not due to any 'collectivist trend' in public opinion at the time.[28] It was a consequence of the combined force of the organized working class and the enlightened bourgeoisie, both acting in their own interests. Supporters of legislation amongst the factory inspectorate and the business community did not see the limitation of the working day as a basic challenge to the capitalist system: it was regarded as a necessary condition of the operation of the 'free' market under the stage of economic development that had been reached. The factory inspectorate thus wrote in 1850; 'The proceedings have afforded, moreover, incontrovertible proof of the fallacy of the assertion so often advanced, that operatives need no protection, but may be considered as free agents in the disposal of their property which they possess – the labour of their hands and the sweat of their brows.'[29] In 1863 the inspectorate insisted that the absence of legislation to restrict the working day did not simply 'permit' the working class 'to work 14 hours a day without meals' but was 'tantamount to compelling' them to do so.[30] In 1864 they defined, in one short sentence, the practical limits to *laissez-faire* in regard to labour: 'Free labour (if so it may be termed) even in a free country, requires the strong arm of the law to protect it.'[31]

The interventionist state thus arose because the market system was incapable of expressing the *collective* interests of capital in regard to reduction of fatigue and the development of skills amongst the working class. No group of capitalists could bring about the necessary reform: the enforcement of legislation was necessary to protect the more progressive capitalists against the abuses of the backward. Thus individual capital does not always promote or achieve the interests of capital in general. Here the state has to step in, and the market, to some degree, is pushed aside.

The same principle can be illustrated by reference to the development of the education system in Britain. There is little doubt that systematic state education was introduced in 1870 because the authorities realized that there were considerable advantages in having a better-educated labour force to work in offices and factories and fight in wars. In addition there was a concern to ensure that the working class was compliant and versed in establishment ideology, subsequent to the extension of the franchise in 1867. The market mechanism would not have brought about systematic education of the entire population: this had to be done by the state. Furthermore, there were good arguments why even the most *laissez-faire* of capitalists should accept the reform. The skills of the work-force would be improved by basic education. Strict school discipline and time-keeping would provide a foretaste of what was to come in the factory.

Thus there are clear reasons why it was that all capitalist countries accepted a considerable degree of state intervention in the nineteenth century, despite the existence of a strong pro-market ideology in every case:

> Victorian England and the Prussia of Bismarck were poles apart, and both were very much unlike the France of the Third Republic or the Empire of the Hapsburgs. Yet each of them passed through a period of free trade and *laissez-faire*, followed by a period of antiliberal legislation in regard to public health, factory conditions, municipal trading, social insurance, shipping subsidies, public utilities, trade associations, and so on.[32]

The development of capitalist industry meant an expanding market system and a growing pool of employable labour. As soon as capitalism had moved beyond the most primitive form of factory production it required the state to protect, regulate, subsidize, standardize and intervene. This process has continued in earnest into the twentieth century, where the state is involved in every sphere of economic life.

The countries that have been most successful in terms of economic growth in recent decades are the ones that have relied most heavily on state intervention, regulation and planning. Two prime examples are France, with its central planning agencies and state control of finance, and West Germany, with discriminatory subsidies, massive public expenditure, and a coordinated industrial banking system.[33] The state has been central to the Japanese 'economic miracle' as well. In the 1950s the Japanese Ministry of International Trade and Industry rejected the advice of *laissez-faire* economists to concentrate solely on the existing traditional industries where there was an alleged 'comparative advantage'. Instead they promoted new industries, namely steel, synthetic textiles, electronics, industrial machinery, motor cycles and motor cars.[34] Japanese, French and West German industry did not expand so massively simply as a result of free competition and market forces: in each case economic growth was spearheaded, guided, and largely financed by the state. In contrast, in Britain and the United States, where there has been less state intervention and an absence of overall planning, there have been lower growth rates of output and productivity and a massive loss of share in export trade since the Second World War.[35] But even in these countries state intervention has not been absent: it has been frequently demanded by business in times of difficulty.[36]

Andrew Shonfield and others have argued that it was widespread state intervention and large public expenditure which reduced the amplitude and violence of oscillations in the 4- to 10-year trade cycle after 1945, facilitating a period of worldwide economic expansion. The case for this argument is strong. The modern theory of the trade cycle has failed to discover an automatic self-righting mechanism to enable recovery from recession in a capitalist economy with little or no sustained government expenditure. In his erudite survey of trade cycle theory, R. C. O. Matthews shows that while there might be good reasons to suppose that a boom is likely to come to an end, a slump, in contrast, can go on forever in the absence of government intervention or uplifting exogenous forces.[37] The central proposition in the economics of Keynes, that there is no automatic self-righting mechanism in a capitalist market economy, appears to be vindicated. Capitalism requires the crutches of government intervention and public expenditure to avoid the possibility of economic collapse. (However, collapse could still result from the anarchy of the world trading and banking system, in the absence of sufficient institutional intervention at the world level.)

Capitalism and the Impurity Principle

The arguments in this chapter have important consequences and are central to the development of the main conclusions of this book. Here they relate specifically to the capitalist socio-economic system: in the next chapter they are extended and stated in more general terms. It has been shown that it is impossible, in both logical and practical terms, for the market mechanism to pervade the entire capitalist system: although it is dominant, it does not encompass all. It cannot completely pervade the family, the education system, the internal organization of the firm, and the creation and regulation of money. In addition, the process of capitalist development requires the active intervention of the state. Capitalism has to accommodate within itself other forms of organization and regulation: typically the family, planning within the firm, and the state. We shall call these forms *impurities*. The idea that they are necessary to the capitalist system we shall call *the impurity principle* (as applied to capitalism).

A precursor of this principle appears in the writings of Rosa Luxemburg. From an analysis of Marx's schemes of expanded reproduction in *Capital* (the forerunners of modern input–output analysis) she claimed to show that the sustained growth of the capitalist system was impossible in pure terms. Capitalism, in her view, existed alongside other more primitive forms of production which it required to sustain its expansion at the same time that it was undermining them. Thus the very processes of capitalist expansion and imperialist aggrandizement would lead, at the limit, to the collapse of the entire system. As she put it:

> Capitalist production as proper mass production depends on consumers from peasant and artisan strata in the old countries, and consumers from all countries; but for technical reasons, it cannot exist without the products of these strata and countries . . . Thus capitalism expands because of its mutual relationship with non-capitalist social strata and countries, accumulating at their expense and at the same time pushing them aside to take their place. The more capitalist countries participate in this hunting for accumulation areas, the rarer the non-capitalist places still open to the expansion of capital become and the tougher the competition; its raids turn into a chain of economic and political catastrophes: world crises, wars, revolution. But by this process capital prepares its own destruction in two ways. As it approaches the point where humanity only consists of capitalists and proletarians, further accumulation will become impossible. At the same time, the absolute and undivided rule of capital aggravates class struggle throughout the world . . .[38]

Since its publication, Rosa Luxemburg's theory has suffered fatal criticism from, among others, Nikolai Bukharin[39] and Joan Robinson.[40] The 'technical' problem which formed the foundation stone of her theory is not a problem at all: it results from a hopeless confusion of concepts, compounded by arithmetical errors.[41] In addition, Luxemburg has a rather fatalistic view of capitalist economic development, informed by her vision of future collapse or catastrophe. She does not deny the importance of human action, but she insists that if revolution fails to overthrow capitalism it will inevitably reach an impasse. However, there is no valid theoretical basis to this assertion. Also it leads to a key political mistake: the underestimation of the capacity of the capitalist system to recover from its own crises.[42] It is evident, furthermore, that Luxemburg fails to notice the non-capitalist forms of production and non-market mechanisms of regulation which exist, of necessity, within even the most advanced capitalist system. To a considerable extent the primary responsibility for this error lies with Marx, who, from the structure and content of *Capital*, seems to assume that the capitalist mode of production has the capacity, in its pure form, to conquer all. However, Luxemburg did have an important insight when she recognized, in contrast to Marx, the essential external role of non-capitalist forms of production in supporting capitalist expansion. It is an assertion of the impurity principle in a different and limited form.

In a recent book,[43] Mike Prior and David Purdy give a vivid account of the different 'modes of production' within modern capitalism, thus highlighting the existence of impurities. However, they emphasize only one type: what they call 'social collectivist' forms, such as rudimentary state planning and a National Health Service (i.e. socialized medicine). Political struggle, they argue, is closely related to the antagonism between the dominant and capitalist social relations on the one hand, and 'social collectivism' on the other. This analysis has implications for political strategy: emphasis is laid on the growth of 'social collectivist' forces in a way that is reminiscent of the politics of traditional social democracy.[44]

Much of the analysis and description in the book by Prior and Purdy is useful and acceptable, and some similar points have been made here. However, it is not enough to single out one impurity: at least four sets of antagonistic social relations have been identified in this chapter. Consequently the transition from a capitalist to a socialist society will be much more complex than the tug-of-war between private and collectivist forms that Prior and Purdy describe. Second, the different sets of social relations within any socio-economic system are in fact (according to the impurity principle), in certain combinations, indispensable for the survival of the system as a whole. There is mutual support as well as mutual antagonism: a structured combination of dissimilar elements: a symbiotic rather than a purely conflicting relationship.

In the analysis of Prior and Purdy the idea of a structured totality is lacking. Dissimilar 'modes of production' co-exist like ingredients in a soup: the objective of the political 'cook' is to change their balance by adding one and removing another. In contrast, with an emphasis on the structured totality it is evident that the efficacy of partial adjustments is limited. The character of the system does not change merely by adding one element and removing another: it is the nature of the symbiosis that must be transformed, or, to use the other metaphor, the structure as a whole. The role of each impurity within the system is contradictory and ambiguous: we cannot simply assign a positive moral sign to some elements and a negative one to others. The evaluation has to be in terms of the system. In particular, the extension of collectivist forms of property (emphasized by Purdy and Prior) is in fact a secondary issue. The character of the system as a whole is determined by the general pattern of *relations of power*. The primary objective of a radical and socialist programme is to rebuild these relations in a democratic mode.

What other conclusions follow from the analysis in this chapter? There are several, some positive, some negative. On the negative side there are important critical consequences for the New Right and others who regard market competition as the panacea for all economic and social ills, and state collectivism as the source of all problems. It has been shown above that an extension of the market mechanism to all spheres of economic activity is a theoretical and practical impossibility. Furthermore, the very existence and development of a market economy requires non-market forms of production and regulation in several key areas. Supporters of capitalism are bound to defend a mixed economy: they have no alternative within a capitalist framework. The fact is that the political programme of the New Right is incapable of realization.

The positive conclusions are equally important. First, according to the impurity principle there is conflict within the system between different forms of production and regulation, including, for example, the family and the state. Such conflicts are additional to, and as important as, the traditional Marxian class struggle. The question of the sexual division of labour in the household, and conflicts over public policy within the state apparatus, are just as real and significant as the struggle between capitalists and workers. The issues raised by the feminist movement are just as important and consequential for radical and socialist politics as the demands and aspirations of the trade unions.

Second, the emphasis on the structured totality makes it possible and necessary to talk of supra-class interests, and to affirm the reality of notions such as 'the nation' or 'the people', without either reducing them to purely class terms, or abandoning the concept of class.[45] Furthermore, one must concede the existence of supra-class objectives such as 'democracy'. Such goals become part of a political programme for the transformation of the socio-economic system in its entirety.

Third, it has been shown that state intervention is essential to capitalist development, and is not confined to the interests of one social class. Certain reforms may benefit workers as well as capitalists. Hence a crude class-instrumentalist view of the state is unacceptable. The Leninist conception of the state as an instrument of domination of one class by another fails to recognize the contradictory nature of the state itself.[46]

Finally, one of the most important consequences of the impurity principle is to challenge a crude view of socio-economic reality in which one economic structure is seen to prevail and all that is relevant is the class struggle within that one structure. Politics is not reducible to the interests of a single social class: this is as true for the Left as it is for the Right. Any feasible political programme must span the disparate structures and elements within society. The appeal of the New Right to the concept of the individual does not relate simply to the capitalist mode of production, or even to the market in its general form. The individual is a more pervasive notion, albeit with forceful and particular expression in a market society. The appeal of the Left has to be in equally pervasive terms. It is here that the ideas of social cooperation, popular sovereignty, and, above all, democracy, have a central part to play.

The important consequences of the impurity principle for political theory and practice will be elaborated later. Our first task is to demonstrate that it does not relate only to capitalist society: its significance is more general and enduring. However, the critical outcome of the argument of this chapter should be emphasized: A pure capitalist or market system is impossible; the state is essential to capitalist cohesion and development; and the apparent goal of the New Right – a system completely regulated by the market and private enterprise – is totally unrealizable.[47]

Seven

Economic Pluralism

A complex system generating high variety must be controlled by requisite variety.

Stafford Beer, *Decision and Control*

The hierarchical order is never simple. All societies are diversified pluralities. They are divided against themselves and such division is probably intrinsic to their nature.

Fernand Braudel, *The Wheels of Commerce*

If the impurity principle applies to capitalism, does it also apply to other socio-economic systems? Capitalism exhibits a variety of economic structures: can the same be said of the slave system of classical antiquity, the feudal system of the middle ages, and the social formations of the Eastern Bloc today? Is a form of economic pluralism evident in all the major socio-economic systems in the history of civilization to date? Can the impurity principle be elevated to a general law?

A comprehensive study of these socio-economic systems is beyond the scope of this work. Neither is it possible to give a detailed account of the relevance of the impurity principle in the process of transition from one system to another. But an attempt can be made to show that the impurity principle has some general relevance to the study of socio-economic systems. If such a point is established, there are clear and important implications for the theory of democracy and for political practice in general. We are forced to rethink our vision of a socialist future.

In this examination of socio-economic systems we are again dependent on the work of Marx and of later Marxist historians.[1] Outside Marxism, social science has contributed very little to the theory of such systems. However, there are some weaknesses in the orthodox Marxian approach. In particular, it is rarely considered that a given system may not be able to function in a pure form, and political concessions to economic pluralism are lacking. As we shall see, these defects have important political consequences.

The pre-capitalist history of Europe stretches, of course, over many centuries. But two types of socio-economic system stand as great landmarks over intervening periods of flux and chaos. We commence with the greatest and most enduring of these two systems: that which prevailed in classical Greece and in the Roman Empire. Subsequently we shall examine the feudal system.

Classical Antiquity

The economic structure of Ancient Greece and Rome was built upon slavery. Typically, the slaves worked on large estates (*latifundia*) owned by rich families who provided the minimal necessities of life. The slaves produced much more than they received: in other words they created a large surplus product over and above what was necessary for their sustenance. Part of this surplus product consisted of goods and services which enriched their masters. Much of the remainder went to the upkeep of the state and military apparatus. Most production in the ancient world, particularly at the zenith of classical antiquity, depended on slave labour. There were as many as four or five slaves to every free citizen.[2]

In terms of basics such as food, clothing and shelter the *latifundia* could be virtually self-sufficient. There was no necessity to sell the bulk of the product on the market. The owners were out to accumulate wealth and power: they did not have to make a monetary profit in order to survive. Moreover much of their wealth could be amassed directly from the labour of the slaves on the estates, without recourse to the market. Although markets existed and were well developed, in marked contrast to the capitalist system they did not regulate and dominate the economic structure. Under capitalism, profit is the criterion of survival; in classical antiquity there were many other, non-market mechanisms of distribution and regulation.

Nevertheless, there is no doubt that market relations were essential to the functioning of the system as a whole. First, it would be inefficient and in some cases impossible for each estate to produce the entire range of products and services: some trade was necessary. In fact merchant trade, particularly along the Mediterranean sea-routes, was extremely important within the Roman Empire. In this way the slave estates were loosely linked together by extensive market ties. Second, although slaves were bred or reared on the estates, it was unreliable, and sometimes too costly, to rely on procreation as a source of increased labour, and owners would usually purchase it from the traders in living human flesh. The slave market was a key element. For these and other reasons, market relations played an essential role, despite the fact that the economic structure of slavery was not, in direct or necessary relation to production itself, a market system.

The 'impurities' within this socio-economic system consist of more than the existence of markets and mercantile trade. The commanding edifice of classical antiquity was the military and state apparatus: slave labour was used to build the road network and military defences, for example. But most administrative and soldiering activities were not carried out by slaves, who, on the whole, were uneducated and illiterate. They were not trusted to carry arms, for fear that they might revolt. Slave labour, therefore, was not central but auxiliary to the functioning of the state. But while the state did not reflect the predominant (master–slave) relationship within the sphere of production, it did play a crucial role in the whole economic formation. First, it defended the system from attack from outside. Second, it organized the complex socio-economic infrastructure (notably, in Ancient Rome, the road system). And third, it provided the most important means of obtaining new slaves: by expansion and the conquest of outlying communities. The state was not only the largest single consumer within the Roman Empire, it was also the mainspring of expansion. The *latifundia* required the military apparatus to provide new slaves. The military apparatus required the *latifundia* to provide food and other necessities for the army and the state. They were interlocked. At first sight the slave estates seem self-sufficient economic units. On closer inspection, the military and the state played a basic, dynamic role. As Perry Anderson has put it:

> For some two centuries, the tranquil magnificence of the urban civilization of the Roman Empire concealed the underlying limits and strains of the productive basis on which it rested. For, unlike the feudal economy which succeeded it, the slave mode of production of Antiquity possessed no natural, internal mechanism of self-reproduction, because its labour force could never be homeostatically stabilized within the system. Traditionally, the supply of slaves largely depended on foreign conquests, since prisoners of war probably always provided the main source of servile labour in antiquity.[3]

Military expansion was thus one of the main regulatory mechanisms of the socio-economic system. The overall development of the economy, whether it be in a phase of expansion, stagnation, or decline, depended on military fortunes at the periphery. Once Imperial Rome had drained the coastlands of the Mediterranean and most of southern and western Europe of its manpower, it had exhausted its ready source of slaves. It then moved into a period of recurrent crises, and for this and other reasons it slid towards its demise.

In addition to developed markets and the military apparatus there are other 'impurities' within this socio-economic system. Under Roman law, property in slaves and goods was absolute. Unqualified property rights were vested in individuals, as under capitalism but in marked contrast to feudalism. With a developed market, wage-labour and commodity production were bound to emerge alongside traditional slave labour. In the urban centres non-slaves were often employed to work for other citizens, as under capitalism today. Wage-labour was more suited to skilled craft production than slavery. A large number of employed and self-employed persons thus produced goods and services for sale on the market.

Within the socio-economic system as a whole there were, therefore, relations of a different type from those normal and dominant upon the slave estates: a market, wage-labour, and the military apparatus were essential for the survival and regulation of the system. The existence of these necessary impurities is a confirmation of the impurity principle for the slave civilizations of classical antiquity.

Feudalism

In Ancient Rome humanity was divided into two groups, citizens and slaves, each with its own status and its own legal rights. Under the feudal system, as in Norman England, there were not two primary divisions but several. The entire society was ranked hierarchically into distinct groups, each with defined powers, privileges and duties. At the pinnacle of power was the king. Below him came the earls, then the barons, followed by the knights, and, at the base of the pyramid, a mass of serfs. The entire structure was based on land. Feudalism differed from the slave society of Ancient Rome and from present-day capitalism in that there were few absolute property rights. Most adult male persons had feudal tenure on a parcel of land, and each tenure involved defined rights and duties, depending on rank.

The serfs were normally bound to the manor in which they were born. Their duty was to work on the land and serve the lord of their manor, who had the right to extract a surplus product in the form of rent. More was exacted as taxes or tithes. The remainder stayed in the possession of the serf and his family: it could be consumed directly or traded on the market. As well as his right to a part of the surplus product, the lord had a duty to protect his serfs, and sometimes even to provide for them in hard times. The serf too had rights as well as duties: although he was bound to the land, he was a legal person, and above the status of a slave.

Typically the lord of the manor would not have absolute property rights in the land of his domain. He would be invested in them by a superior noble to whom he would owe knight-service: i.e. he would have a duty to fight for him in times of war. His manorial estates were (in legal parlance) held as a fief.[4] The superior noble (or liege lord) would in his turn be a vassal of a baron, earl or king, bound to provide military service. This chain of relations of feudal homage, involving rights and duties for each party, extended upwards to the king. According to the ideology of the time, the monarch was the supreme guardian of the land as a divine right bequeathed by God. In return he had duties: to God, to the land itself, and to all his subjects.

Unlike classical antiquity, feudalism did not have to conquer adjoining territory to import labour-power: it was more self-sufficient. However, it was still strongly militaristic, since the hierarchy was based on knight-service. But there was rarely a standing army, and the military apparatus was decentralized and under the control of various lords. Characteristically, throughout the feudal system power and sovereignty were parcellized.

However, feudalism was not held together simply by the use or threat of force. The simplistic picture in some historical writing of serfs labouring under the lash of a whip or at the point of a sword does not square up with the facts. The military apparatus impinged upon the sphere of production only rarely. The serf did not normally work under the glare of armed guards, as in Ancient Rome: it was only in periods of rebellion that military force was deployed. It was always present, often covert rather than overt, but the system required much else in order to function. It was the church, for example, that served to buttress and reinforce the whole social structure. The ultimate justification of feudal rights and duties, and of the entire hierarchy, rested in religion. Unlike the Roman Empire before Constantine, in feudal Europe each person was obliged to believe in a single and all-powerful Christian God.

The church apparatus was extensive and well organized. Like the secular hierarchy, it held a great deal of land; it exacted tithes and it accumulated vast wealth. Through its powers, rituals and proceedings it perpetuated the view that the feudal system was the natural order of things on earth. Church and state constituted a dual structure which pervaded every tier of the hierarchy, from the adjacent local administrations of parish and manor at local level, to the two supreme powers of pope and sovereign. The spiritual arm served to legitimate the system of liege-homage and serfdom in the secular world.

Although the feudal system was relatively cohesive, the church was probably necessary for its survival. The church institutions, staffed by bishops, priests, monks and nuns, were an important impurity, partially demarcated from the feudal hierarchy as such. The violent reaction of the established church to heresy and witchcraft, and later to Protestantism, is an indication of its importance in reproducing and stabilizing the feudal order.

An impurity may be necessary for the self-reproduction of a system, or it may arise to deal with problems and crises in its development. The church fits into the former category, most of the additional impurities under feudalism into the latter. The feudal system was impressive in that it combined a rigid hierarchy with a considerable degree of decentralization. Its stability was attained by an emphasis on routine and established precedent. It saw itself as a natural and unchanging order. But it was, in fact, quite dynamic, for reasons we shall examine below. Additional impurities evolved and became established, enabling the system to cope with unrecognized dynamism and progress.

There are numerous minor examples of these emerging additional impurities. One is the existence of communal forms of organization and property. As Marc Bloch notes:

> The feudal West universally recognized the legality of individual possession, but in practice the solidarity of the kindred was frequently extended to community of goods. Throughout the country districts there were numerous 'brotherhoods' – groups consisting of several related households sharing the same hearth and the same board and cultivating the same common fields. The lord frequently encouraged or even enforced these arrangements, for he considered it an advantage to hold members of the 'communal households' jointly responsible, willy-nilly, for the payment of dues ... Many petty lords ... particularly in central France and Tuscany, practised parcenary just as the peasants did, exploiting their inheritance in common, living all together in the ancestral castle or at least sharing in its defence.[5]

Another example is the development of the contract system for recruitment of armies, during and before the Hundred Years War. Recruitment by summons, based on liege-homage, was unreliable and uncertain, and often the monarch would find himself served by an inadequate army in a time of crisis. Routinized military service was often inefficient and ineffective. The contractual method of raising troops bypassed the old system. Recruitment was based on a direct appeal for military service in return for wages or other rewards. It enabled a quick and more controllable response to a crisis or war.[6]

However, the above minor impurities were not vital to feudalism. Before we discuss some of those that were, we have to examine the source of the system's inner dynamism. This dynamism was in the sphere of production. Compared with classical antiquity there was much more rapid technical progress during the feudal epoch. Why was this so?

As noted above, the serf was obliged to pay a rent to his lord. This rent took the form of labour-services in the early feudal period: the serf would work on another piece of land for three days a week for the lord, leaving three days to work for himself and his family. Later there was an almost universal adoption of money-rents, paid by the serf and his family by means of working for six out of seven days on one piece of land. In both cases the serfs had a good deal of autonomy: they had considerable control over their own work, and they received a sizeable share of the product.

In contrast to slavery there was thus an incentive to improve efficiency and experiment with new techniques. The serf, unlike the slave, would reap some of the benefits of any improvement. The slave received at his master's whim. There were few technical innovations related to production in the entire period of classical antiquity. Under feudalism, technical advance was evident. Innovations in agriculture included the three-field system and the iron plough, leading to a dramatic increase in output and of the average standard of living. Despite the static and tradition-bound nature of the social structure, the feudal economy was dynamic and innovative.[7] Thus enormous tensions were created within the system.

In comparison to the Roman Empire, the market and merchant trade played a less extensive role in the two centuries after the Norman conquest of England. What was critical, however, was the rapid expansion of market trade in response to the impressive dynamism of the feudal mode of production. Initially, of course, the feudal manor could be as self-sufficient as the slave estate. In principle, no part of the agricultural output had to be distributed *via* the market mechanism. Some social division of labour was inevitable, however, and, as under the slave system, the market stepped in and formed a network of trade although, in the absence of strict and absolute property rights, it was antagonistic to the dominant social structure. However, it always played a necessary role which increased enormously with the improvement in agricultural technique and the associated transition from labour-rent to money-rent. Now a greater and greater proportion of the economic product was brought to market for sale, for the conversion to money-rents meant the trading of a significant part of the serf's produce in order to pay them. Thus the adjoining market was both essential in a basic sense, and a necessary buffer and regulatory mechanism, given the dynamism of the feudal economy. In the social conditions of the time it is unlikely that any other institution could have fulfilled this function.

Throughout the feudal epoch, therefore, two important institutions, different in key respects from the central feudal structure, played an essential, adjoining role: namely the church and the market. The one legitimated the ranked division of humankind and made God the measure of all persons; the other regulated the social division of labour and made money the measure of all things. Each helped to maintain the social structure, one by sanctifying rigidity, the other by accommodating variety and change. Yet each also played a part in feudalism's erosion and downfall. The church spawned Protestantism. With the growth of the market came the expansion of the towns, of overseas trade, and a separate and independent merchant and urban culture. But that is another story.

Compared with the slave mode of production, the feudal structure was less pluralistic in its composition. Yet even here there is evidence to support the impurity principle.

State Collectivism

Capitalism has been dealt with in the previous chapter. Now – jumping several centuries from the previous section – we move to the period after 1917. In that year the Bolsheviks began to establish a new order. Russia's later economic development cannot concern us in detail here: we must focus on its social system, which has been duplicated, with important variations, in Eastern Europe and China. Many would wish to call this socialism. A recent fashion has been to insist on the 'utopianism' or 'idealism' of any alternative description. For example, the renowned economist D. M. Nuti believes that 'in political economy there is no room for utopias, "nowhere" to be found'.[8] He thus, albeit in a qualified manner, insists on calling the Eastern Bloc countries 'socialist'. Other writers argue that to do anything else is to counterpose 'ideal norms' to 'existing reality'.

However, all social science has to define ideal 'norms' or 'types' at the outset, as Max Weber argued long ago. To attempt otherwise is to descend rapidly into an unstructured and useless empiricism. Moreover it is historically inaccurate to state that political economy has had no room for utopias, unless we are to dismiss the works of William Godwin, Thomas Hodgskin, Pierre-Joseph Proudhon, John Ruskin, William Thompson, and even some passages in the works of Marx and Engels, as outside the realm of 'political economy'. Even the political economists of the Right, such as

Milton Friedman and F. A. Hayek, propose their 'utopia' where markets regulate all, and state power is diminished to minimal proportions. From a radical perspective, political economy *should* be concerned with utopias, as well as attempting to conform with scientific guidelines. To do otherwise is to dismiss the realm of the future from political economy, and to concentrate exclusively on the present and the past. For the future does not emerge automatically: it depends on our making. This means that there is undoubtedly a place for ideal norms.

If we define socialism as essentially a democratic system, then it is clear that the Eastern Bloc countries are not socialist. To assert that they are involves a different definition of socialism. As Ernest Mandel argues: 'What is opposed is not "ideal norms" to "existing reality", but two different definitions of socialism.'[9] Definitions are unavoidable. But there is no necessary superiority or analytical advantage in choosing one which happens to conform with an existing system. After all, before 1917 there was no such system for socialists to invoke. Socialism has always involved the vision of a utopia.

Although one's choice of definition does not necessarily imply a moral judgement, it can (as in the case of the New Right) often lead to one. Those that insist that the Eastern Bloc is 'actually existing socialism' may or may not approve of the type of socio-economic system to be found in that part of the world. If they do, my point is made. If they do not, then they as well are impelled to counterpose a view of 'what socialism *should* be like' to the existing situation in the East.

In this work the Eastern Bloc countries are regarded as examples of 'state collectivist' socio-economic systems. Other labels are possible. Leon Trotsky described the Soviet Union as a 'degenerated workers' state'.[10] Max Shachtman saw it as an example of 'bureaucratic collectivism'.[11] There is also a popular view that Soviet-type societies are 'state capitalist' in nature.[12] It is because of important theoretical differences among all three of these perspectives that the 'state collectivist' label is preferred.[13]

The key features of state collectivist societies are state ownership of most of the means of production, with the major exception of peasant holdings; and the existence of an extensive bureaucracy which directs and plans the economy on a centralized basis. The market has a limited role, confined, on the whole, to the distribution of consumer goods and the sale of agricultural materials and equipment to the peasantry. According to this definition, the Soviet Union, China, Cuba, Vietnam, North Korea, Eastern Europe (excluding Yugoslavia), and perhaps a few other countries in the Third World, are state collectivist.

The existence of structural impurities in these Eastern Bloc countries is proved by the survival of legal, as well as 'black', market mechanisms. Orthodox Marxists see the continued existence of the market as a hang-over from the 'bourgeois' past, which can over time be gradually displaced by the wider use of planning. Some would go further and argue that the introduction of 'workers' democracy' is necessary within the planning process and elsewhere, and that the survival of market forms, as under capitalism, makes such democratic planning difficult or impossible. In their view, therefore, both markets and bureaucracy are unnecessary impurities: both are 'deformations' in what are otherwise regarded as 'workers' states'. If the Trotskyists and others are correct in this assessment, then the impurity principle does not apply.

However, it has been argued, forcefully and effectively (as summarized in a very important article by Alec Nove[14]), that both orthodox Marxism and its Trotskyist variant are profoundly mistaken. Nove convincingly denies the very possibility of any form of completely centralized planning, at least in an advanced industrial society, because of the enormous complexity and variety of the system. According to Soviet estimates, there are at least twelve million different types of product, and even these do not take into account all the possible variations in quality and type. Even with the most sophisticated electronic computers imaginable it is beyond the realms of possibility to evolve a finely detailed plan to cope with all these goods, issue the appropriate instructions to different sectors, and deal with the delivery problem for every single product.

Consequently, the central planners have to deal with aggregate targets, and they have to assert priorities. In some sectors of the economy, central planning works well. For example, electricity presents no problems of quality variation (as Nove puts it, a kilowatt-hour is a kilowatt-hour is a kilowatt-hour). And central planners are arguably in a better position than a local company in a market economy to estimate electricity needs in the future. This, in Nove's term, is a good example of 'planability'.

Elsewhere serious problems can arise. Overworked planners have to issue instructions to sectors of the economy in aggregate terms: so many pieces of footwear, so many square metres of cloth, so many car tyres, and so on. Incentives and bonuses have to be formalized in terms of the achievement of aggregate plan-fulfilment norms, with less attention to the quality of the products. Even with the best will in the world, and the highest commitment to collectivist and social goals, the manager and worker at local level cannot and does not know, in complete detail, what is 'really needed'. Some sort of ordering of priorities has to be established. For example, a worker might quite reasonably conclude that it is best to produce the target number of pieces of footwear, even at the cost of quality, finish, and so on. Thus the problem is not one simply of bureaucracy, individualism, and the absence of workers' control: it is one of limited access to relevant knowledge and limited means to establish rational priorities. Bureaucracy, social fragmentation, and cynicism in the Eastern Bloc compound these difficulties enormously. But they would remain in any centrally planned, state collectivist, system.

The very complexities of centralized planning enforce some degree of bureaucracy and hierarchy. It is impossible to deal with the details of planning and to make decisions on priorities through some ubiquitous system of voting or democracy. In contrast, many socialist critics of the Eastern Bloc countries believe that

> there could now exist a 'real' socialist democratic planning system which would dispense simultaneously with market, bureaucracy and hierarchy, based on some undefined form of mass democracy. Those who hold this view are usually quite unaware of the complexities of the modern industrial structure, with its innumerable complementarities and interdependencies. It is not clear where, in this process, is the place for political democracy as an alternative to both market and bureaucracy. Democratic procedures are indeed essential, but these cannot be meaningfully applied to multiple-millions of micro-economic decisions: an elected assembly can vote on broad priorities (e.g. more for primary education, or housing, or developing a region), but hardly on whether three tons of construction steel should be allocated to this or that building site, or that production of red dyestuffs be increased by 3 per cent.[15]

Most of the Eastern Bloc countries have suffered tremendous privations, before, during and after their transition to state collectivism. All had a legacy of some degree of industrial backwardness, notably China and the Soviet Union. Many have undergone invasion and prolonged civil war. History has not made things easy. But it is unconvincing to suggest that none of these problems would have arisen if history had been more generous: it is more likely that major distortions and problems are inherent in centralized planning itself.

It is clear, for example, that the Soviet Union – despite persistent efforts to establish rational and successful central planning – has always had to rely on structural impurities within the system. These impurities are complex and numerous. We may briefly mention six: the legal market for consumer goods, the survival of an employment relation, other legal markets, illegal 'black' markets and deals, peasant agriculture, and trade with the capitalist West. These impurities fill the gaps where the central planning system fails: they provide cohesion where the central bureaucracy would threaten to disrupt the entire socio-economic fabric. The periodic attempts to limit or remove them have often been followed by a greater tolerance and relaxation of constraints when it is realized that hundred-per-cent central planning, or close approximations to it, cannot function and would spell collapse. Thus the economically disastrous period of 'War Communism', with its military conscription of industrial labour and forced appropriation of food produced by the peasantry, was followed in 1921–8 by the New Economic Policy, with its broad tolerance of the market mechanism and small private firms. Then when the private sector began to move from the grip of state regulation and control there was a lurch towards collectivization and central planning, with the introduction of the first five-year plan in 1928. However, even during the 1930s and 1940s the impurities survived and played a necessary role. The peasants were allowed private plots to produce food for sale. Markets for consumer goods and trade with the West persisted. After Stalin, Khrushchev first tolerated, then to some extent restricted, the private sector. In 1965 reforms were introduced under Brezhnev to reduce the number of compulsory planning indicators passed down from the centre, to increase managerial autonomy at plant level, and to enhance the use of indices of 'profitability' as criteria of success. By 1970, much of this policy had been reversed. However, in the late 1970s there was a much greater explicit reliance on, and tolerance of, peasant private agriculture than in any period since the 1930s, and trade with the West, including the importation of advanced technology, was showing a marked increase. The economic history of the Soviet Union is very much a story of changing boundaries and relations between centralized planning and its systemic impurities.[16]

There is little sign that state collectivism is evolving into a type of private-enterprise, capitalist economy. Nor is it moving towards complete centralization, hundred-per-cent public ownership, and effective and comprehensive planning. Whatever its limitations and instabilities, it is an enduring system in its present form. But its survival and reproduction have depended on its impurities. Alternative methods of economic regulation have always stepped in to fill the gaps which – though here exaggerated by the excessive bureaucracy and lack of industrial democracy – would exist in any system of centralized planning. The problem is one of 'planability': the potential and limits of planning itself.

Thus we should resist the temptation to regard bureaucracy, inefficiency and corruption in the Soviet Union solely as a product of the privations of history, or the exercise of tyranny, or the lack of a democratic past, or the legacy of backwardness. The weight of evidence is to the contrary. Examples are so numerous that one hesitates to provide a list. Basically, the central plan gives exclusive emphasis to production targets in terms of single quantities. As a result, the individual enterprise is often ignorant of precise requirements. For example, plan-fulfilment targets in terms of square metres in the textile sector can lead to the production of an excessive amount of thin, fragile cloth. The firm tries to achieve the target in quantitative terms, knowing or not knowing that the cloth is too thin. If the target is expressed in terms of weight, the tendency will be to produce cloth that is too heavy. Such distortions could occur in the most democratic of centrally planned systems.

In a less perfect world, more serious distortions can occur. In China, for example, a composite production index was evolved for the textile industry, in which 'quality' was an important element. 'Quality' was defined as the absence of imperfections in the cloth. At least one enterprise responded by cutting out all the imperfections so that every length of cloth was dotted with holes.[17] Plan-fulfilment targets are bound to cause distortions where large variations of type, dimension, weight, quality, etc. are possible:

> Thus when window-glass was planned in tons it was too thick and heavy; so they shifted the plan 'indicator' to square metres, whereupon it became too thin. Common sense tells us that glass should be thick or thin according to the circumstances of its use, but such detail is not and *can not* be within the cognizance of the central planning organs. Aggregation is a 'must' if next year's plan is to be drafted before the end of the century.[18]

An over-centralized planning system tends to create shortages of certain types of goods, particularly high-quality ones. It can lead to waste and inefficiency. The areas in which its performance is impressive have been accorded high priority, or are easily 'planable' due to the nature of the product. In response, either an extensive black market has arisen to plug the gaps, or the state collectivist system has actually legalized a more extensive role for the market (as in the Soviet Union under the New Economic Policy, or in Hungary since 1968[19]). In no country has centralized planning worked efficiently on its own.

Of course it is impossible to measure the extent of the 'black economy' in the Soviet Union. All the indications are, however, that it is enormous. A short visit is sufficient to confirm this opinion. We are not simply talking of a black market for goods in short supply, or a lust for Western consumer goods: a whole stratum of Soviet society survives and prospers by filling the gaps in the centralized planning system. The full-time occupation of several thousands, possibly even millions, of people nicknamed *tolkachi* consists of obtaining materials, spare parts, etc., and expediting supplies, for which they receive an illegal commission. *Tolkachi* will often pretend to have another job, and officially draw a salary elsewhere, but become prosperous through a backhand income from plant-managers and officials. They flourish throughout the economy. In one year, in the town of Dnepropetrovsk alone, there were several thousand visits to factories by *tolkachi* on corrupt business.[20] Facing continuous pressure to reach production targets, and the lack of even a few essential parts and supplies, a manager is often forced to use illegal methods. The overworked planners at the centre cannot deal with all the many shortages. The manager will be tempted to use crude political or personal influence, or to go direct to the black market, or to bring in a *tolkach*. The higher committees of the bureaucracy may instigate periodic campaigns to reduce corruption and illegal practices of this sort, but there is a widespread and well-informed opinion in the Soviet Union that without such illegal methods production would not be able to function in many sectors of the economy.

In the state collectivist societies there are legal as well as illegal markets. An important example of the former is the market for labour-power. Although the labour market does not create periodic mass unemployment (as in the West), employment in return for a money wage has been retained. Another important legal market is for consumer goods. Despite the occasional use of rationing, money remains the main medium of exchange for both labour-power and consumables.

Socialists have often referred to the abolition of money as a desirable and practical objective.[21] Be that as it may, to do so in a state collectivist society would lead to a deterioration of the conditions of the majority of the population. Although he does not recognize all the limitations of centralized planning *per se*, Ernest Mandel comes to a similar conclusion. Writing of the Soviet Union, he argues that

> money, by retaining the possibility of a certain degree of choice on the part of the consumers, constitutes a safeguard – limited but real – against total invasion by regulating bureaucratism. Money likewise remains the simplest device for measuring the efficiency of enterprises by means of a comparison between costs of production; it is indeed the most flexible instrument for economic measurement in all spheres.[22]

In one obvious sense a state collectivist society cannot become a pure form, and collectivize everything. The complete collectivization of labour would imply a reversion to a quite different form of society, for the ownership of labour-power by the state, under the control and direction of the bureaucracy, would in fact mean the institution of a form of state slavery. Apart from the concentration camps of the Gulag, this has not yet occurred.

Thus, even in the highly organized and regulated societies of the Eastern Bloc there is evidence to support the impurity principle. There is private production and reproduction of labour-power in the family, as well as other forms of private production and both legal and illegal markets. Elements of economic pluralism are found in even the most centralized socio-economic systems. While state collectivist societies are not socialist, this discussion has important implications for democratic socialism which will be developed later.

General Observations on the Impurity Principle

The discussion of different socio-economic systems in this chapter has been brief and sketchy. However, it is possible to derive some principles which, although they cannot be proved here, are of quite general significance. Slavery, feudalism, capitalism, and state collectivism have together spanned more than two thousand years of human history. If these general principles apply to these four socio-economic systems, then it would be dangerous to assume that they do not apply to the conceivable future.

The first general principle has been defined in loose terms already: the impurity principle. It means that all socio-economic systems of necessity exhibit a variety of social relations and structures. Examples of social relations are those of slavery, employment, or market exchange. A social structure is a set of social relations which together can produce some proportion of goods and services. Examples are the domestic economic structure; a community of self-employed producers linked together by the market (i.e. simple commodity production); capitalism; feudalism; and slavery. A socio-economic system may be dominated by one particular economic structure, but differ from it in being capable of producing all necessary goods and services and reproducing itself over time. Thus there is a distinction between a capitalist economic structure and a capitalist socio-economic system. Each of the four socio-economic systems discussed in this chapter includes a domestic economic structure and one or more forms of commodity production, as well as other economic structures.

The statement that economic structure X is *necessary* for the functioning of socio-economic system Y is open to different interpretations. It could mean that X was necessary because there was no alternative. Or it could mean that X, or an alternative W, was necessary. In this chapter the impurity principle is asserted in a general sense. It is impossible to clarify the precise meaning of the word 'necessary' in each case without a much more detailed examination of the systems involved. Thus to say, for example, that market relations are necessary for a particular system to function does not rule out a plausible alternative; it will depend on the individual case.

The fact that stronger or weaker conclusions can be drawn from the impurity principle does not mean that it is devoid of substance. For example, it is much stronger than the statement that 'all social formations in history have included a variety of economic structures'. The impurity principle asserts that some of these economic structures were *necessary* for the socio-economic system to function over time. For this reason, our account of different socio-economic systems has omitted some impurities which do not seem to be positively necessary for them to survive. Slavery, for example, persisted in medieval England. According to the Domesday Book about ten per cent of the population were slaves. The use of slave labour in the early years of capitalist expansion is well known. Another survivor of classical antiquity, feudalism, and capitalism is simple commodity production. Although all these impurities are important, it is not clear that they were necessary for the systems involved. A more precise evaluation will have to await further theoretical work and study.

The second principle has been implied but not stated explicitly. It will be called the 'principle of dominance' – that is to say that socio-economic systems generally exhibit a dominant economic structure. Classical antiquity is characterized by the economic and social dominance of slavery, and of the master–slave social relation. In contrast, slavery existed but was not dominant under feudalism and early capitalism. Under feudalism the lord–vassal relation was part of the dominant economic structure. The capitalist economic structure is now dominant throughout the Western World.

The notion of dominance requires further elaboration; in particular, the role of the dominant economic structure in the transition from one socio-economic structure to another has to be clarified. Over what period of time and through what process does one dominant structure give way to the next? Precise answers cannot be given to this question, but there is much work by Marxist and other historians which would point the way.[23]

Using the notion of dominance it is possible to rephrase the impurity principle by saying that every socio-economic system includes at least one non-dominant economic structure. Furthermore, every dominant economic structure requires at least one other structure for the system as a whole to function. It may be possible to conceive of systems where two or more economic structures are rivals for dominance, perhaps accompanied by social and economic instability; but they would be exceptions to the principle of dominance. As far as we can see, there are no exceptions to the principle of impurity.

Marx did not imply or formulate an impurity principle. In fact it could be argued that the structure and content of *Capital* effectively deny it. The impression is given that the dominant capitalist economic structure could in principle encompass social life in the process of expanding and destroying all adjacent economic structures. Marx paid little attention to the domestic economy, for example. He seemed to believe that the family would dissolve under the pressure of the capitalist system. In addition he failed to emphasize the important fact that under capitalism the production of labour-power is logically impossible. This failure to recognize the existence of impurities within capitalism forces Marx to place all faith in its perishing through its own inner contradictions. Little attention is given to the possibility of creating harbingers of socialism within capitalism itself.

In contrast, notions both of dominance and of structured combinations of heterogeneous elements are found in Marx's writings. Take an important passage in the *Grundrisse:*

> In all forms of society there is one specific kind of production which predominates over the rest, whose relations thus assign rank and influence to the others. It is a general illumination which bathes all the other colours and modifies their particularity. It is a particular ether which determines the specific gravity of every being which has materialized within it.[24]

This passage amounts to an acceptance of the principle of dominance but not of that of impurity. He recognizes the co-existence of impurities, but not that at least one non-dominant impurity is necessary for the system as a whole. This mistake leads him to isolate completely the capitalist economic structure which, according to him, must be 'the starting point as well as the finishing point' of the analysis.

Cybernetics and the Impurity Principle

The establishment of the impurity principle, and the principle of dominance, has not been a matter of *a priori* theoretical proof. Some may want to dismiss them for that reason. That would be too rash and formalistic. Although these two principles are empirical in character, and thus capable of refutation, many other important laws and principles in the real world have a similar theoretical status. Consider, for instance, the law of gravity or the entropy law. In the same manner, neoclassical economists cling to the law of demand (which asserts that the lower the price, the greater the quantity of the product demanded by consumers). Each one of these laws is capable of refutation, and some are more vulnerable than others. But they are each interesting and important generalizations. I would argue that such empirical laws and principles tell us more about the real world than many *a priori* theorems and that they are necessary for any theoretical system which would be of some use in practice. Who would deny the importance of the law of gravity in physics, or the entropy law in thermodynamics?

The real inspiration for the impurity principle comes from the Marxian and post-Marxian discussions and analyses of social formations in history and from the science of cybernetics. Some brief discussion of the latter is warranted. In his pioneering work, W. R. Ashby asserted the principle or 'law' of 'requisite variety'.[25] The shortest and most frequently quoted version of this law is 'only variety can destroy variety'; that is, if a stable target outcome is to be attained, then the variety of the controlling system must be at least equal to that of the activity which it is directing. For example, an air-conditioning system which is meant to keep both the temperature and the humidity of the air within a desired range must have two or more controlling instruments, namely a thermostat and a hygrometer. One instrument will, in general, be insufficient to keep two elements in target range.

Ashby's law is familiar to economists in a form associated with the name of Jan Tinbergen. In his study of the theory of economic policy, published in the same year as Ashby's original work, Tinbergen showed that, in general, the number of policy instruments (e.g. government expenditure, taxes, etc.) must be equal to or greater than the number of policy targets (e.g. full employment, balance of payments equilibrium, etc.).[26] Strictly, Ashby's law and Tinbergen's rule are not identical, and the former is a more general statement than the latter. But the near-simultaneous publication of very similar ideas based on the same core of formal reasoning is one of those uncanny happenings which have occurred at times in economics and other sciences.

Basing himself on Ashby's work, Stafford Beer has applied 'the law of requisite variety' to management science.[27] Beer argues that in a complex system, such as a capitalist firm, management must deal with all types of behaviour and a multitude of unpredictable problems by means of many and various organizational structures, methods, and strategies. Beer gives a number of case studies and examples to show the usefulness of this approach. Its relevance to the design or control of complex management structures is in no doubt.

However, the assumption that Beer is using the strict 'law of requisite variety', as propounded in Ashby's work, has been challenged.[28] It has been argued that variety is not always required to meet certain types of variety. For example, a variety of people in a restaurant may be hungry, and the single and uniform response of providing them with a meal may be sufficient to relieve that (varied) hunger. It all depends what we mean by variety. Raul Espejo and Nigel Howard have shown that it is always possible to classify phenomena into varieties so that the 'law of requisite variety' will hold. Ashby's law, they argue, is thus a mathematical truism, provable by a theorem, without recourse to experience or empirical facts. The same could be said of Tinbergen's rule. Beer, they claim, is using a more interesting but potentially falsifiable 'law', which they call the 'law of insufficient variety', which amounts to saying that for every single system there is a disturbance for which there is no response that will lead to a target outcome. In other words the variety in the environment will generate a threat to the system: there is a possibility that it will be unable to adapt or respond. In economic terms, it would mean that there is an ever-present possibility of crisis and malfunction within a single economic system. The law of insufficient variety is not provable in the same way as Ashby's law. It is not *a priori* but *a posteriori*: an empirical law rather than a mathematical theorem. The weight behind its assertion is derived from an analysis of real world systems.

If the analysis and arguments of Espejo and Howard are accepted, then the impurity principle is a special case not of the 'law of requisite variety' but of the 'law of insufficient variety'. It has been argued, in establishing the impurity principle, that no structure can function in an economic system without adjoining structures and social relations. In other words, given the variety present in any social formation (i.e. varied goods, services, consumer preferences, information, ideas, etc.) malfunction is immediately pressing in a 'pure' system, and adjoining systems are required to help. The similarity to the law of insufficient variety should now be evident. The impurity principle is a special case in at least two senses: first it is applied to economic systems, and second it is implied that malfunction in a pure system is immediate.

In particular, in a capitalist system there is a variety of fundamentally dissimilar or diverse commodities. Labour-power is essentially different from material goods and other services, and money is essentially different from both. Although markets are a powerful regulator, and capitalist relations are dynamic in character, a pure capitalist system cannot cope with this variety; other systems and structures, including state intervention in the economy, are required.

It has been argued here that a pure state collectivist system would have insufficient variety to cope with quality control, large numbers of products of different types, diverse consumer preferences, and so on. All these examples are manifestations of the law of insufficient variety. Cybernetics, it would seem, has a great deal to contribute to our understanding of economic systems, as well as providing the ultimate generalization of the impurity principle in all (including non-economic) systems.[29]

The policy conclusion of this analysis is clear. Some form of structural economic pluralism is unavoidable. Neither a pure market economy nor a completely planned economic system is feasible. However, as is emphasized throughout this work, this is not a wishy-washy argument for the type of 'mixed economy' which is attractive to some economists and politicians. The economy must indeed be mixed, but by the principle of dominance one economic structure is likely to prevail. Something approaching a half and half, public/private mixture is no solution: it is an unrealizable utopia of the political Centre, just as the extremes of pure planning or pure market systems are unrealizable. We have to choose which economic structure is to dominate the whole: it can be the market, or it can be planning, but it cannot be both.

Eight

Capitalism and Democracy

Either poverty must use democracy to destroy the power of property, or property in fear of poverty will destroy democracy.

Colonel Thomas Rainsborough, speaking at the Putney Debates of 1647

Are capitalism and political democracy compatible? Do they serve each other as enduring complements, or are they in a war of attrition, one against the other? In implicit terms at least, these questions were raised in the debates within the Cromwellian army held in Putney in 1647. The army leaders, such as Cromwell and Ireton, and the Leveller radicals, such as Rainsborough and Sexby, seemed to agree that true democracy and full liberty were incompatible with the concentration of wealth and property in the hands of a few. But Ireton and Cromwell saw this as a reason to restrict democracy, whereas the Levellers began to challenge propertied interests for the sake of liberty and democracy.[1]

Over three hundred years later the dilemma posed by Ireton and Rainsborough is still with us. In the twentieth century we have seen growing socialist movements aiming at greater equality in the distribution of wealth. Quite often, in reaction, propertied interests have supported fascism or military dictatorships in order to protect their property. (This has happened in Germany, Italy, Spain, Indonesia, Brazil, Bolivia, Argentina and Chile, to name but a few.) Even in the apparently stable democracies of advanced capitalism we have seen proposals from eminent and 'moderate' sources to limit severely the powers of democracy. Perhaps, for over three hundred years, we have witnessed the battle of capitalism *versus* democracy: a battle which may well be decided in this century.

Perhaps not. Liberal opinion would have it otherwise. Distinguished liberal theorists, from Jeremy Bentham to Milton Friedman, have argued that capitalism is the only secure basis for democracy. In this view, the two systems are not only compatible: democracy positively needs capitalism in order to survive. The most famous presentation of this argument in the twentieth century is F. A. Hayek's *The Road to Serfdom*.

What is enduring in the classic liberal tradition is this belief that democracy cannot be secure except within a capitalist or market system. However, the degree of commitment to democracy varies from one liberal to the next. The classic liberals of the New Right agree that it requires the soil of capitalism to grow and flower, but at the same time they are in favour of a drastic pruning. It is evident that they would prefer capitalism to democracy if the two come into conflict. Like many earlier liberals, they would limit democracy to the parliamentary sphere. They are clear that its extension to the running of the economy would interfere with the cherished 'rights' and 'freedoms' of the minority that control industry. The argument of the classic liberals and the New Right is in fact that *parliamentary* democracy cannot be secure except within a capitalist framework. Following Samuel Bowles and Herbert Gintis we shall call this 'the compatibility thesis'.[2] The question of the compatibility of capitalism with a wider democracy will be dealt with at a later point in this chapter. Initially, democracy will be considered in a narrow parliamentary sense.

The Compatibility Thesis

It is commonplace to divide the world into three camps: (1) the state collectivist countries of the Eastern Bloc; (2) the advanced capitalist countries; and (3) the less developed capitalist countries. What is remarkable is that parliamentary democracy is almost entirely confined to the second of these three camps. It is effectively absent from the Eastern Bloc, and present in very few of the less developed countries. A close relationship between parliamentary democracy and developed capitalism would appear to be confirmed.

However, such casual empiricism does not clinch the argument. It is necessary to examine the mechanisms in history which have connected capitalism to parliamentary democracy. As we have seen, a limited form of parliamentary democracy pre-dates capitalism in Britain by several centuries. In addition, the struggle for the sovereignty of Parliament in the seventeenth century was conducted well before the rise of industrial capitalism. There was, however, an extensive web of market trading relations, and a large number of merchants and self-employed producers. Agriculture had been integrated into the market system long before 1640. Much of the economic output was distributed *via* the market. Commodity production was well developed. As a consequence there had already emerged 'a group in society with an independent economic base'.[3] It was the development of such an independent group that Barrington Moore regards as a crucial instrument for the establishment of liberal democracy. Without it, democracy would have been unable to challenge the absolutist state with success: it would have been bonded to the old order.

However, the very independence of this social group depended on the existence of a developed market system. Its social practice was connected to the world of contract and trade. Its economic independence and prosperity were based on its labour and above all its private property. Thus, while this group of merchants and small producers was an effective instrument against absolutism and for democracy, it was also wedded to the market system and private property. These formed the basis of the full development of capitalism itself. There is no necessary connection between capitalism and markets on the one hand, and parliamentary democracy on the other: the association is historical rather than logical.[4]

To extend this market system based on private property, traders and progressive landowners had to confront much of the restrictive apparatus of the absolutist state. Many of the disputes with absolutism, as in England in the 1640s, and in America in the period leading up to the War of Independence, were over the payment of taxes by the business community to an autocratic state. The limitation of such arbitrary powers, and the removal of other obstacles to the development of markets, turned out to require legislation as well as revolution. Parts of the old state machine had to be destroyed; the rest was to be used but contained.

In Britain business and trading interests had early and established access to a parliament. After the revolutions of 1642–9 and 1688, parliament became a crucial instrument to use and contain the state. The process in France was similar in some respects after the Revolution of 1789–93, except that the threat of invasion by foreign powers was much more serious, the business community did not have as developed an economic base, and the parliamentary system was interrupted by Bonapartist and monarchical regimes. In Germany and Japan there was lacking a group with an independent economic base and with sufficient weight and strength to accomplish an enduring democratization of the state before the First World War. The eventual outcome in both cases was fascism.[5]

There is a germ of truth, therefore, in the New Right idea that democracy is more likely to survive in a system where there is a plurality of economic power. The development of parliamentary democracy in the West has depended on the existence of relatively autonomous producers.

However, it has not been demonstrated that democracy in any form is necessarily linked to a market system based on private property.

In Britain, as we have seen in Chapter 6, a dynamic was unleashed in the nineteenth century which led to the growth of the interventionist state and the limitation of *laissez-faire*. The liberal state had been consolidated and stabilized by the widening and rationalization of the franchise in the Reform Bill of 1832, which had the support of the under-represented industrial capitalists and a wide section of the population. The strongest economic force in the reform movement at that time was growing industrial capital. However, no sooner had the Bill become law than there were appeals from the newly enfranchised middle classes, as well as from sections of the old aristocracy, for the limitation of the horrors of industrial capitalism. Democracy was the sorcerer's apprentice: once the franchise had been widened, the way was open for all sorts of interest groups to press for economic as well as political reform. Thus sections of the capitalist class combined with organized workers to campaign for the limitation of the working day. As the trade union movement grew in strength in the late 1800s, and after the franchise had been widened still further in 1867 and 1884, the working class became an independent political force in its own right and there was irresistible pressure to bring market forces under some sort of social control. The state began to intervene once more. Democracy helped to remove some of the fragments of the absolutist state; but once established it helped to build up a state machine which would intervene more and more in the market economy.

Thus democracy was the child of a developed market system but it led to the end of *laissez-faire*. Not long after the triumph of classic liberalism in 1832 this creed became an anachronism. Most liberals were forced to do a U-turn and accept a more interventionist role for the state. Thus in Britain and the United States a 'liberal' became a person who supports some state regulation, argues for a welfare state, and is enthusiastic about democracy. Ironically, it is the 'conservatives' who now support much of the classic liberal ideology. They argue for the retraction of the state from the economic sphere, and the sovereignty of markets. Notably, they are less enthusiastic about democracy than those who did the U-turn long before. To some extent, it would seem, a choice was posed between the welfare state and democracy on the one hand, and *laissez-faire* on the other. A bifurcation occurred in liberal thought. The Liberal Party in Britain, for example, chose the former. The New Right chooses *laissez-faire*.

This would appear to undermine the compatibility thesis. There is, however, another side to the picture. Parliamentary democracy has helped to stabilize the capitalist social formation in many countries. Take Britain in the nineteenth century. There were persistent conflicts of interest between the aristocracy, large capital, small capital, the self-employed, and the growing working class. Parliamentary democracy served as a political and economic mechanism of regulation. In a distorted manner it reflected the shifting balance of group interests and class forces. It was not a faithful representative of popular opinion, but most people believed it was or could be so. Thus, despite its shortcomings, parliamentary democracy had the support of the majority. They were held together through fear of an absolutist alternative. Parliamentary democracy partly expressed and strongly reinforced the social consensus. The result has been more than a century of civil peace.

After parliamentary democracy had helped to create a stable political and social environment, private investors were inclined to take a more optimistic view of the economic future. Stability in politics helped to foster economic expansion. However, as we shall see below, there are arguments from the Left as well as the Right that parliamentary democracy is now an impediment to capitalist economic advance: by helping to push up wages and welfare spending, for example. These arguments will be considered in the next section.

There is strong evidence, however, that parliamentary democracy has made a significant contribution to the development of capitalism in the past. With very few exceptions (such as, perhaps, India and Venezuela) all parliamentary democracies are located in developed capitalist countries. This appears to show a contribution by parliamentary democracy to capitalist development.

As suggested above, the reverse is probably true as well: the growth of capitalism has, to some extent, promoted parliamentary democracy, for every single developed capitalist country has this form of government at the present time. However, this second feedback loop, from capitalism to democracy, is weaker than it would appear at first sight. Despite some economic development since the Second World War, most Third World countries have remained as military or other dictatorships. After two centuries of capitalist development, democracy is still the exception not the rule. Furthermore, full parliamentary democracy, based on universal adult suffrage, was not present in more than a dozen countries until after the Second World War.[6] Thus the process of feedback is long and slow. In addition it may be weaker than some pro-capitalist ideologists suppose.

In summary, there is evidence of a degree of positive feedback in two directions. To some extent capitalism has assisted the development of parliamentary democracy. Also, parliamentary democracy has helped capitalism to stabilize and expand. However, in both cases these feedback loops are not as strong as supposed in classic liberal and New Right theory. Furthermore, the processes involved may take many decades to have effect. In addition, the interaction is made more complicated by elements of negative as well as positive feedback. Finally, the interaction depends a great deal on historical and international circumstances which can alter its pace and direction. There is an element of truth in the compatibility thesis, but in its simplistic form it is unacceptable.

The Incompatibility Thesis

Bowles and Gintis have argued that 'the compatibility thesis' is false. Their conclusion is that 'capitalism and democracy have reached a parting of the ways'.[7] It would be appropriate to refer to this as 'the incompatibility thesis'. The idea that democracy and capitalism have become incompatible is found in the works of a wide variety of authors. Arguments tend to focus on the way in which democratic institutions allegedly promote state expenditure and foster the growth of powerful trade unions, which leads to a squeeze on profits and investment. Thus there are four actors in the drama: capital and democracy, plus the working class and the interventionist state. The very expansion and industrialization created by the capitalist system has pushed the working class on to the stage. In addition, the process of capitalist development required state intervention in the economy. This has been true for all capitalist economies, without exception. These developments have become most pronounced since the Second World War.

Let us consider the arguments behind the incompatibility thesis in more detail. The script is as follows. To maintain its legitimacy, or for other reasons, parliamentary government has had to respond to growing demands from working people for social welfare provision, better education, trade union rights, and so on. The extent of state intervention within advanced capitalist economies has created still further opportunities for the articulation of such demands. As the state becomes involved more and more in the economy, it is subject to greater and greater pressure from interest groups. If an interventionist state is supposedly under democratic control, then to maintain its legitimacy it has to respond to such pressures.

Furthermore, the adoption of Keynesian measures of demand management created near-full employment for a quarter of a century. This allowed the trade unions to grow in membership and strength. Real wages were pushed up, taking up a greater and greater proportion of national income. The combined result of extended state intervention and policies for full employment is growing public spending and an increasing share of the national cake going to the working class. Some writers then conclude that the result is an inevitable squeeze on the level of profits and investment. Others argue that the main deleterious result is inflation. All are agreed that state intervention plus a responsive democracy bring about a crisis of the capitalist system.

Bowles and Gintis write:

> A significant portion of the customary standard of living of the working class – between a fifth and a third of the total wage bundle in all advanced capitalist countries except Japan – is now allocated through political mechanisms in the form of medical care, income support, public schooling [i.e. state schooling] and the like. Most significant, perhaps, democratically won gains in social expenditures – what *Fortune* charmingly terms 'social drag' – appear to constitute a significant obstacle to the capitalist growth process.[8]

In his significantly-titled book *The Zero-Sum Society*, Lester Thurow argues that citizens of the United States 'have to be willing to make greater sacrifices in our personal consumption ... But the need to cut consumption creates strains in a democracy that do not exist in a dictatorship.'[9] Even more graphically, Ian Gough writes:

> Capitalism, which ... has permitted the development of the productive forces, political democracy and social rights in the post-war period, may no longer be capable of achieving all three simultaneously. In that case, either accumulation and economic growth or political and social rights must be sacrificed.[10]

A number of common assumptions underlie these arguments. First, they reflect the belief that productivity growth in advanced capitalist countries is under some sort of severe constraint, making a substantial and general increase in the average standard of living difficult or impossible. Second, one of the most notable constraints is the degree of social and welfare expenditure that has been forced upon these economies. And third, the existence of democratic institutions has been instrumental in facilitating this expansion of the welfare state. In short, the main economic effect of democracy has been to increase wages and social spending which, in turn, has constrained economic growth.

The above arguments bring democracy into a picture which has, in part, been sketched out before. There is the famous study of Andrew Glyn and Bob Sutcliffe which appeared to show that pressure for higher wages had resulted in a falling share of profits in national income.[11] A little later, Robert Bacon and Walter Eltis put forward the argument that social welfare and other public spending has led to falling investment in industry and declining production.[12] These analyses have many features in common. None of them is devoid of key insights or elements of truth.

What is striking, however, is that the counteracting influences are ignored. Only the negative effects of democracy on the capitalist economy are considered. For the writers of the Left this is in an attempt to show that capitalism must be transcended if both democracy and trade union rights are to survive. For the writers of the Right this is in an attempt to show that trade unions and democracy must be limited or dismantled in order to save the capitalist system. The political conclusions are different but they share the same premises.

It is not suggested here that the counteracting influences are necessarily stronger than the negative effects. What is suggested is that both positive and negative effects should be considered together. First take the positive contribution of parliamentary democracy to capitalist economic development. To some extent this has already been discussed. What could be termed the 'productivity effects' of democracy have to be included. By its promotion of open debate and discussion, democracy helps to raise the level of education and culture. This may have a slight effect on productivity and economic growth. Parliamentary democracy may also help to encourage wider participation in decision-making, and there is considerable evidence that worker participation leads to improvements in productivity.[13] Although these positive 'productivity effects' are not overwhelming, they continue to be of significance. In one sense democracy is a burden, but in another it is an engine of progress.

There is also a 'taxation effect'. The prophets of doom lay exclusive emphasis on the way in which democracy may lead to increases in public expenditure. There is a strong case for presuming that democracy may also facilitate increases in taxation. The extension of democracy has helped to legitimate the attempts by government to increase tax revenues. By being nominally 'answerable' to the electorate, the government is able to raise taxes on the grounds that its policies are approved by the population. Thus heavier taxation does not meet the resentment or political resistance that it would if it were carried out by a dictatorship. Opposition to taxation in capitalist democracies is significantly more muted than the opposition to the much lower levels of the seventeenth to nineteenth centuries. How many Boston Tea Parties would there have been in 1773 if taxes were then at 40 per cent? How much more invective would Prime Minister Gladstone have raised against income taxes in 1874 if they were at 30 per cent instead of the actual 0.8 per cent of the time, before universal suffrage and the welfare state?

Social expenditure itself has positive effects on productivity and economic growth. Expenditure on education and welfare helps to create a trained and healthy workforce. According to Keynesian economic theory, both high wages and state expenditure constitute effective demand in the economy. Effective demand in the form of private investment is less reliable and sustained. In contrast, public expenditure constitutes a continuous and effective stimulus to the economy, helping to raise both employment and the level of average productivity. These techniques of demand stimulation have their problems and limitations: the negative effects should not be ignored. But in addition the positive contribution of public expenditure and relatively high wages to economic expansion and development should be recognized.

In fact the doom-laden diagnoses of democracy are reminiscent of pre-Keynesian attitudes to increases in wages. Keynes's economic adversaries saw only the negative aspect of the wage bill: it was a cost to private firms. However, wages are also an element of demand in the economy as a whole, as Keynes pointed out. Similarly, the modern prophets of doom see only the negative aspects of democracy, ignoring its positive contribution to the economy. Public expenditure is merely a drain on resources; it is not recognized as a stimulus to demand and production. Keynes criticized his adversaries for making the 'Ricardian' error of assuming that effective demand and employment were at a steady level. Modern writers tend to assume that the level of productivity is either constant or severely constrained. Let us consider this last point in more detail.

If we were to believe the orthodox economics textbooks, with given labour, capital and technology the level of output is fixed and pre-determined. Production is seen as a mechanical result of given inputs. The evidence shows that this view is untenable. Output per worker is about three times higher in the USA than it is in Britain. In West Germany and France it exceeds that in Britain by about 50 per cent. Comparisons of productivity between plants in different countries with very similar labour and capital, and identical technology, still show large differences.[14] These variations have to be accounted for by historical, cultural, political and organizational factors.[15]

Above all, production is not a 'black box' whose output is determined merely by its inputs: it is a purposeful activity, dependent on social and human relations. As an illustration of the effect of political and other factors on productivity, consider the three-day week imposed by the Heath Government in Britain in early 1974. Despite the fact that working time had been reduced to 60 per cent of its former level in manufacturing, output was reduced by only 10 per cent. Thus labour productivity per hour increased overnight by 50 per cent. It is therefore quite wrong to regard the level of productivity as under severe constraint. Political and democratic influences can lead to a substantial increase.

Apart from variations in productivity resulting from political, cultural and organizational factors, there is a new technology waiting in the wings. The computer, the microprocessor and the robot threaten to take over jobs, both on the shopfloor and in the office, at the rate of between 10 and 20 per cent per decade. This will of course bring about a huge increase in the average level of output per employed full-time worker. The social effects will be equally dramatic. Unless other work is created (for example in the education and leisure sectors) or existing jobs are shared (through systematic part-time work, a reduced working week, and early retirement) the result will be an unemployment epidemic. This, indeed, could pose a threat to parliamentary democracy. Riots on the streets and counteracting repressive measures will become commonplace. Unemployment will feed the authoritarian state.

But there is no reason why this should necessarily occur, even under capitalism. Some advanced capitalist countries show signs of adaptation to the technological revolution. Britain, of course, remains a conservative nation, seemingly incapable of making adjustments until it is almost too late. But in some European countries (particularly Belgium and Italy) the combination of longer holidays and a shorter working week means that the average number of hours put in by a full-time worker in a year is about 20 per cent less than in Britain.[16] In Scandinavia there are extensive experiments in work-sharing and systematic part-time working. We should not underestimate the capacity of capitalism to adjust, and retain its democracy.

Admittedly there are problems with finite resources on planet Earth. But in many cases, such as coal and oil, these are a long way from being exhausted.[17] Although resource constraints are ultimately a problem, their effects in the last decade or so have been exaggerated. In addition it has to be emphasized that much productive activity does not require intensive inputs of raw material or non-renewable resources. Productive output consists of services as well as material goods. The service sector is a considerable fraction of the economy in all advanced capitalist countries. There is also the growing importance of information-related technology and services. For example, a piece of software may take a great deal of the time of a computer programmer to produce, but the quantity and value of the physical resources required may be minimal.

Thus, despite resource constraints it is possible to envisage economic growth in the capitalist system in the future. Growth rates of productivity per worker of 5 per cent or more per annum are commonplace in West Germany, Italy, France and Japan, even in recent years of world recession. Despite growing unemployment in these countries, overall output has continued to increase.

The arguments here are not that such growth is desirable or undesirable, but that within the existing and democratic capitalist systems there is still much potential for economic expansion. If this argument is correct, then the analyses of Bowles, Gintis, Gough, Thurow and others are found wanting. As Stanislaw Gomulka has pointed out, the Bacon–Eltis theory of a public sector squeeze on marketed output loses much of its force if higher growth rates in productivity and output are considered. Gomulka points out that if in the 1950–74 period the growth rate in productivity in the UK had been as high as it was in France or West Germany, output in 1974 would have been as much as 70 per cent greater than it actually was. In these circumstances a reduction of employment in the manufacturing sector (much lamented by Bacon and Eltis) would not have posed such a problem. Employment could have been directed elsewhere, or there could have been a reduction in the working week without loss of income. Welfare provision could have been increased without any squeeze on manufacturing.

> The maximum social wage which the public is prepared to finance by taxes is also likely to be positively associated with the output of marketed goods per person. Had productivity been 70 per cent higher, then the real wage could well have been sufficiently high to be (again politically) consistent with the tax rate that is required to support the present social wage.[18]

Similar arguments apply to the profits squeeze hypothesis of Glyn and Sutcliffe. If the growth of productivity in Britain had been similar to that in other advanced capitalist countries, wages would not have squeezed profits in the way suggested by their theory.[19] Substantial increases in real wages would have been compatible with a constant or even increasing share of profits in national income. The theories of both Bacon and Eltis on the one hand, and Glyn and Sutcliffe on the other, concentrate on the effects of a phenomenon rather than its underlying causes. Both theories ignore the potential for capitalist recovery which has been exhibited to some extent elsewhere.

Close scrutiny of 'the incompatibility thesis' has uncovered several defects in its argument. The conflict between capitalism and the social movements promoted by democracy is not as cataclysmic as it is sometimes portrayed. This does not mean, however, that there are not germs of truth in these theories. The growth of democracy and public expenditure can sometimes pose both a political and an economic threat to the capitalist system.[20] The emergence and mobilization of a strong groundswell of opinion for a more participatory and accountable democracy is bound to challenge capitalist relations of production and property.

But this process could take decades rather than years. There is always a temptation to depict emerging conflicts as the beginning of a final showdown. We live in an unstable and crisis-ridden world, but that does not mean that catastrophe is necessarily our fate. In addition, the worsening crisis is largely due to international factors, rather than resource or other constraints within the national economies. The long postwar boom was due, in the main, to the stable international trading system under the hegemony of the United States. When that system began to break down in the early 1970s the economic boom came to an end.[21] The current crisis has much less to do with the scale of public spending or the existence of democracy.

The 'Uncomfortability' Thesis

Nevertheless, the grains of truth in both the compatibility and the incompatibility theses should be nurtured. Consider the schematic relationship in the figure below. We assume, for simplicity, that democracy can be measured on a quantitative scale: zero implying its absence, parliamentary democracy attaining a moderate score on its own, and a higher index for full, participatory democracy. There are also quantitative measures of the amount of resources devoted to social welfare (including health, education and social services), and the total output of the capitalist economy. Thus we have three inter-related quantities, say D, W and Q respectively.

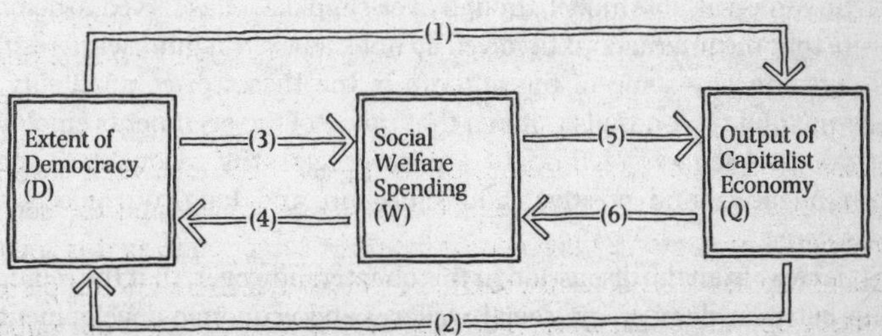

Proponents of the compatibility thesis stress the two connections (1) and (2) between D and Q. They assert that both influences are positive. It has been argued here that although these influences probably are positive, their effects are weak and spread over a long time. Proponents of the incompatibility thesis stress connections (3) and (5). They argue that (3) is strong and positive, but (5) involves a negative correlation, so that increases in W lead directly to decreases in Q. In this argument short-run and long-run effects are sometimes confused. An increase in social welfare spending (W) may well have a short-term negative effect on total output (Q) by, for example, diverting resources from investment. But the long-term effects are likely to be positive. Once supply bottlenecks have been overcome, W will make a contribution to effective demand in the economy. Furthermore, there will be positive economic results from having an educated, healthy, and socially secure workforce. There is no inconsistency between having a negative short-term relationship and one which is positive in the long run. It is easy to express this mathematically, such as in a difference equation with some negative and some positive coefficients.

In fact, all six influences in the figure could be expressed in difference equation form. Some of the difference equations would have coefficients of different sign, some would be all positive, and some might be all negative. There would then be six difference equations expressing (lagged and unlagged) relationships between D, W and Q in terms of condensed mathematical formulae. This dynamic relationship could be oscillatory, stable or explosive. There are a large number of possible forms of dynamic behaviour. They would be similar to the phenomena generated in that branch of economics known as trade cycle theory.[22] Without further and much more specific information it is impossible to determine whether the relationship between D, W and Q will be stable or unstable, or if the overall connections in the system imply compatibility or incompatibility between these elements. Things are a great deal more complicated than many writers suppose.

The three-variable model, though over-simplified, has served to demonstrate that the interactions involved do not lead to straightforward results, as presumed by some of the authors of the theses of compatibility or incompatibility. It has also shown that many of the arguments employed by the two schools of thought are not necessarily inconsistent, once both negative and positive, and short-run and long-run, effects are considered.

It is clear from the discussion in this chapter, however, that the relationship between democracy, social welfare, and economic development is not necessarily harmonious or stable. There are important elements of antagonism. There is the contrasting combination of short-run and long-run effects, and the juxtaposition of negative and positive influences. These combinations, amounting to a range of dynamic behaviour in the system as a whole, create enormous potential variety. Mutual reinforcement, symbiosis, or crisis: all are possible.

Charles Lindblom has summed it all up as 'the close but uneasy relation between private enterprise and democracy'.[23] Perhaps the term 'the uncomfortability thesis' could be coined to express this dynamic combination of antagonism and mutual reinforcement. Democracy and capitalism have had a long love affair: a courtship lasting centuries, but stormy rows and a rather tense period of living together in the twentieth century. It is a potentially unstable and insecure association which can cramp the development of production and the advance of more participatory forms of democracy.

Taking the long historical view, we are forced to recognize the elements of mutual reinforcement, and the germ of truth in the compatibility thesis. However, in an increasingly unstable world, our eyes are focused on the fragility of the relationship, and the emerging threats to democracy. While it is incorrect to assume that an enlargement of democracy is impossible within capitalism as such, some developments in the twentieth century bode ill for it. The incompatibility thesis is unacceptable in a bald form, but some of its arguments are valid if placed in the proper context. The incompatibility is not predetermined or inevitable, but it is possible that future developments will lead to the erosion or end of the limited democracy that survives within capitalism.

There are a number of ways in which this could happen. In Italy and Germany in the 1920s and 1930s, against a background of social and economic crisis, fascism emerged as the victor after the turbulence and dislocation of the First World War, a number of failed insurrections from Right and Left, and a class war in which no side was able to triumph. Such circumstances are unlikely to recur in the present period, but there are forces pushing in the direction of authoritarianism and dictatorship. After all, explicit plans have been made in Britain that, in the event of nuclear war, parliamentary democracy shall be dissolved, civil liberties shall be extinguished, and arbitrary power of life and death shall be placed in the hands of appointed regional despots. If such atrocities can be planned in advance, what could be the result of the *unconscious* forces of capitalist development?

The postwar growth of multinational firms has concentrated both economic and political power in the hands of a few large corporations.

To a large extent these multinationals can act without being accountable to parliament. They can readily shift resources across international frontiers, creating unemployment in one place for the sake of investment in another. The mechanism of transfer pricing – the use of artificially low prices in the internal sale of the products of one subsidiary to another – can be used to avoid taxation of their profits.[24] The multinational firms have set up professional lobbying organizations to influence Parliament in Britain and Congress in America. Such a concentration of economic power is bound to have serious repercussions and be harmful to any form of democracy.

This concentration of private economic power is not tamed by the market. Although international competition, even between large firms, has not diminished, the scope of corporate decision-making has been enlarged. The market economy is being managed by the large firm and the state. Private ownership and competition remain, but the state and the large corporation have assumed greater powers of control. Thus there has been steady development of corporate capitalism, involving the state, big business, and the trade unions in patched-up deals to manage and sustain the capitalist system. This trend is evident, to some extent, in all advanced capitalist countries.[25]

Under a corporatist or semi-corporatist capitalism the regulatory properties of the market are partially supplanted by undemocratic, interest-group politics at the level of the state. The state bureaucracy proliferates. An army of officials and committees grows up to regulate the system and take over some of the functions of the market. There is no guarantee, of course, that this growing central administration will use democratic procedures, or even refer all its more important decisions to parliament. Thus grows the dictatorship of bureaucracy and unelected committee, the repression of dissent against corporate wisdom, and the gradual development of a totalitarian state.

The New Right desires to take us in a different direction. An attempt is made to shift the initiative back to the market, and to reduce the power of the state in the economic sphere. In the process, however, there is massive deflation in the economy, a decline in industrial production, and a large increase in unemployment. The solidarity and cohesion of society is eroded, both by the recession and by the abrasive competition of the market. There is social disclocation and urban riot. In accord with most New Right thinkers, state expenditure is transferred from welfare and social areas to the forces of law and order. Repression becomes the only expanding industry. The ranks of the police and the army swell in an attempt to integrate the declining and fracturing system. The philosophy of the New Right is turned into its opposite. Instead of freedom from coercion, we are observed and bullied by the repressive arm of the state.

Both scenarios eventually increase and centralize state power. The emphasis is different, however. Corporatism first centralizes economic control; the New Right espouses strong and authoritarian government. Neither variant is inevitable. Both, in fact, are partially unstable, as it is impossible to ensure permanent social and political equilibrium by either authoritarian or corporatist means.

Neither do these two variants exhaust all the possibilities. We have found no reason to exclude a difficult but progressive process of democratization under capitalism, leading to its transformation into a socialist system. There have been a few signs of the beginnings of this process in the 1960s and 1970s in Western Europe and the United States in movements for greater political participation, the growth in the number of worker cooperatives, the re-emergence of the women's liberation movement, the wider awareness of ecological issues, the campaign against nuclear power, and so on. Such movements have been prominent in every advanced capitalist country. It is possible that they will lead to a greater and more powerful political force which can begin a radical transformation of society.

We make the future ourselves through our own actions. All theory can do is to offer appropriate warnings and explore the more positive possibilities. Democracy and capitalism are uncomfortable bedfellows. Through either corporatist controls, or mass unemployment and the growing authoritarianism of the state, democracy can eventually be excluded in its entirety. Alternatively, it can grow, first within capitalism, and then beyond it. Or, in some prolonged and unsatisfactory way, it can survive an era, leading an insecure and stunted existence, as part of the capitalist system. Just as the demise of capitalism is not assured in our lifetime, neither is the end of democracy.

The preservation and extension of democracy is a worthy end in itself, and a task that cannot be postponed to a future beyond capitalism. It is a matter of applying democratic leverage to the existing system to the point where a fundamental transformation of society is effected. We have to determine in practice how and where capitalism and democracy reach a parting of the ways.

Part Three

PRACTICAL SOCIALISM

Nine

Economic Arguments for a Participatory Democracy

[Economic] development does not start with goods; it starts with people and their education, organization and discipline. Without these three, all resources remain latent, untapped, potential.

E. F. Schumacher, *Small is Beautiful*

At times, radical ideas can be acceptable, even fashionable. Everyone seems to nod in agreement, but not in every case is there the real force of conviction. We find supporters of 'worker participation' on the Left, Centre, and Right of the political spectrum. A small measure of worker participation is law in the European Economic Community. Its virtues are argued by management experts in the United States.

It is much the same with worker cooperatives, and the financial participation of workers in the ownership or profits of the firm. In the past, cooperatives have received a good deal of favourable comment. The economist Alfred Marshall argued that 'associations of labourers ... could not but succeed'.[1] Earlier, John Stuart Mill had written in his *Principles of Political Economy*:

> The form of association, however, which if mankind continues to improve, must be expected in the end to predominate, is not that which can exist between a capitalist as chief, and workpeople without a voice in the management, but the association of the labourers themselves on terms of equality, collectively owning the capital with which they carry on their operations, and working under managers elected and removable by themselves.[2]

Some support for worker cooperatives has been shown by leading members of the British Conservative Party such as Sir Keith Joseph. More articulate and consistent support has come from Peter Jay[3] (former Economics Editor of *The Times*) and members of the Liberal and Social Democratic Parties, as well as from the Left. Appeals for worker cooperatives and an extension of worker participation have come from the Catholic Church, notably from Pope John Paul II.[4]

In the socialist movement, of course, the ideas of worker cooperation and participation have a long pedigree.[5] From the idea of John Bellars for a cooperative 'Colledge of Industry' in 1695,[6] through the Shaker and other cooperative communities in the New World in the eighteenth and nineteenth centuries, the nineteenth-century experiments of Robert Owen, the birth of the modern British Cooperative Movement in Rochdale in the 1840s, European syndicalist movements, and the inventive ideas of Guild Socialism, cooperative and participatory ideas have survived and developed. The world-wide radicalization of the 1960s brought these issues to the top of the political agenda.[7] Most, if not all, socialist parties were affected, and various forms of worker participation and self-management appeared in their political programmes and manifestos.

In Britain, for example, the Labour Party published a report on *Industrial Democracy* in 1967, and this was approved at the annual conference in 1969.[8] This pamphlet called for powers to force companies to divulge vital and important information to trade unions, and for a measure of worker participation as an extension of collective bargaining. Similar ideas were repeated in *Labour's Programme 1973*, which later became the basis of the so-called Alternative Economic Strategy.[9] *Labour's Programme 1982* went slightly further and endorsed a central idea of the ill-fated Bullock Report on Industrial Democracy (1977) for the statutory representation of workers on the management boards of firms. In addition there was a brief discussion of industrial democracy in the 1982 Report produced by the TUC–Labour Party Liaison Committee.[10]

However, in such literature, in Britain and elsewhere, there is scant recognition of the economic necessity of such proposals. They are usually treated as moral ideals, or merely as a short logical extension to trade-union collective bargaining. The economic policies of political parties on the Left, Right and Centre remain obsessed with crude macroeconomic variables such as the balance of payments, the money supply, and the level of the exchange rate. In concentrating on such surface aggregates, the key underlying problems are ignored. As things stand, an extension of worker participation is low down the list of economic priorities.

The 1982 TUC–Labour Party Report is not that significant in terms of its detailed proposals, but it is one of the few statements to recognize that 'accountability in economic decision-making is not an inefficient luxury but is essential for improving ... economic performance'.[11] However, this point is not elaborated in detail.

It is contended here that a restructuring of industry on democratic lines is necessary for our future economic and social well-being. Worker participation should not remain a moral gesture of token and minimal consequence. Industrial democracy is essential, not merely desirable. The sooner we recognize that our problems are deep-seated and require radical action, the better. Many economic policy-makers would have us believe that serious problems can be solved by a manipulation of the exchange rate, or by controlling the money supply, or merely by increasing aggregate public spending. I suspect that the public at large are sceptical of these arguments. They are right. Our problems are fundamental, and they require a major reorganization of industry, work and leisure. Adjustments at the level of the market or the public purse will not bring about the necessary changes. Intervention is required to re-structure the economy along democratic lines.

Worker Participation

It is necessary, first of all, to clarify some terms. There are a number of different and contradictory definitions of 'industrial democracy', 'worker participation' and 'workers' control'. Usage can vary from author to author and is in some cases highly idiosyncratic. For example, Hugh Clegg has taken 'industrial democracy' to mean merely trade union power. In some other cases 'worker participation' means little more than a worker representative on the board of directors. Following more recent usage, such narrow definitions are rejected here. In particular, the term 'worker participation' is used in the following rich and broad sense, involving a number of different degrees or forms:

> *Worker participation* at the firm level is the ability of workers to directly influence or form the management and work process in an enterprise. Inherent in this definition is the notion of power, i.e. worker participation necessarily entails the wresting of some prerogatives from management or capital by the workers. It follows that participation occurs at many levels and in many forms ... To begin with, we may distinguish several 'forms' of participation: grievance; collective bargaining; information and consultation; veto; and participation through minority, parity, and majority representation on decision-making bodies.[12]

Thus different degrees of worker participation are possible, from grievance procedures at one extreme, to majority worker representation on the management board at the other. It is argued here that a high degree of participation, involving substantial representation on decision-making bodies, is an economic necessity in advanced industrial societies. The connection between worker participation within the enterprise, and other forms of popular participation within the community and society as a whole, will also be discussed.

Production is a social process, involving a number of people organized together. The modern firm requires, in one form or another, a division of labour, breaking down a complex and extended production process into a series of discrete tasks. The followers of Frederick Winslow Taylor, advocating the principles of so-called 'scientific management', aimed to analyse each task, measure the standard time taken to complete it, and erect a system of rewards and penalties for its completion or non-completion. Under this system the worker is subject to external control, and works under standards and for targets which are formulated away from the shopfloor by management. He or she is treated like a machine, devoid of much decision-making capacity. Taylorism thus tries to render production a reliable, efficient and *mechanical* social process.[13]

Taylorism worked to some extent, largely in the early and primitive stages of industrialization. When people are short of food they do respond to the inducement of extra wages, and to the deterrent of their reduction. To some degree the stick and the carrot still work in an advanced industrial society. But, in addition, other influences and motivational factors have become both relatively and absolutely more important. Work is more than a purely laborious task, and more than simply a means to monetary remuneration. From it, people derive a sense of self-esteem; it is a source of self-identity and self-actualization.[14] Work fulfils important human needs apart from the achievement of reward. Its social character adds another dimension. At the workplace one can interact with one's colleagues, fulfil social roles, and derive a sense of personal worth and position. Much of our waking experience is at work, so it is not surprising that it has this function.

These needs and roles are not considered in the Taylorist approach. But workers are not like machines – they are people with complex needs, acting purposefully in a social context. For this reason, hierarchic control from above is never satisfactory or completely effective. In the workplace, informal structures and networks of communication spring up which, as several studies show, play a significant part in the process of production. Yet they are beyond the direct and complete control of management.[15] Thus Taylorism has its limits. It fails to increase productivity beyond a certain point.

Uncertainty or partial ignorance also contribute to the failure of Taylorism to work effectively within a complex industrial society. No-one can know exactly what is being done, and what is possible. Information regarding technology, availability of materials, machine defects, personal skills, and so on, is scattered throughout the enterprise. Thus management can never, at least on its own (and short of complete automation), plan and direct production to perfection: it has to rely to some extent on the initiative and decision-making capacity of its employees. Furthermore, informal and formal channels of communication between workers play an important part in disseminating information and dealing with unforeseen eventualities. Management cannot manage on its own, no matter how hard it tries. For this reason some degree of formal or informal worker participation is essential.

An example of what can happen when these channels of communication break down has been given by Tony Lane.[16] Sifting through the Joint Works Council minutes of the now-closed Dunlop tyre plant in Liverpool, he came across a case where a shop steward had raised the same item at almost every monthly meeting for more than a year. The management had complained of poor productivity on case-making machines (the last stage of production before a tyre goes into a mould and gets its tread). The senior steward of the section had always given the same reply: 'There aren't enough rings and stands.' He referred to the simple pieces of equipment which ensured that the tyre cases kept their shape; if they were simply piled up straight off the machine they became deformed and worthless. New case-making machines had been introduced with a much higher output than the old ones, but the number of rings and stands had not kept pace. So, rather than produce for scrap, the men stopped working when all the existing ones were full. Despite continuous complaints to management from the shop steward, nothing was done. Productivity remained at about one-third of its potential with the new machines.

It is examples such as this which together form an impressive case for worker participation and democracy within industry. In contrast, much recent writing (especially by American Marxists) has asserted that hierarchical organization or Taylorist methods play an essential role within capitalism. This applies to the classic work by Harry Braverman,[17] and a more recent study of the labour process by Richard Edwards.[18] Rebutting the excessive emphasis on Taylorism in some American studies, Andrew Friedman has argued that Braverman

> must be criticized for confusing one *particular strategy* for exercising managerial authority in the capitalist labour process with *managerial authority* itself. Just as strict disciplinary rules were a particularly popular managerial strategy of top managers in the early years of the first industrial revolution, so strict work measurement and minute division of tasks have been popular managerial strategies, particularly during the first decades of the twentieth century. But Taylorian scientific management is not the only strategy available for exercising managerial authority, and given the reality of worker resistance, often it is not the most appropriate strategy from top managers' point of view.[19]

It is not, however, simply a matter of worker resistance to exploitation; it is also to do with the complex nature of production itself. As well as Taylorism, hierarchical control is not necessarily efficient. Quite often it is cultural factors and ideological misconceptions which prevent management from seeing this. It would be wrong to assume that people in power always act in their best interests and know what is optimal from their position. In general, people are not as rational as some analyses of the capitalist class imply. However, as we shall see below, it is also likely that hierarchy is supported by management to maintain their control, rather than to increase the efficiency of the firm.

Another possible objection to the argument in this chapter is to assert that modern technology necessarily involves the de-skilling of the workforce, leaving little room for worker decision-making and the enhancement of production by extended participation. Let us consider an example. In some factories the skilled lathe operator is being replaced by the computer-operated machine tool. Human beings then have the more menial task of overseeing several computer-operated lathes, without using much skill. A computer programmer works elsewhere to produce programs for the machines. However, the new technology does not necessarily impose this division of labour, with the consequent de-skilling of the operative. Recent research at the University of Manchester Institute of Science and Technology has shown that a more humane as well as efficient configuration is possible by which the skilled operative produces the component in the normal way and the computer, linked to the lathe, monitors the work and indicates any necessary adjustments. The record of machine operations (typically on a punched paper tape) can then be used to produce any number of additional components automatically. There is no need for a computer programmer in the office, and the operative acquires greater, not less, skill. In addition, it has been shown that the machine is far more efficient in terms of production and electrical power because a skilled worker can monitor the entire operation and make necessary adjustments directly. There is an interaction between operative and machine, unlike the one-way instructions on the computer program. Thus the new technology does not impose a single, necessary form of work organization. De-skilling is not inevitable. The same objections to hierarchy and one-way control remain: they are not invalidated by the new technology.[20]

Participation and Productivity

There is overwhelming evidence that increased worker participation reduces work alienation and raises productivity. To illustrate this, we shall first quote an example from the literature on the subject.[21]

Eight young women workers were employed in an American toy factory. Their job was simple and repetitive: to spray paint on each wooden toy and then place it on one of the overhead hooks moving by at constant speed on an endless belt which carried the toy into an adjacent drying oven. Despite a wage bonus system, productivity was low, and many hooks on the belt went by empty. Morale was bad, and there was much absenteeism and turnover of staff. The women complained that the room was too hot due to the proximity of the drying oven; and that it was impossible to keep up with the speed of the belt, set by engineers. Management therefore brought in a consultant and advised the foreman, against his will, to confer with the operatives. After a series of meetings, a ventilation system was introduced, at the suggestion of the workers but against the advice of the foreman and engineer. The improvement was a success, and the operatives became more interested and involved in the organization of their own work.

Subsequent meetings turned to the question of the 'excess speed' of the belts. The episode with the ventilation system had raised the heresy of wider participation in decision-making. After much discussion the operatives made the proposal that they should be able to adjust the speed of the belt, depending on how they felt. The foreman and engineer were horrified, and prophesied disaster. Eventually, however, the principle was conceded. The workers developed an elaborate schedule of when during the day the belt would be operated at slow speed, when medium, and when fast.

The result of this innovation was startling and ironic. The original complaint of the operatives was that the belt moved impossibly fast; but under their own control the average speed of the belt was actually increased. As a result, productivity rose between 30 and 50 per cent, morale reached an all-time high, and for the first time there was some evidence of satisfaction with working conditions. The first moral of this story is clear: increased productivity and reduced alienation are both possible through an increase in worker participation, and without repression, authoritarianism, increased exploitation, or a further subdivision of labour.

As we shall see below, there are many similar examples of greatly improved productivity arising from increased worker participation. In an aware and rational world, this should make its extension a priority for managers, economists and politicians. But, despite some lip-service to the idea, it has not been introduced on an extended and widespread basis. Economists continue to ignore the issue, concentrating instead on market phenomena. The tendency is to complain of wages being too high, rather than worker participation being too low. There is a widespread belief that the way productivity will be raised is through the competitive pressure of the market. The obvious, humane and democratic alternative has been neglected.

Why is this so? In part it is due to prevailing ideologies and practices. But there are other factors involved. Returning to the example of the American toy factory, a further reason why management have not introduced large-scale worker participation becomes clear. Earning a high productivity bonus, the eight young women workers began to receive wages in excess of those of the nominally skilled workers elsewhere in the plant. In addition it became evident that the role and prestige of the engineer and the foreman had been challenged by the experiment. In response to these new 'problems', management decided to end worker control of the speed of the belt. Productivity fell off immediately, and within a month six of the eight paint shop operatives had left the company. This example shows that the prerogatives and security of management can be threatened by the introduction of even a small measure of worker participation. The introduction of industrial democracy may be 'rational' from the point of view of increasing productivity, but it is not necessarily 'rational' from the point of view of maintaining management security within existing structures.[22] In the United States and elsewhere, many experiments have been ended precisely and explicitly for this reason, as for example in the 1960s in the Polaroid company. The training director complained:

> It was too successful. What were we going to do with the supervisors – the managers. We didn't need them any more ... The employees' newly revealed ability to carry more responsibility was too great a threat to the established way of doing things and to established power patterns.[23]

Thus while some hierarchy may be necessary, management has additional vested interests in preventing participation from below. The Belgian socialist Henri de Man saw this clearly a long time ago: 'hierarchy ... embodies, apart from the control necessary for the guidance of labour, also motives of private gain, on the one hand, and motives of social dominance, on the other.'[24]

Management power enables them to reward themselves with higher salaries. It carries with it status and prestige on the basis of its concern with 'important' and 'high-level' decisions. In addition, as Stephen Marglin has argued, a function of the hierarchy within the firm is to establish managerial control of production, technology and investment largely for its own sake. The economy is a system of power relations which cannot be justified simply in terms of prevailing technology: technology alone does not explain or justify hierarchical control.[25]

It should also be noted that many trade unionists have strong reservations about worker participation. Even Left-wing trade union leaders have resisted the idea.[26] Some trade union officials have regarded an extension of participation as a threat to their role in the collective bargaining process and their exclusive right to represent the workforce. At the other end of the scale there is a fear that worker participation involves taking responsibility for what are regarded as exclusively management matters. Ironically, in these cases trade unionists and management seem to unite in support of the maxim: 'It is the exclusive right of management to manage.'

Much of the trade union resistance to worker participation results from the more common adoption of cosmetic schemes which do little to increase the real decision-making power of the workforce. Substantial extensions of participation are rare: in general, management attempts to introduce it have been timid and reluctant. As a consequence, many workers – not surprisingly – have reached the conclusion that such schemes are of no positive advantage. It is extremely unfortunate that the preference of management for half-hearted measures which relinquish little or no control over the decision-making process has given worker participation a bad name, for the case for its substantial introduction is very powerful, and it should appeal especially to workers and trade unionists. The American socialist Paul Blumberg surveyed seventeen experiments in worker participation and reached the following strong conclusion:

> There is hardly a study in the entire literature which fails to demonstrate that satisfaction in work is enhanced or that other generally acknowledged beneficial consequences accrue from a genuine increase in workers' decision-making power. Such consistency of findings, I submit, is rare in social research.[27]

Blumberg has been criticized for basing his argument on experiments which were mostly short-lived and involved only minor increases in participation.[28] However, a large body of supplementary evidence, including long-term studies of both worker cooperatives and private firms, covering many countries, supports his conclusion.[29] In a recent and particularly impressive study, Juan Espinosa and Andrew Zimbalist have developed a taxonomy and index of worker participation and have shown that under Allende's socialist government in Chile in 1970–73 there was a strong positive correlation between labour productivity and worker involvement in decision-making. After an updated survey of the literature they remark: 'In summary, a wide-ranging group of studies are virtually unanimous in concluding that real participation has a positive impact on productivity. Our results for Chile corroborate these earlier results.'[30]

As the toy factory example shows, big gains in productivity are possible even within capitalism. In the Pacific North West of the United States there are plywood cooperatives with a level of productivity much higher than that of non-cooperative firms. The average difference is reckoned to be between 30 and 50 per cent, and in some cases it is much greater. A recent researcher has pointed out:

> Much of the productivity stems from flexibility of job assignment. Most plywood co-operative members learn to do most jobs in the plant and can be shifted as needed... These measures (similar to those recommended by management experts for combatting job 'alienation') eliminate idle time and need for some positions, as well as improving job satisfaction and performance by relieving the boredom of monotonous work.[31]

Within the capitalist sector of the United States economy there are further examples. In the claims and invoices departments of American Telegraph and Telephone a minimal participation scheme increased productivity by 27 per cent. In the assembly section of Non-Linear Systems a participation scheme led to a doubling of output in two years. Texas Instruments achieved an even more spectacular increase in one section of 330 per cent in a year, through a similar increase of worker participation. In Britain, ICI has registered a 30 per cent increase in output in its Gloucester synthetic fibre factory, with a reduction of supervision and a breakdown of the old division of labour.[32]

In West Germany, John Cable and Felix FitzRoy constructed a simple index of worker participation relating to forty-two private firms using industrial partnership schemes. Seven decision-making areas were identified: the wage system, production methods, job design, bonus system determination, product design, price policy, and investment policy. A 'score' of 0, 1, 2 or 3 was recorded for, respectively, 'no participation', 'observer', 'adviser' and 'active participation' by the workers in each of the decision-making areas. A maximum score was thus 21, which very few of the forty-two firms achieved. A statistical analysis of the relationship between this index of worker participation and (value added) productivity was carried out. It was discovered that the relationship was statistically significant, and on average a rise in productivity of 1.5 per cent was associated with a 10 per cent increase in the participation index.[33]

To indicate the importance of this observed relationship consider the following hypothetical application of these results to Britain. From experience I would suggest that very few firms would score as high as 8 on the Cable–FitzRoy participation index, given the fact that disclosure of information relating to most decision-making areas – which would be necessary to achieve 'observer' status – is not widespread. The implementation of the proposals of the Bullock Report would bring 'active participation' into all seven areas. Assume, in fact, participation is raised from 8 to an index level of 16. According to the parameters of the Cable–FitzRoy study, this increase would rapidly lead to a growth in productivity of 15 per cent.

The much-trumpeted 'success' of the Thatcher government in raising productivity pales into insignificance by comparison. In three years, from 1979 (second quarter) to 1982 (second quarter), British manufacturing productivity per person rose by only 3 per cent overall, and manufacturing productivity per person-hour by only 6 per cent. It took nine whole years for manufacturing productivity to exceed its 1973 level by as much as 15 per cent.[34] We can conjecture that similar increases would have occurred after the introduction of the proposals of the ill-fated Bullock Report on Industrial Democracy in a matter of months, if the Cable–FitzRoy results are taken as a guide.

Clearly there is very strong evidence to support the conclusion that substantial increases in productivity are possible through extended worker participation in decision-making. In addition, participation is associated with a reduction of worker alienation and a noticeable increase in job satisfaction. In spite of considerable hostility, especially from management, to an increase in worker participation, it has been shown that such a reform is possible, viable and beneficial. On what basis can its introduction be resisted?

Objections to Worker Participation

The debate around the issues of worker participation and cooperation has been going on for more than a century and it is impossible to do justice to it here. However, it is possible to pick out a few key themes that recur in the critiques and dismissals of industrial democracy.

The first objection is that participation and cooperation encourage shirking. According to two New Right writers:

> Membership of a team implies that any individual does not bear the full cost of his actions. Thus the opportunity and incentive is created for 'shirking' behaviour. The output of the firm will consequently be less than it could be. If such shirking is to be controlled, a monitor must exist who has sufficient incentive not to shirk himself. This incentive could be the right to residual rewards [a polite term for profits – G. H.]. Thus to minimize shirking behaviour ... a bundle of property rights must be invested in the monitor ... This bundle of rights defines the ownership of the traditional free-enterprise firm.[35]

Behind this first objection lies the familiar classic liberal assumption of an entirely egotistical individual, concerned only with his or her immediate costs and benefits. With any form of cooperation and joint worker decision-making the individual is encouraged, it is argued, to become a free-rider and to 'shirk'. But the objection would be open to doubt if there was the slightest demonstration of 'team spirit' and commitment to some of the collective interests of the group as a whole. It is not necessary to assume that people are entirely altruistic to reach this conclusion: the merest hint undermines the presuppositions of the classic liberal. And as the Prisoner's Dilemma (see Chapter 4 above) and other examples illustrate, in the absence of perfect knowledge of, and trust in, the actions of one's fellows, an individual may well choose an outcome which is non-optimal from the point of view both of the group and of himself. The dogma of the entirely selfish individual is not only without justification; it does not necessarily lead to the conclusion advocated by the New Right.

The second assumption is that it is possible to invest the ownership of the entire firm in a single individual (i.e. the 'monitor'). As soon as the possibility of a partnership or a joint-stock operations is admitted, we are on a slippery slope down to a workers' cooperative. Thus the ambiguous use of the term 'traditional free-enterprise firm' obscures the fact that we are talking about exclusive individual ownership which has rarely existed in the history of industrial capitalism. Partnerships, family holdings, and joint-stock companies were common in Britain in the nineteenth century, all involving 'team' ownership and thus creating the 'opportunity and incentive' to 'shirk'. We are being asked to return to an impractical golden age which never, in fact, existed. The separation of ownership and control in the modern enterprise, noted by Berle and Means in the 1930s,[36] is another fact of modern capitalist life wished away by the New Right. In recent decades there has been increasing ownership of stocks and shares by large financial institutions, making the capitalist firm even more remote from the individualists' ideal.

Even if individual ownership of the modern capitalist firm were conceivable, it is highly unlikely that a single 'monitor' could control and direct the entire process of production. The complexity of the modern enterprise is such that an army of overseers would be required for continuous supervision. To a considerable extent the worker inevitably has to be trusted to get on with the job. Given that complete supervision is impossible, anyone monitoring those directly beneath in the hierarchy is working in a situation of uncertainty and partial ignorance, relying to a significant extent on the initiative of those both above and below. Thus the well-known defects of a hierarchical bureaucracy arise: distortion of information, information 'noise', inadequate information, over-routinized procedures, and so on. We are faced with a cornucopia of inefficiency.

It is noticeable how often the New Right fail to consider the wealth of evidence showing the relative efficiency of participative structures. In addition, worker cooperatives are performing quite well even in circumstances of extreme competition and economic recession. Their number has risen dramatically in Britain in recent years, to about five hundred at the time of writing.[37] It has been shown that, on the average, produce cooperatives have a superior survival record to private firms of similar size.[38] All this the advocates of hierarchy and private ownership conveniently ignore.

The 'property rights' argument against worker participation and cooperatives assumes the same view of human relations that is implied in the Taylorist approach. The fact that it has been generally rejected for many years by management experts, organization theorists, and social psychologists is, once again, ignored. It is sufficient to quote from the critique of Taylorism in *The Social Psychology of Industry* by J. A. C. Brown, first published in 1954:

> The researches of Taylor and his successor Frank B. Gilbreth came to form the basis of what is now known as Time and Motion Study ... It is clear that the psychologists and efficiency experts of this period had accepted the attitudes of management which arose during the early stages of the Industrial Revolution and these tended to form the background to all their investigations. Behind each experiment there lies the tacit implication that human nature is possessed of certain fixed properties which decree that most men find work distasteful, are naturally lazy, solely motivated by fear or greed (a motive now described as 'the carrot or the stick'), and always do as little work as possible for the largest possible wage. Economic man – for that strange perversion of human nature devised by the Physiocrats is the origin of this picture – is a rational creature who uses his reason primarily to calculate exactly how much satisfaction he may obtain from the smallest amount of effort, or when necessary, how much discomfort he can avoid.

> 'Satisfaction' does not mean pride in one's job, the feeling of having accomplished something, or even the regard of others; it refers only to money. Similarly 'discomfort' refers, not to failing one's task, or losing the respect of one's comrades ... Economic man is naturally competitive, basically self-interested, and in the battle of life strives hard to outwit every other man; so far from helping the weak or underdog, his sole concern is with his own survival ... Finally, the hypothesis assumes that man is a machine ... [In] this view of mankind ... every detail is almost completely fallacious. There is no such thing as a fixed human nature, either good or bad, which determines minutely how people shall behave. There is no evidence that men are naturally competitive or self-interested, and there are many things which are more important to the worker than his wages. Human beings are not machines in any significant sense of the word, nor does a good physical environment, in itself, make them happy. In fact, any truth the picture may contain relates solely to the peculiar conditions in certain highly industrialized countries during the nineteenth and early twentieth centuries. Yet it is probably quite safe to say that the management of most factories ... is still based on these outmoded assumptions.[39]

How tragic it is to note that what J. A. C. Brown said of management styles in the 1950s is probably still true today. Furthermore, the fallacious assumptions of 'economic man' have re-emerged with a vengeance in the economic policies of the Thatcher and Reagan governments of the 1980s.

The second objection to cooperatives and worker participation is that under the market system any firm will be forced into line by the pressure of market forces, and thus behave no differently from a conventional, hierarchic and private firm. This second objection is found, in different versions, on both the Left and the Right. Thus the orthodox Marxist economist Ernest Mandel writes:

> There have been many examples of workers' cooperatives that went wrong; there have been some that 'succeeded' – in capitalist terms that is! All that they have succeeded in, however, is transforming themselves into profitable capitalist enterprises, operating in the same way as capitalist firms.[40]

Mandel wants it both ways. If cooperatives fail he is proved right, and workers should not set them up. If cooperatives succeed he is proved right: all the workers have done is to turn themselves into good little capitalists.

Two neoclassical economists, J. T. Addison and A. H. Barnett, have called into question the view that 'internal organization matters' within the firm.[41] They suggest that external competitive pressure is the primary determinant of performance. It forces a firm to 'choose' which type of organization (hierarchic or participatory) is best for minimizing costs.

Then a process of 'natural selection' emerges: the firms which do not choose the organizational form which is relevant for minimizing costs will be wiped out by competition. The 'best' form of organization survives. In a capitalist world all firms thus behave in an identical capitalist way. We are led to conclusions similar to those of Mandel.

Such views have been effectively demolished in a recent work by Jim Tomlinson.[42] He notes, first of all, that the neoclassical and the orthodox Marxist arguments are very similar in their view of the firm and its market environment. They both depend on the idea that firms act to maximize their profits (or act 'as if' they are doing this). Marxists often invoke the 'law of value', without explaining what this means in clear terms. It appears, however, that the 'law of value' is very similar to the neoclassical idea that market forces impel firms to maximize profits. This 'law' is never expressed rigorously, or proved theoretically. But it is said to show that worker cooperatives and participatory firms are compelled to act in the same way as other capitalist firms.

Tomlinson shows that this neoclassical–Marxist account is false. He does not deny that market forces are important. The rejection of the neoclassical–Marxist account does not mean that we have to assume that all firms have the scope to act as they wish; there are indeed real and pressing constraints on the activities of all economic agents. But it does not follow that all agents are forced to behave mechanically in the same way. There is no good reason why high-profit firms must necessarily perform more dynamically than firms with lower profits. The level of profits is not a mechanical regulator of economic performance. This point is confirmed by investing institutions, who do not treat the level of announced or perceived profits as the major criterion for investing their funds in an enterprise. In addition, Tomlinson points out that even if all firms did attempt to maximize their profits, since there is no single way of doing so, this does not point to uniform behaviour. Each firm has its own strategy, 'a term which itself implies room for manoeuvre, room for diverse calculations, room for diverse practices to be brought to bear on the objective'.

Both the observation of firms in practice, and the extended controversy within economic theory as to 'the' objectives of the firm, support the view that there is a diversity of objectives and strategies. Some firms are hierarchic and authoritarian. Others are more participatory. Many are paternalistic. Some firms stress sales maximization and low profits per unit sold. Others use product diversification, or appeals to the 'up' market, to reap large profits on small quantities. Some firms focus on technological developments and long-term expansion; others lay greater emphasis on sales techniques and capturing a dominant position in the market. None of these strategies, as Tomlinson puts it, 'has been unambiguously successful or unsuccessful in maximizing profits – profit maximizing is an extremely speculative business rather than an objective with simple logical implications for the way to run a firm'.

The implications of this analysis should be clear. There is scope for the extension of real worker participation, and the survival and multiplication of workers' cooperatives under capitalism. Although such forms will face real problems and pressing constraints, this does not necessarily mean that they will be pushed into extinction. Cooperatives, for example, may face greater problems in obtaining finance than a capitalist firm. But this does not mean that they are destined to fail. A cooperative, furthermore, does not have to behave in the same way as the average private firm. It may have to make profits to survive, but it does not have to maximize them. There *is* room for manoeuvre within capitalism. There are problems and dangers connected with the democratization of work, but that does not mean that it should not be attempted.

There is both theory and evidence to support these arguments. The view that all firms will be forced to act in the same way is countered by recent evidence from Britain, published by the Department of Employment, which shows that there are wide variations of productivity within industries. Reviewing this evidence, J. M. Ball and N. K. Skeach imply that there is room for cooperative or participatory forms of organization: 'The wide variation in productivity within plants in the same industry indicates that there might be scope for increasing the output of the less productive plants ... by ... rearranging working practices.'[43] Such increases could be achieved by the introduction of worker participation, or by turning some of the firms into worker cooperatives. This would not mean that these firms will all be forced to behave in a similar and capitalist way. Neither will the democratic firms necessarily be driven out by competition. There is a place, perhaps an uncomfortable one, for such impurities. We do not have to wait until 'after the revolution' before such forms of organization and ownership can be introduced.

The third objection to worker participation comes, most often, from the Left. It is argued that participation strengthens management by co-opting the trade union or workforce leadership, that it is a means of securing the compliance of labour to capital, that it is largely a symbolic or cosmetic change, and that it involves patching up a compromise between workers and capitalists whose interests are fundamentally incompatible.[44]

The first counter-argument to this objection is to point out that if it were correct it would apply, to a similar if not greater extent, to all forms of trade unionism as well. In fact there is a strong opinion among sections of management that trade unionism is necessary to secure the compliance of the workforce. In South Africa today many white employers, with no radical intentions, are supporting widespread and forceful moves to unionize black workers. Similarly in the United States some management theorists believe that trade unionism improves labour relations and leads to increases in productivity.[45] There is considerable substance to this view. Trade union organization can provide a framework of consultation between management and workers, a means of reaching agreements that avoid confrontation, and a means of giving workers 'symbolic' participation in lesser decisions. In fact, it could be argued that the majority of trade union activities are directed towards compromise, and result in partial co-option, rather than leading to conflict. In Britain, for example, despite the unionization of over half of the employed workforce, strikes are limited to a small minority of plants.[46] In the practice of trade unions, compromise rather than confrontation prevails.

On the Left there is a romantic view of 'free collective bargaining' which is at variance with the facts. In reality, the wage-bargaining process generally involves compromise and often results in workers giving up a certain degree of power in return for higher wages. Arguably, it has done little to enhance the power or influence of the working class as a whole.

In several capitalist countries in recent years trade unions have been instrumental in securing compliance to government policies on incomes and economic austerity. Such corporatist-style agreements between trade unions, big business and the state have been common in Western Europe since the Second World War, particularly in countries with a government of social democratic hue.[47] To be consistent, supporters of the third objection to worker participation should reject trade unionism as well.

In reality, however, there are contradictions and opposing tendencies within both trade unionism and worker participation. Each can act in the direction of compromise, or of confrontation. The outcome depends, in part, on the balance of class forces, the nature of the leadership, and the political and institutional context. The result is not predetermined. A realistic strategy involves the exploitation of contradictions in both trade unionism and worker participation to maximize economic democracy, and to mobilize people for a wider and more egalitarian transformation of society as a whole. Without the example of economic democracy in microcosm, it is unlikely that popular support for such a wider transformation will be forthcoming. There are clear dangers in this strategy. But those who say of worker participation 'leave well alone' are condemning the democratic socialist movement to isolation and impotence.

The third objection assumes that the initiatives for an increase in worker participation generally come from management, with the intention of manipulating the workforce. In fact, however, many have emanated from the labour movement. One writer has depicted worker participation as being solely imposed from above, in conspiratorial fashion, in response to cycles of worker dissatisfaction. Thus he treats the Bullock Report, and its proposals for sizeable workforce representation on company boards, as being initiated by employers and business interests.[48] This is a very blinkered reading of the facts. While token 'participation' schemes were to be found in many places at that time, all the major and substantive initiatives for industrial democracy came from the labour and trade union movement.[49] The Bullock Report of 1977 was itself a result of growing pressure from a number of trade unions and sections of the Labour Party (inside and outside Parliament) for democracy in industry. In addition, it marked the re-emergence and development of a strong labour movement tradition for worker participation and worker control.[50] It was opposed vociferously by the Confederation of British Industry, most managers, and newspapers of Right-wing views.

There is no clear evidence that the level of class consciousness or the extent of labour organization have been undermined by even minimal schemes to increase worker participation. In contrast, its significant extension is seen as a clear threat to the autocracy of management: in evidence we can cite the active hostility of some managers to participation schemes, and the failure to introduce extensive participation in all advanced capitalist countries. If substantial worker participation is so effective in keeping the workers quiet and in their place, why is it so conspicuous by its absence?

There is a sectarian tendency in the socialist movement which rejects compromise out of hand, and shies away from the dangers in all real struggles, which are generally limited and confused in the world as we find it. We are told to wait for the day of revolution when the workers will rise and reject all halfway measures. In criticizing the ideas of one such revolutionary romantic, three members of the Institute for Workers' Control referred to one Joe Budgett, a veteran socialist of the nineteenth century.[51] A more principled and consistent revolutionary socialist than Budgett could not be found. In interviewing him on his deathbed, George Bernard Shaw discovered to his horror that Budgett had opposed the 1832 Reform Bill on the grounds that it favoured the middle classes and denied the vote to working people. He also opposed Chartism because it did not contest the state and the system of private property. The Factory Acts were rejected because they legalized and legitimized exploitation. And the Education Act was also seen as a retrograde step because it was designed to teach children to submit to authority and be efficient slaves to their masters in the factories. Given that all real reforms have been fudges and compromises, it is difficult to conceive of any advance or improvement which could not be rejected on such grounds. The sectarian revolutionaries are forced to deny all progress. They ally themselves with conservative forces in their criticism of reform. In effect, they are conservatives in revolutionary clothing, even to the point of using similar arguments and analyses to support their position. George Orwell once wrote perceptively: 'every revolutionary opinion draws part of its strength from the secret conviction that nothing can be changed.'[52]

Economics is about People

Taking the apparent commitment of most political theorists to democracy seriously, Carole Pateman has argued that a wide participatory system is necessary for democratic government to work effectively and efficiently. In a concise and stimulating study she produced evidence to show that democracy at work was necessary to develop the political education and democratic competence of the population. Participatory democracy is politically necessary, to involve people in decisions and to set up learning processes to enhance decision-making. Without democracy at work, she maintains, there can be no full democracy in society as a whole. 'It seems clear from this evidence that the argument of the participatory theory of democracy that an individual's [politically relevant] attitudes will depend to a large extent on the authority structure of his work environment is a well-founded one.'[53]

The political arguments for industrial democracy that Pateman provides supplement the economic arguments to be found in this chapter and elsewhere. It has been propounded here that worker participation in decision-making is necessary to increase productivity. However, it should be emphasized that high productivity is not the be-all and end-all; neither is it a panacea for all economic problems. There is an additional, more fundamental, argument for worker participation and a wider participatory democracy.

Economics is not simply concerned with the production of more material goods. It is concerned with the means by which *all* human needs can be satisfied. There are basic needs, such as for food, clothing and shelter. But in addition there are a number of social, relational and specifically human needs. This point has been presented and elaborated by Abraham Maslow, who posits a 'hierarchy of needs'.[54] The higher needs include the needs for belongingness, love, self-respect, self-esteem, and what Maslow calls the need for self-actualization. In a developed society it is not sufficient simply to survive and to satisfy basic biological needs; it is also necessary to satisfy the higher needs, otherwise the society will show symptoms of tension and frustration. A sane and healthy socio-economic system will give people the opportunity for autonomous growth in their own personality. It will rest on the full development of the inherent potentialities of every individual.

Work is an important means by which some of the higher-order needs can be partially satisfied. There are, of course, negative features associated with it: drudgery, authority, exhaustion, blood, toil, tears and sweat. But it has positive features as well. The workplace is a major forum for social interaction, and all the evidence indicates that people regard it as such. Work is a means by which people can take a (perhaps limited) part in a process of creation. And it is a means through which people can obtain a sense of position and value in society. In part, it can satisfy the needs for belongingness, self-respect, self-esteem and self-actualization. The importance of these needs, and the function of work in partly satisfying them, is indicated by what happens when people are made redundant. The unemployed person is devalued, losing access to a creative process and a sense of personal worth. This is an important reason why people fear and resent unemployment: it is not simply the loss of a monetary income.

If work was democratized, so that workers had much more say about its conditions and objectives, much of the drudgery, and the risks to life and health, could be removed. Furthermore, there would be greater satisfaction of the higher-order human needs. The social character of work would be recognized and reinforced through participation in decisions affecting the work process. Ideally, this would take place in a society which put a high value on varied human creativity, and made the satisfaction of higher-order needs a priority.[55]

It is important to recognize that economics is not simply about the needs that people may have for material goods, and the means by which these goods may be produced. It is also about the production and reproduction of social relations, and in addition the satisfaction of non-material needs. Very few economists have paid serious attention to these issues. Exceptions are Mark Lutz and Kenneth Lux, who in a recent book have attempted to construct a 'humanistic economics',[56] and

E. F. Schumacher, whose work on the economics of less developed countries emphasizes the fact that human relations must develop simultaneously with the expansion of production of material goods, and as a necessary condition for the building of a poverty-free society.[57]

Worker Participation and Common Ownership

So far we have avoided a question which must be of concern to both advocates and critics of worker participation: to what extent is it compatible with a private enterprise, capitalist economy?

The hostility of many sections of management would suggest that a significant extension of worker participation was not possible within a capitalist framework. Despite growing pressure from progressive management and the labour movement, in no advanced capitalist country has participation compromised the ultimate control of managers or owners. But, on the other hand, it has rarely been tried on an extensive scale.

What of the worker participation schemes that *have* been tried? In a careful discussion of the issues, Espinosa and Zimbalist first accept the arguments of some Left critics. But they then go on to qualify these arguments:

> it appears that work humanization, far from threatening capitalist control over the production process, promotes labour's identification with capital and fortifies capitalist control. But this is true only as long as the initiative and direction of the programmes remain with the capitalists. There's the rub. There is ample evidence that, once given a taste of control over their work, workers go after more. If this occurs, the capitalists' control over the programme is lost and their control over the entire production process becomes threatened.[58]

Thus worker participation is a Pandora's Box. It may unleash forces beyond the control of the existing captains of industry. On the basis of this discussion, Espinosa and Zimbalist suggest

> an ultimate incompatibility between industrial democracy and private ownership of industry. The capitalist maximizes profits or surplus, subject to one crucial consideration – the ability to control surplus appropriation. When control over the work process is recovered by the workers, a major justification for private surplus appropriation is called into question. A generalized movement toward workers' control cannot be absorbed by a capitalist society. It must be resolved either by harsh repression and a return to industrial autocracy within a capitalist or Soviet-type society or by a transition to a democratic socialist society.[59]

In its essentials this argument cannot be flawed. Capitalist organization and direction of production is indeed ultimately incompatible with a large degree of worker participation in decision-making. Democratic control of production does challenge capitalist hierarchy and private ownership and appropriation. Capitalism and worker participation are in contradiction to one another. The problem, however, is to determine the force of this conflict and the time-scale involved. For how long can significant worker participation co-exist with capitalism?

It should be pointed out that capitalism contains many internal conflicts, some of which could be described as ultimately threatening the system itself. Take the existence of trade unions, so vigorously resisted by employers in this century and the last. The taxation of firms interferes with the private appropriation of profit, and is seen by some economists as a threat to the survival of capitalism. A similar verdict has been pronounced on government intervention in the economy. Yet it would be rash to regard these factors as bringing about the immediate downfall of the system. It would seem reasonable to suggest that capitalism could survive with trade unions, taxation, and government intervention for a considerable period of time. It is far too tempting to identify a real and important conflict and then predict the Apocalypse.

It is impossible to identify in advance the position where extended worker participation and capitalism will come into final conflict. Maybe capitalism can live with enlarged worker participation in decision-making for a while. In the absence of sufficient data, we do not know. Of two things, however, we can be sure. There is, first, a sound economic case for a large increase in worker participation and the development of real industrial democracy. Second, the sustained existence of significant worker participation in decision-making will bring private ownership of the means of production under threat, and eventually lead to an extension of common ownership. Only by attempting to bring about a participatory democracy in practice will we be able to see the extent and nature of this transformation of property relations.

But what of the nature of this practice at the present time? Hilary Wainwright and Dave Elliot have criticized the traditional socialist view of state intervention, in which an extension of public ownership is seen as the first step, *before* any extension of participatory democracy. They argue that the transformation of work relations is an end or goal, not simply a means. They assert

> a very different relationship between ownership and workers' power. Put it this way: the extent to which public ownership is an advance towards full socialism depends on the extent to which workers *create* a changed relationship between themselves and management in the course of achieving public ownership.[60]

This very different emphasis from that found in orthodox socialist thinking may prove crucial in countering the prominent but mistaken view that socialism is simply about the extension of public ownership and the advance of state power[61] – a view that has enabled the New Right to make electoral gains with populist rhetoric against 'socialism'. The mistake has to be rectified, in part by a stress on the necessity and desirability of a participatory democracy.

It is beyond the scope of this study to give a detailed plan of the structures of a participatory socialist society. Two points, however, have to be made clear. First, worker and popular participation is not simple and one-dimensional; its nature and quality should depend on the circumstances. In the case of an industry which is strategically central and vital to the region or country concerned, there is a case for elected representatives from outside the industry on the management boards, as well as elected and accountable worker representatives from inside it. To represent the wider popular interest, participation has to be wider than the firm itself. It is naive to assume that workers within an industry will (even under socialism) fully identify with national or international interests. Are crucial decisions, such as to whether the production of nuclear bombs and nuclear power plants is to be continued, to remain solely with the workers in that industry? Clearly they should not. It is democratic to include wider popular participation in the running of industry, as well as worker participation.

Thus co-management, rather than pure workers' management, is sometimes more democratic, especially when conceived within the framework of a democratically constructed national or regional plan. Co-management gives the opportunity for the representation of national, regional, municipal, community, and industrial, as well as plant-based interests. Worker participation does not necessarily mean majority representation on company boards in all cases; there may be arguments for the representation of other interest groups as well. On the other hand it is obvious that there are dangers in minority worker representation, for it is possible that their legitimate aspirations and interests will be swamped. It is also possible that the worker representatives will change their outlook and fail to serve their colleagues. For these reasons it is essential that they are accountable to those that elected them, and are under some system of recall.[62] But these measures in themselves do not solve all problems and cure all ills. It has to be pointed out that complete worker self-management is compatible not with a planned society, but with a Yugoslav-type market system, in which the workers have control over the allocation, as well as the production, of the product.

Thus, in a sense, there is a conflict between even democratic planning and self-management. Some sort of compromise has to be worked out.

The second qualification is to note that a general and substantial extension of worker participation, though both necessary and desirable, does not mean the abolition of some form of hierarchy. Although authoritarian elements will be removed, different tiers of organization are necessary to gather and process information, and to coordinate production. The task of management will remain, but managers will become accountable both to the workers and to the community at large. In some cases they may be elected by the workforce; in others they may be appointed by representative and participatory company boards. Ultimate power will shift to the grassroots, not to the top of a hierarchical system.

Participation is not the creation of single-tiered structures, with votes on everything by everyone. Such a system is unworkable. Participation is about the dispersion of power to ordinary people, so that they may have some sort of real control over their lives and their environment. It is about the removal of controlling elites, rather than the complete abolition of hierarchy *per se*. A hierarchy may indeed give rise to the re-emergence of elites, but this danger can be avoided if the mechanisms of accountability are substantial and well designed. It should be pointed out that lack of organization can also be dangerous. What some anarchists forget is that the lack of structures can be tyrannical and authoritarian; for example, a meeting without a chairperson can be nasty, brutish and short.[63]

Conclusion: Towards a Participatory Democracy

Participation will be all the more successful if it is generalized within society as a whole. As Pateman has noted, an increase in worker participation will interact positively with the development of a wider political democracy. Democracy is a learning process which helps people to understand their needs and abilities and which will be the more effective the wider its scope and domain. Democratic participation in the sphere of work is perhaps the first priority, given that work dominates the lives of a large number of people, but it should later be extended to the community, to the home, and to political institutions. A participatory society requires a generality of participatory structures[64] – indeed, it requires a participatory culture. The acceptance of authority and the practice of deference have to give way to the prerogative of involvement.

Thus, although isolated attempts at the introduction of worker participation are important and valuable, they are under constraint without a political and social context of democratic participation.[65] It seems reasonable to assume that there is positive feedback between advances of democracy in one sphere and those in another. This 'virtuous circle' is likely to set off a cumulative process, eventually challenging and transforming relations of property and power. We should not therefore condemn current and proposed schemes of worker participation for their limited effectiveness. The participatory socialist society of the future has to be prefigured within the capitalism of the present. Without examples to point to, people will never be generally convinced of the viability of socialism.

Ten

Political Pluralism and Economic Planning

Complete liberty of contradicting and disproving our opinion is the very condition which justifies us in assuming its truth for the purposes of action.

John Stuart Mill, *On Liberty*[1]

In orthodox social science there is a chasm between economic and political analysis. This gulf in theory reflects an alleged separation, in the real world, between the economic system and political institutions. Only in recent years, as we have seen in previous chapters, has the New Right attempted to bridge the divide. For example, in the writings of Milton Friedman a positive correlation between private ownership and political freedom is proposed. It has been noted, however, that Friedman's conception of political freedom has more to do with the existence of 'individual choice' in the marketplace, and the absence of overt political coercion, than with the development of pluralism and democratic government.

There is a parallel in the attitude of some members of the Left who assert that it is possible to introduce real political democracy in the Eastern Bloc countries without any major modification of the centralized planning process other than to diminish bureaucracy. This proposition is found, in various guises, in both Trotskyism and Eurocommunism. The mistakes and defects of centralized planning are written off by reference to 'the bureaucracy', or to the years of material deprivation and civil war, with no examination of its innate shortcomings. Furthermore, from this characteristic viewpoint, in terms of the reforms that are required to 'democratize' the economy, political pluralism is not given a sufficiently high priority; it is seen as an optional extra, rather than an essential component of a healthy, planned economy.

The central thesis of this chapter is that some form of political pluralism, typically in association with a parliamentary democracy, is necessary for the functioning of a healthy socialist society where common ownership and control of the economy prevail. Initially we may take the word 'pluralism' as meaning the existence of two or more political parties, each with the means of spreading ideas and obtaining power through the electoral process, without an absolute constraint on the formation of further parties, and without constitutional priority being given to any one party over its rivals. Clearly, the Soviet Union is not pluralist according to this definition, as one single party, the Communist Party, is endowed with a 'leading' or 'vanguard' role within both the political constitution and the planning structure of that country. Reforms which fall short of removing this special status, such as the admission of factions within the Party, do not themselves give rise to pluralism. It is suggested here that the frequent undervaluation or rejection of pluralism by sections of the Left is related to a misconception of the nature of social reality in general, and to an implausible account of how a healthy socialist economy could work in practice.

Towards the end of this chapter a multi-dimensional extension of the notion of pluralism is suggested, to deal with the problems that have been outlined. Arguments for a wide participatory democracy that have been raised in the previous chapter will be supplemented and reinforced.

Uncertainty and Planning

A distinction has been drawn between *risk* and *uncertainty*.[2] Risk covers events which may or may not happen, but to which we may assign a meaningful probability. If we throw a die, there is a 50 per cent risk that we shall get an odd number. In contrast, an uncertain event, such as the prospect of a Third World War, or a revolution in South Africa, is one for which it is impossible to calculate a probability which is anything more than a guess. In the words of John Maynard Keynes, who gave uncertainty a central part in his economic theory: 'We simply do not know.'[3] In contrast, most orthodox economic theory covers nothing more than risk: it does not embrace uncertainty.

This defect succours a mechanistic view of the economy, in which economic development is seen as an automatic or probabilistic outcome of factor inputs (i.e. labour, capital, etc.), tastes and preferences, and either market forces (under capitalism) or the planning process (under socialism). The economy is seen as a more or less rigid machine. In particular, production is regarded as an automatic process in which given inputs are transformed into a predetermined quantity of output. Prices, when they exist, are governed by the 'law of value' (orthodox Marxism), or by marginal relations in general equilibrium (neoclassical economics). Both traditional Marxism and neoclassical economic theory are dominated by a mechanistic paradigm. In part this results from the mutual neglect of the concept and reality of uncertainty.

A conceptual distinction between uncertainty and risk has been made. It is also necessary to distinguish between the type and degree of uncertainty which prevails under socialism, or, more generally, a planned economy. The capitalist system is dominated by market relations, and the private and uncoordinated decisions of individuals or business corporations. This state of affairs gives uncertainty under capitalism a special dimension. As Keynes showed in *The General Theory of Employment, Interest and Money*, in the absence of ameliorating remedies such a system is prone to market shocks and adverse forces which can bring about a cumulative process of economic contraction, leading to full-scale slump. The market itself provides no automatic self-righting mechanism for recovery. The very structure of capitalist society gives uncertainty a prominent and forceful role.

However, uncertainty is not peculiar to capitalism. Obviously, under any economic system of which we can conceive in present circumstances, natural shocks or catastrophes (such as floods or earthquakes) will occur with little forewarning. More significantly there are other non-natural and continuous sources of uncertainty. (The term 'partial ignorance' which is sometimes used in relation to a planned economy[4] is here passed over in favour of 'uncertainty', in order to emphasize the scale and the common features, of the problem, in a planned as well as a market society.)

In an extensively planned society, the central agency draws up comprehensive and detailed plans, and directs the allocation of resources. Then, in theory, the output is distributed according to needs and social priorities. Part of it goes to the consumer; another part is invested in production. Many socialists have assumed that the management of a planned economy is, despite its complexity and scale, fundamentally unproblematic. Thus Lenin wrote:

> Accounting and control – that is *mainly* what is needed for the 'smooth working', for the proper functioning, of the *first phase* of communist society ... *All* citizens ... should work equally, do their proper share of work, and get equal pay. The accounting and control necessary to do this have been *simplified* by capitalism to the utmost and reduced to the extraordinary simple operations – which any literate person can perform – of supervising and recording, knowledge of the four rules of arithmetic, and issuing appropriate receipts.[5]

Unfortunately, this ignores the sheer scale of the planning process and the degree of uncertainty and complexity involved. The processing, interpretation and summarizing of the vast quantities of accounting information necessary to formulate the plan are not discussed. Instead, a naive 'labour accounting' method is proposed which is supposed to homogenize all the variables. The problems involved in such a valuation are sidestepped. How are different types and intensities of work, carried out by integrated groups as well as individuals, to be treated? How are products of different type and quality to be valued? The amount of 'socially necessary' labour performed by each worker and embodied in each product is not readily measurable. A massive computer calculation, taking years rather than hours, is involved. It is not explained how the 'average' amount of 'socially necessary' labour time is to be determined without reference to a control mechanism such as the market. (It is not possible to determine this for every commodity by committee decision or democratic vote.) Critics of the labour accounting proposal have shown that even if such labour-values could be determined, they would lead to a choice of production technique which was non-optimal by established (Marxist or other) criteria.[6] In the socialist movement there is a complacent neglect of the problems involved in planning, and of the detailed structures and necessary features of a future socialist society.

There are a number of sources of uncertainty in a planned economy. The first is from within the sphere of production. Contrary to the neoclassical 'production function', in which inputs such as 'labour' and 'capital' are automatically and mysteriously transformed into an output, production is a social rather than a mechanical process.[7] It involves social change and conflict. Under capitalism, of course, conflict between workers and management flows directly from the antagonistic and unstable nature of the system. But to some degree such conflict is also bound to exist in a socialist society, and could account for significant variations in output. Furthermore, levels of productivity are continuously changing, at vastly different rates, in different enterprises, industries, and countries. If the mechanistic view of production is rejected, and instead production is conceived as a process in which labour, as the conscious and active agency of production, acts upon the materials and instruments of work,[8] then such differences and variations in output and productivity are more readily understood, even if they cannot with any accuracy be predicted. A central planning agency must deal with a situation in which output is essentially variable, even with given resources and labour-power. The level of production in the future is always to some extent uncertain.

Second, uncertainty over levels of production will result from the fact that performed labour depends upon the level of skill of operatives, and the acquisition of skills takes place to a large extent during production itself. This acquisition of skills is sometimes predictable, particularly with routine tasks, sometimes not, especially when insight and cognitive development are crucial. Production is a learning process, subject to the same sort of variation in attainment as education at school or university. In addition, the learning that takes place during production may well involve innovations in the method, practice or technology of work. As Karl Popper has pointed out,[9] future knowledge cannot be predicted. If it *were* predictable we would know it already, and it would not be future knowledge. This is one reason why Popper, quite rightly, concludes that all social processes are essentially unpredictable. The fact that production involves continuous learning and innovation means that an additional level of uncertainty is involved.

The third source of uncertainty is just as ominous. It is to do with the determination of consumer needs, and the consequent division and distribution of the economic product. In the Soviet Union there are only limited channels for the popular expression of preferences and need. In the absence of such sources of information as consumer councils and popular representation on the various planning institutions, the central planning agency has to estimate needs and determine priorities in a darkened pit of ignorance. But even if there was a vast extension of participatory democracy, including workers' control of production, there would still be uncertainty in the determination of social needs. Such needs are not static: they evolve through time. Furthermore, their evolution is not a passive reflection of circumstances but an active process in which people learn and innovate from their own perceptions, and their own interpretations of their experience. This process of need formation and evaluation is only partially open to prediction.

All this highlights another strange parallel between the economics of many orthodox Marxists and neoclassical theory. The former is associated with the proposal for a centrally planned economy. The latter has most often been used to justify a market economy. Yet both incorporate a mechanical model of the economy in which problems of uncertainty or partial ignorance are absent. Recognition of the significance and reality of uncertainty is incompatible with most of the underlying neoclassical theory of markets, and much of the economics that has gone under the name of Marxism.

Planning as a Non-Mechanistic Paradigm

If it were the case that production was a machine-like and an automatic process resulting from given inputs, and needs were fully perceived by the central planning authority, and the problem of uncertainty was easily surmountable, then planning could be a simple computational process. It would involve known mathematical techniques such as linear programming and input–output analysis. The main problems would be the (known) production and resource constraints that were faced within the economy and the quantity of information involved.

However, this is not, and cannot be, the case within any real society. Planning involves uncertain and only partially accurate estimates of existing resources, essentially arbitrary margins to allow for mistakes, estimates of future productivity with again arbitrary margins for error, and good or bad estimates of social priorities and needs. Even in the most healthy and democratic socialist society, planning is not a purely mechanical process. Any plan involves a set of estimations that may be false. It is more like a refutable hypothesis about the future than a target that can be reached with certainty. In short, every plan is fallible.

When a plan is being implemented, how can its failure, partial or otherwise, be known? Primarily, failures will be registered in terms of shortfalls in production targets. But even the published production figures may conceal some manipulation by local managers and others. They may reach the target of the plan, and reap the prescribed bonuses and rewards, by sacrificing quality for quantity, or by presenting goods from stock and claiming that they were produced during the current period. Second, a failure will exist if there is a vast discrepancy between popular needs and preferences, and those decreed or achieved by the plan. Such failures are numerous and extreme in the Eastern Bloc: most visibly the failure to produce Western-style consumer goods, for which there is evident demand. In a state collectivist system, many needs are not given the means of popular expression, and thus, quite often, they will not be perceived by the central planning authorities.

In contrast, within a democratic socialist society such wants and needs will be expressed more easily. Complaints and misgivings will have a legitimate voice. But that is not enough. A democratic socialist society must also have means of rectifying failure. Effective planning must deal with the contingencies of production shortfall or unrecognized need. It is not simply a question of expressing needs 'democratically' and then treating planning as a mechanical process in which subsequent failure is not considered likely. The permanent possibility of failure has to be recognized in the objectives, methods, structures and other aspects of the plan.

Even in the most simple and conventional planning models there is a 'degree of freedom' which defies mechanical determination. It is the well known trade-off between current consumption and future economic growth. Should resources be used to raise the standard of living now, or be diverted to investment for an even greater projected standard of living in the future? An infinite number of variations is possible. No faultless mechanical method exists, either for the central planning authority to calculate an optimal mix between current consumption and investment, or to determine the exact wishes of the population regarding the trade-off between the two. The attempt to determine such preferences is indispensable, but the planning authority is still essentially taking a leap in the dark, or, more appropriately, in inadequate illumination.

To recapitulate, therefore, the mechanistic view of the economy is inappropriate both for the capitalist and for any form of planned economic system. Mechanistic conceptions within the Marxist tradition are based on a loosely specified 'law of value', and often an idea that it is possible to establish a 'real social cost', defined independently of the socio-economic system involved.[10] Some Marxists believe that these notions apply to socialism and state collectivist societies as well as to capitalism. Neoclassical economists emphasize the idea of equilibrium, attained through the competitive forces of the market. These two approaches have much in common. In contrast, more realistic models of the capitalist system, such as those of oligopolistic or imperfectly competitive markets, or of firms which do not necessarily act to maximize profits, often yield indeterminate solutions for output and prices. (For similar reasons they would not yield determinate embodied labour values within Marxian economics.) For these reasons, such realistic models are banished or ignored by neoclassical–Marxist orthodoxy.

However, there are a growing number of critics of this orthodoxy, from varying viewpoints. For example, Nicholas Georgescu-Roegen has written of irreversibility and uncertainty in economic processes: 'Every change through which the economic process goes leaves its imprint upon that process ... [It] is not a mechanical process. It is an evolutionary process which continuously produces novelty.'[11] Other critics include Janos Kornai, Brian J. Loasby, Joan Robinson and G. L. S. Shackle.[12]

A better analogy than the machine is the game. Under capitalism, a game-like process is involved, played with a number of persons, some with much more power than others, and some with the exclusive ability to change the rules at will. In a socialist and planned economy elements of cooperation between 'players' are more prominent than they are within capitalism. There is more trust and open discussion. The elements of competition for egotistic ends are correspondingly subdued. Although the structure and content of the capitalist and socialist 'games' are different, in each case the analogy is apposite. Both have an indeterminate outcome (as there is no perfect and complete knowledge), and there is no single optimal strategy or set of strategies for the players. What may be the best course for one player at one point in the game will depend on what other players decide to do, and how they act.

There are at least two important objections to the mechanistic paradigm within economics. One is that it assumes that processes through time are reversible: ruling out novelty and evolution in the system. The irreversibility of a game is clear. Actions in the present depend upon an assessment of an uncertain and unknown future. If time was reversible the future would become as knowable as the past. The very attraction of a game is that it produces novelty and surprise. The other objection is that the mechanistic paradigm does not account for imagination and will among the individual agents. In her novel *Felix Holt*, George Eliot uses the analogy of a chess game to show the inadequacy of a 'mathematical' (i.e. mechanistic, or deductive-rationalist) conception of society when individual wills are involved:

> Fancy what a game of chess would be if all the chessmen had passions and intellects, more or less small and cunning: if you were not only uncertain about your adversary's men, but a little uncertain also about your own; if your knight could shuffle himself on to a new square by the sly; if your bishop, in disgust at your castling, could wheedle your pawns out of their places; and if your pawns, hating you because they are pawns, could make away from their appointed posts that you might get checkmate on a sudden. You might be the longest-headed of deductive reasoners, and yet you might be beaten by your own pawns. You would be especially likely to be beaten, if you depended arrogantly on your mathematical imagination, and regarded your passionate pieces with contempt. Yet this imaginary chess is easy compared with the game a man has to play against his fellow-men with other fellow-men for his instruments.[13]

Pluralism and Planning

We are now in a position to discuss some of the political consequences of the above remarks. They apply to socialist movements both in a planned society, and in an advanced society in transition to socialism in which planning may be at the formative stages, and capitalist relations may still hold sway.

The key point is this: in such political circumstances no individual or party can be justly certain that any particular political strategy or economic programme is the best, or even adequate: all are possibly false and governed by a degree of uncertainty. This fact confounds the closed and secretive type of government which is found in most advanced capitalist democracies, and more authoritarian forms such as Stalinism and fascism. Closed, secretive government relies on the advice and amenability of carefully chosen 'experts'. It is subject to the pressure of unrepresentative and powerful interest groups behind the scenes. It exacerbates the problem of uncertainty and incomplete information by failing to create open and informed debate.

But the problems are most serious under authoritarian regimes, which crush all opposition and put a stop to any critical evaluation of policy in society at large. Flows of accurate information from subordinates are closed off, for fear that they might be deemed critical or unconstructive. Such regimes can, by mobilizing the population behind a single ideology, create spurts of more rapid economic growth. On the whole, however, the dead weight of authoritarianism and the monolith of dogma prevent the achievement of an economic performance which parallels even that in the modern capitalist West.

Under liberal-democratic capitalism, alternative nodes of political organization and expression allow a greater articulation of wants and needs, but even this is far from adequate or fully effective. Political pluralism is not a panacea – it should not be overrated or divorced from other necessary measures. It is however necessary for any healthy form of socialism.

In brief, the argument is as follows: any politico-economic strategy for the transition to socialism, and any economic plan within socialism itself, is based on inadequate information, suffers partial distortions, and embodies faults of a more or less serious nature. This ever-present potential for failure means that alternative plans and strategies must be given scope for political expression. The most suitable way of achieving this is through some form of political pluralism.

It may be suggested that all that is necessary is scope for the expression of different points of view in select committees, planning boards, and so on: political parties need not be involved. This view would be unconvincing. Without means to appeal to the population at large, a minority point of view would have to adapt to the approach of the dominant elite. Even if this elite is subject to personal election, a one-party system of government inevitably narrows down the political debate, closes off options, and is subject to the danger that candidates and officials will be vetted and manipulated. The key feature of a multi-party system is that the approach of an entire political grouping is periodically put to the ultimate test: approval or disapproval by the electorate.

With the electoral test, the means of legitimation are partly external to party organization instead of being almost wholly internal. In contrast, authoritarian and one-party states tend to cover up mistakes and claim a mythical infallibility in order to shore up their power. The mere existence of a multi-party state does not, of course, guarantee open political debate, or a government's acceptance of fallibility. The argument here is that pluralist political structures are not sufficient for full economic and social development; but they are necessary.

The argument in favour of pluralism can be extended beyond the issue of multiple political parties to industry, the community, and the institutions of economic planning, as well as the national parliament. Rival means of political expression are desirable at every level.

Consider a democratic socialist society in which there is a large measure of decentralization, as well as central planning. There would be tiers of decision-making under some system of democratic control, as well as considerable local autonomy. The central planning authority cannot however be infallible, for it does not have sufficient information to appreciate all the consequences of a policy at a more local level. Within limits, there has to be some sort of institutionalized feedback process to allow some modification of high-level plans. Similarly, in some circumstances it may be necessary for high level authorities to overrule the policies of a lower level. (Such as, for example, the fishing policy of a coastal community which may threaten to deplete stocks for others, and the nation as a whole.) This vertical pluralism involves elected councils at all important levels, in all localities, and in all relevant spheres of major social activity. Furthermore, it involves powers of upward and downward modification of policy, within realistic and acceptable limits. It is a hallmark of democratic socialism that it exhibits a healthy vertical pluralism, as well as the horizontal pluralism of the political parties found in a capitalist society.

If vertical and horizontal pluralism are necessary for a healthy socialist economy, a number of important analytical consequences follow. First, a sharp division between politics and 'the economy' is undesirable: the point has been made elsewhere in this book that economy, polity and society are entwined. Second, it becomes clear that democracy, in addition to other elements such as planning and common ownership, is an end as well as a means. Remarkably, there is little recognition of this in socialist and Marxist writing, even from authors who consider themselves democrats.

Ernest Mandel, in his famous two-volume work *Marxist Economic Theory*, devotes an entire chapter of thirty-six pages to the 'socialist economy'. Such detailed discussions of the socialist future are rare, and

Mandel should be given credit for this one. Much attention is given to the question of needs under socialism, but as to how such needs are determined and evaluated there is silence. Democracy, and democratic structures in any form, are not mentioned. The performance of social democratic theorists is little better. C. A. R. Crosland, in *The Future of Socialism*, pays lip-service to democracy, but gives it no major or essential role in the planning of the economy.

To sum up, the socialist economy cannot be considered in isolation from political and democratic structures. Socialism is not simply planning for human need; it is planning within a system in which the determination of those needs can be criticized and scrutinized from alternative viewpoints. Without a wide and pluralistic democracy there is no socialism.

Socialist Politics and the Acceptance of Uncertainty

The argument in this chapter has consequences for immediate political practice, as well as for a future socialist society. The concepts of fallibility and uncertainty have a bearing on the past and present practices of many socialist organizations. Consider first the traditions that derive from Bolshevism (i.e. Leninism, Stalinism and Trotskyism). Lenin and Trotsky thought that factional organization within the revolutionary party was generally desirable, in contrast to Stalin during his period of rule; but an important central feature of all types of Bolshevism is the politics of *the line*. Discipline, and the need for fidelity of the party member to established policy, are emphasized at the expense of setting up political structures which allow alternative policies to have effective voice.

It is not argued here that the attempt to construct a coherent or general political position is without value. What is argued is that the promulgation of a line, and practical adherence to it, should not squeeze out debate and dialogue within the party. Furthermore, it should be openly admitted by the party leadership that such debate and evaluation is necessary because the predominant line could be incorrect. The acceptance of fallibility and the promotion of dialogue should be institutionalized in the structure and practice of the party, and in relation to other organizations. Whatever the intentions of their founders or leaders, the practice of Leninist, Stalinist and Trotskyist parties has been quite different. In fact, on occasion Trotsky perpetuated the myth of party infallibility:

> In the last analysis, the party is always right, because the party is the sole historical instrument that the working class possesses for the solution of its fundamental tasks . . . I know that no one can be right against the party.[14]

As I have suggested elsewhere,[15] much of the intolerance and dogmatism in the Bolshevik tradition stems from a mechanistic and deterministic view of history, in which the party is seen as an agent of inevitable change and predestined socialist victory. Consequently, with history allegedly pushing at the rear, democracy, internal debate and political pluralism become luxuries, diversions, a waste of time and resources, and an interference with the historical process which in any case is 'inevitable'.

In contrast, reformist socialism has generally given greater verbal support to pluralism and parliamentary institutions, though not on the whole on the grounds put forward in this essay. Indeed one of the hallmarks of reformism is an over-emphasis on parliament as the exclusive arena for the resolution of debate, and as the main agent of social change. Democratic movements and participatory institutions outside parliament are ignored or belittled. The role of a socialist party is to obtain a majority in parliament, and then to hand down reform from above – a paternalistic and elitist conception which pays insufficient attention to the fallibility of a particular policy or reform. The party 'knows what people need' and does not see the urgency for institutionalizing means of popular expression and debate, such as workers' and consumers' councils, which can act as a check or counterbalance to parliament. In the reformist conception, pluralism is accepted in narrow parliamentary terms only, not in terms of mass participatory power.

Concluding Remarks

The purpose of this chapter is both to show the economic necessity of a pluralist democracy and to reinforce the arguments put forward elsewhere that economics and politics cannot be separated. Democracy is not simply a means to an end: it is part of the end in itself. Wlodzimierz Brus makes a related point concerning reform in the Eastern Bloc:

> it is not 'depoliticization of the economy' but 'democratization of politics' that is the correct direction for the process of socialization of nationalized means of production ... the problem of socialization turns into the question of the democratic evolution of the state, of the political system.[16]

In short, there can be no socialist economy without a democratic polity. Political pluralism is not a luxury; it is an essential part of the socio-economic structure of any healthy planned economy. It is no accident that the number one aim of the Polish trade union movement Solidarity at its national congress of September–October 1981 was the achievement of a political pluralism. It demanded before anything else 'political pluralism of opinions and transformation of the economy and the state according to the spirit of democracy'.[17] Thus Solidarity's achievement was not only the construction of a free trade union, but to establish that there is no true socialism without democracy. Martial law and repression cannot remove this indelible mark on our history.

Eleven

Socialism, Decentralization and Markets

Freedom consists in converting the state from an organ superimposed upon society into one completely subordinate to it.

Karl Marx, *Critique of the Gotha Programme*

Let us reflect for a while on a feasible socialist society of the future. It has been established in the two preceding chapters that a considerable measure of democracy would be necessary. What would be the socio-economic structure to which a pluralist and participatory democracy related? What degree of decentralization would be necessary and desirable? Would a measure of market regulation be required? While no socialist society has yet emerged on this earth, immediate discussion of these questions is vital for a socialist movement wishing to maintain its sense of direction.

The aversion to such discussions which is prevalent on the Left has two sources. The first is the leaning within the trade union movement, which is not confined to the Left, towards class-against-class confrontation. Politics is basically the battle of 'them' against 'us'. Little thought is given to the structure of a future socialist society in which – since working people are in control – there is no capitalist class to confront. The politics of 'class-against-class' concentrates on exacting concessions from the employers, rather than on a fundamental challenge to their power. It demands more bread, but it does not strive for control of the bakery. To move in that direction would mean accepting responsibility for 'their' system. Such is the aversion from the basic issues of power and responsibility that hierarchy, authority and the prerogatives of management are not challenged. Democratic socialism is pushed off the agenda, or consigned to the days after the revolution or the 'next' election. Class-against-class provides a comfortable formula within which both Left and Right can operate: there is no fundamental challenge to existing relations of power, neither is it necessary to consider seriously an alternative society of the future.

The second source of the aversion stems from orthodox Marxism. It is well known that Marx and Engels claimed that their socialism was scientific, and opposed the 'utopian socialism' of their day.[1] For them, blueprints were unnecessary; the future society would emerge out of the 'real forces' of the present. Capitalism creates the agency of its demolition, and the future builder of socialism, in the form of the working class. It is thus illegitimate to interfere with this agency and its 'historic' destiny. On the basis of such arguments, much discussion of a future socialist society is curtailed.

A strict interpretation of this orthodox Marxian position would seem to lead to the view that ideas, wills, and conceptions of the future are not 'real forces' in present society. It seems to involve a vulgar and naive view of 'the economy' in which ideas and expectations do not play an active role. This view is untenable. Ideas and expectations do not dominate economic behaviour, but they are essential to it. This point is all the more relevant when we consider the replacement of one socio-economic system by another. It is important to recognize that all social change results from a combination of causes based on institutions and social forces as well as the ideas and wills of the persons involved. 'The economy' does not write the script of future history.

The idea that the construction of socialism is the sole prerogative of the working class is criticized in the next chapter. There is no *a priori* reason why the transformation of society should be the sole province of one group or class. Thus we do not 'substitute' for this class if we develop a plan or vision of a socialist future.

The rejection of the vulgar Marxist critique of utopianism does not mean the abandonment of science. Science is necessary to establish what is possible. We may then select from the set of possibilities that which we find most desirable. But socialism, if it is to be a forceful creed, has to be utopian as well as scientific. One reason why utopias should be considered by the Left is that if no clear long-term objective is articulated, the Right is effectively permitted to tar socialism with any brush it chooses. In almost every case the brush selected is that of a centralized, state-run 'socialism' akin to the Eastern Bloc.

To a great extent the Left itself is to blame for this state of affairs. Although several important socialist writers, including Marx and Trotsky, stressed the importance of democratic control, and did not equate socialism with nationalization, we frequently hear today slogans for the 'nationalization of the top two hundred monopolies'. Some people on the Left, who feel that such a slogan is inopportune and somewhat simplistic, still agree with large-scale nationalization as an objective. In response it has to be pointed out that nationalization is not the only form of common ownership, and in practice it would concentrate excessive economic and political power into the hands of the state. Other forms of common ownership, such as cooperatives and municipal enterprise, allow for a greater decentralization of power and control.

It has been pointed out (most often by Marxists) that many 'reformist' socialists and social democrats hold the naive view that the state and parliament are a potential instrument of the people. Through their elected representatives in parliament, it is presumed that the people can control the state and society. On the whole, the critique of this reformist view is valid. Parliament is not at the apex of power. It cannot change society without massive extra-parliamentary action. However, it is generally not realized that there is a similarity between the reformist view of the state and parliament on the one hand, and on the other the Left's widespread support for large-scale nationalization. They are both based on the premise that the state can represent the people, either at present or in a future society. Nationalization (under socialism) is seen as being synonymous with placing control of industry in the hands of the population at large, through the 'representative' agency of parliament. As Jim Tomlinson has written:

> The very legalistic notions of property inscribed in much of the debate about nationalization have as their counterpart very legalistic (constitutionalist) notions of politics. In the present context this led to a conception of the state as the appropriate body for owning industry because only this body could truly represent the general public as opposed to private interests. Thus nationalization was pursued as a policy despite a strong hostility to the state as an employer, not because the state was conceived of as the central political power but because it was deemed to represent the community.[2]

The mistake, of course, is to regard all social institutions and structures as passive, as instruments of individual social actors or political parties. Hence an over-obsession with mandation, procedure, and even reselection of elected representatives, to the neglect of the struggle to change the structure and character of the institutions themselves. Such mechanisms of accountability are important and valuable, but they should not be considered in isolation from the more fundamental issues of social structure. Discussion of these should not be postponed by the Left any longer.

Arguments for Decentralization

According to the view of the orthodox Left, after the 'commanding heights' of the economy are nationalized there will be planning according to the criteria of need. Some of the problems inherent in a system of centralized planning have been raised in Chapter 7. It was noted that in the Soviet Union there are at least twelve million types of product. This amount of information and complexity would have to be handled within a democratic socialist society.

Are computers the answer? Undeniably they are an extremely useful tool. However, it is unlikely that they will be able to overcome the problems of complexity and uncertainty in a conceivable socialist society. Even a giant central computer will not be able to handle the amount of information involved in a detailed national plan. Consider the modern planning method of input–output analysis. Information is presented in tabular form, and analysed with the use of matrix algebra. These techniques are illuminating and powerful, but they cannot be used for the planning process in all its details and in its entirety. For example, to discover the accounting prices to be used (or the embodied labour values if these are to be mistakenly employed) a manipulated input–output matrix has to be 'inverted', according to a standard mathematical definition of a matrix 'inverse'. For computational purposes there are a number of ways of inverting the matrix and finding the required information. One requires a number of mathematical operations equal to twice the square of the number of products involved. This would appear to be a reasonably efficient procedure. At the time of writing, one of the fastest computers around takes two-millionths of a second per mathematical operation (with floating-point numbers). If there were twelve million products in the economy (and this would appear to be an underestimate), the matrix inversion would take more than eighteen years at this speed. It would thus take about two decades to formulate a single five-year plan! Obviously it would be out of date, in terms both of technology and of economic development, well before it was computed. And we have ignored the amount of time required to gather and check information, and to evaluate what choices there may be in the plan.

It is now realized in the Eastern Bloc that a complex economic system cannot be regulated by some computerized centre of control. This has been clearly demonstrated by a Soviet mathematician: a simple problem involving 2 objectives and 2 variants will have 4 solutions. With 5 objectives and 3 variants we already have 243 solutions. With 500 objectives and 10 variants (still a very simple economic planning problem) the number of solutions is 10^{500} (i.e. a '1' followed by 500 zeros). This is much more than the number of atoms in the entire universe![3]

Thus, it is simply impossible to process this quantity of information on a centralized basis. Some degree of central planning is necessary, but it is compelled to work with crude aggregates. It cannot deal with all types of product, nor with all the possible variations of quality. Neither can the central planner 'know' all the nuances and variations of popular want and need. The first argument for decentralization results from the utter impossibility of completely centralized planning. To handle and process all the information it is necessary to create localized planning structures which can relate to their sphere of influence on a more direct and informed basis. In addition, it is necessary to give each enterprise considerable autonomy to plan its production and work out its requirements. Some degree of centralization and coordination is necessary under socialism. But central planning cannot function without considerable decentralization at the same time.

The point that completely centralized planning is impossible was made first of all by Ludwig von Mises. An important restatement has come from Friedrich Hayek. In an article published in 1945 he wrote:

> What is the problem we wish to solve when we try to construct a rational economic order? On certain familiar assumptions the answer is simple enough. *If* we possess all the relevant information, *if* we can start out from a given system of preferences and *if* we command complete knowledge of available means, the problem which remains is purely one of logic . . . This, however, is emphatically *not* the economic problem which society faces. And the economic calculus which we have developed to solve this logical problem, though an important step toward the solution of the economic problem of society, does not yet provide an answer to it. The reason for this is that the 'data' from which the economic calculation starts are never for the whole society 'given' to a single mind which could work out the implications and can never be so given.[4]

Thus, according to Hayek, completely centralized planning is impossible because the central planning agency cannot possess all the necessary and relevant knowledge, as if it were 'concentrated in a single head'. However, once he has constructed his brilliant critique, Hayek jumps to the conclusion that *no* central planning is desirable. Furthermore, he asserts that it is possible for the market system to deal with all the complexities and uncertainties, and that it alone is the best economic regulator at hand. Hayek makes this jump with the assistance of a highly individualistic and subjective conception of 'knowledge', and a good dose of classic liberal prejudice against the state.

Contrary to Hayek, knowledge does not simply reside in the heads of individuals: it is transmitted and refracted through social institutions. Consequently, the most 'individualistic' economic system available, i.e. the market system, is not the most efficient means of dealing with all knowledge. It is just as absurd to confine all regulatory processes to a single type of mechanism such as the market, as to assume that all the knowledge that is necessary for planning can be concentrated in a single head. It does not follow from Hayek's critique of completely centralized planning that the market should be the dominant regulatory mechanism in society.

The second argument for decentralization is that it would help to devolve real power to ordinary people. A centralized planning apparatus concentrates power in the hands of national politicians, planners and civil servants – a power which is always open to abuse. While there are no grounds for assuming, along with the New Right and the theorists of 'rational economic man', that people are entirely egotistical and selfish, there are none to suppose that they are entirely benevolent either. This would be especially true of people in power. Decentralization does not solve this problem on its own. But it gives it a better choice of solution by offering greater accountability to the community and the locality involved. Moreover, decentralization can help to reduce alienation, increase participation, and improve efficiency. It can make local services more responsive to the needs of the people.[5] It can encourage innovation and creative thinking, as exemplified by the workers of Lucas Aerospace who designed many ingenious and socially useful products in their corporate plan.[6]

However, there is a danger of 'decentralization' becoming another 'nice' word like 'participation', to which many people pay lip-service, but without clarity or real commitment. It is necessary to think through what decentralization means, and seriously examine the problems which have been thrown up in practice.

Decentralization and Markets

The Left seems to have an immobile mental block on the subject of decentralization. Right at the end of a long and valiant attempt to discuss an alternative form of socialist society for Eastern Europe, Rudolph Bahro begins to discuss the 'structural conditions of individual initiative and genuine communality'. He writes:

> What is needed is evidently a certain *combination* between systemic regulation from above (which in terms of information theory is unavoidably hierarchical), and

> the economic initiative of relatively autonomous basic units of combined labour and social life (which by no means function in all circumstances in an emancipatory sense).[7]

But then Bahro is at page 439 of 453 pages of text, and we are given little insight as to the precise structural nature of this 'combination' other than the rediscovery of the 'federative principle' in the very last paragraph. It is like walking twenty miles to a promising restaurant to discover only fish and chips on the menu.

Hilary Wainwright and David Elliot fare no better, but they do not promise a gourmet meal at the outset. In their book on the Lucas Aerospace workers' plan, in which they discuss some of the implications of this important struggle, they write: 'A central government planning department, however well computerized, cannot handle efficiently all the millions of connections which, like a nervous system, make up the economy.'[8] They thus reject the traditional model of Soviet-type central planning. But they also reject the market, as being insensitive to social needs. We are left with nothing but a crude and vaguely specified 'lobbying' model of a proto-socialist society in which working people put 'pressure on public institutions to order the alternative goods to meet obvious needs'. Other than the 'utopia' of perpetual street demonstrations we are given little vision of the structure of a future socialist society. There is no outline of how such a society could function without either prominent central planning or a linking market mechanism.

A few years ago Stephen Bodington began to grapple with the problem of central planning in his book *Computers and Socialism*, advocating decentralization long before it became fashionable. He wrote:

> the potential of modern electronics and of the computer in particular makes it possible for anyone to have immediately retrievable information about sources of supply and about requirements of users and to communicate his responses to this information. Linkages which hitherto have been made through the market may now perfectly well be made through computer-based information systems. This is the crux of the matter.[9]

However, it is still unclear as to how the computer solves the problem. It is certainly possible to use it as a means of distributing and exchanging information, as in Chile under Allende with the assistance of experts such as Stafford Beer and Raul Espejo.[10] However, the exchange of information is not the same thing as the exchange of goods and services, which the computer cannot deal with. It can provide important information and overcome much of the ignorance and uncertainty normally associated with a market economy, but it has not yet been able to do away with the market altogether. The decentralized, computer-based planning system in Chile in 1970–73 did not achieve such a goal. The advocates of decentralization have not provided us with a plausible alternative.

Consider how Bodington's computer-based information system would function without a market. A manager of an enterprise might express a dire need for spare part number 64521 which is in short supply. This information is fed into the computer. The manager of another plant discovers a surplus stock, and communicates this information to the first manager. What, then, do they do? If the second manager is simply allowed to give away the spare part, the door is open to corruption. The manager of a whisky distillery could give away a crate of the spirit to a fellow manager 'in need' in return for 'a favour'. There is no social monitoring process to ensure that goods and services are transferred for legitimate reasons. As many as 98 out of 100 managers may be of the highest character, but the activities of the two others would not take long to undermine the trust and loyalty of the 98.

What social monitoring process is conceivable? An elected (preferably local) committee of Commissars for Desirable Transfers of Goods and Services? If they were to attempt to scrutinize every transfer, they would not be able to find enough hours in a year to evaluate the potential transfers of a single day. Furthermore, the very existence of such a committee would be a centralization of considerable power, which the original proposal attempted to avoid.

It has been noted in the previous chapter that Lenin condensed the planning process to 'accounting and control'. The question then is *how* products are to be valued so that the accounts may be compiled, and *how* transfers are to be controlled so as to minimize waste and corruption. No amount of computer technology solves the problem on its own. Essentially, we must ask, is the valuation process to be centralized or decentralized? And is the control of transfers to be in the hands of the central planning agency, or are enterprises to be allowed some autonomy? The latter course would be tantamount to granting the enterprise rights of possession (if not absolute property rights) over some products. If rights of valuation are conceded, the enterprise is authorized to set the price. We have reached the position where contracts are permitted between enterprises: products can be sold in return for money or other commodities. We have entered the realm of the market. The decentralization of control over industry inevitably means the establishment of a market mechanism: no realistic alternative has been found.

Markets, Capitalism and Socialism

I am aware that I am uttering heresy. Despite the support for some form of 'market socialism' from Wlodzimierz Brus (Poland), Branko Horvat (Yugoslavia), Janos Kornai (Hungary), and the leadership of the Polish trade union Solidarity, it has not been considered seriously by the Left in the West. In fact it is very common for the Left actually to define socialism in terms of the removal of the market (plus the establishment of nationalized industry). For example, in an important debate with Charles Bettelheim, the American Marxist Paul Sweezy explicitly identifies the use of the market mechanism in the Eastern Bloc as a 'turn to capitalist techniques'. The boundaries of capitalism are thus the boundaries of the market.[11] Another notable exponent of this view is Tony Benn. When asked to define socialism he repeatedly answers in terms of the absence of the market.[12] In *Arguments for Democracy*, in a section entitled 'The incompatibility of a strong political democracy with a market economy', he writes:

> democratic power, acquired by working people in Britain through our long campaigns for independent trade unions and the right to vote, is now so great as to be capable of dislocating, or paralysing, the market economy upon which British capitalism still relies for its motive force ... Labour governments, then, have to make one of two choices. They can either implement their manifesto objectives, paralyse the system still more effectively ... or they can abandon their reforms and accept the dictates of a system they were elected to change.[13]

Clearly the *bête noire* here is markets *per se*, rather than capitalist hierarchy in industry, private ownership of the means of production, or the other integral features of a capitalist economic system. In Benn's view, the primary and immediate objective of a Labour government is to uproot the market mechanism and replace it by a vague and unspecified form of democratic planning. This identification of capitalism with the market leads him to dismiss all forms of 'market socialism':

> 'Some Conservatives would like workers to confront directly the disciplines of the market economy through co-operatives. In this way they hope to create a new framework in industry in which capital can withdraw to a banking function, only funding co-operatives that are successful in fighting market forces. This is also what lies behind 'market socialism'. Industrialists who are ready to fund co-operatives see this as a way to withdraw from their role as managers of labour in the front line, letting the workers fight market forces alone.[14]

Benn's identification of markets with capitalism is in fact widespread on the Left. The crude markets/planning dichotomy is based on a mistaken view of the real capitalist economy and an impractical vision of the socialist future. It is the failure to discuss such 'utopias' that allows such errors to be perpetuated.

Interestingly, and once again, a very similar error is perpetrated by orthodox economists. Open any standard introductory textbook and there, in one of the first few chapters, will be an explanation that the fundamental choice is between a 'command economy' and a 'free market' system, with a continuum in between. This one-dimensional continuum is identical to that conceived by the Left. The only difference lies in the point upon it where each side would like us to be. The Left might choose a position towards the 'command economy', relabelling it 'democratic planning'. The orthodox economist is most likely to choose a position nearer to the 'free market'.

There are many things wrong with this one-dimensional conception of the fundamental alternatives. First, all market systems necessarily involve planning. Under capitalism there is considerable planning within the firm. Even the self-employed commodity-producer plans ahead. Thus the essential variation is not the extent of planning *per se.* There are two crucial issues: First, does the market dominate planning? And second, what is the nature of the institution which is doing the planning? Typically, under capitalism the market dominates, and the institution is the privately owned corporate firm. Under state collectivism planning dominates, and the typical institution is unelected and unaccountable. Under socialism, planning will dominate the system, but the planning agencies will be democratically elected and accountable to their 'constituency', be it the community or the nation.

Second, it is possible to conceive of non-capitalist market systems. One example is what Marxist economists call 'simple' (or 'petty') commodity production. This is a hypothetical economic system of self-employed producers. There are private property relations and a market, but there are no employers, i.e. no capitalists. Each person works for himself or herself, producing commodities to be sold. Such a system is a market system but it is not capitalism. Marx makes this point in the following terms. Under capitalism

> commodities are not exchanged simply as *commodities*, but as the *products of capitals* . . . Let us suppose the workers are themselves in possession of their respective means of production and exchange their commodities with each other. These commodities would not be products of capital.[15]

If a full market economy is not necessarily capitalist, where does capitalism fit on the orthodox planning–markets continuum? It does not seem to have a ready-made place. A second type of non-capitalist market economy makes the point even more dramatically. It is a community of producer cooperatives. Each cooperative is owned and run by the workers themselves. Their products are sold on a market. They purchase the required raw materials themselves. There is little or no central planning. We could describe such a system as 'market collectivist'. In some respects Yugoslavia is such a society, although there was a tendency in the 1970s to increase central planning.[16] Market collectivism has received support from such writers as Jaroslav Vanek and Peter Jay, Vanek in particular stressing the view that such a society is necessary to provide working people with self-management over the conditions, processes and objectives of their labour.[17] It is the democratic and participatory character of such a system which is stressed by most of its advocates. In this respect at least, it contrasts fundamentally with capitalism. Marx wrote:

> The labour-process, when it is the process by which the capitalist consumes labour-power, exhibits two characteristic phenomena. First, the worker works under the control of the capitalist to whom his labour belongs ... Secondly, the product is the property of the capitalist and not that of a worker, its immediate producer.[18]

Thus a market collectivist society is not capitalist because both these conditions are defied. The workers are self-managed: they do not work under the direct or indirect control of a capitalist. In addition the workers (collectively) own the product of their labour, which they bring to the market for sale. Thus the single, one-dimensional continuum found in both the orthodox textbooks and in much Left writing is completely flawed. Consider the point in diagrammatic terms. The orthodox view is that all possibilities can be arranged at various points along this single line:

⇐ 'Left' — 'Right' ⇒

A

'planned' or 'command' economy — 'free' or 'market' economy

According to this view the existing Western economies would be round about point A. We have argued that this view is far too simplistic, and at a minumum another dimension should be included. Matters could be developed in the following way:

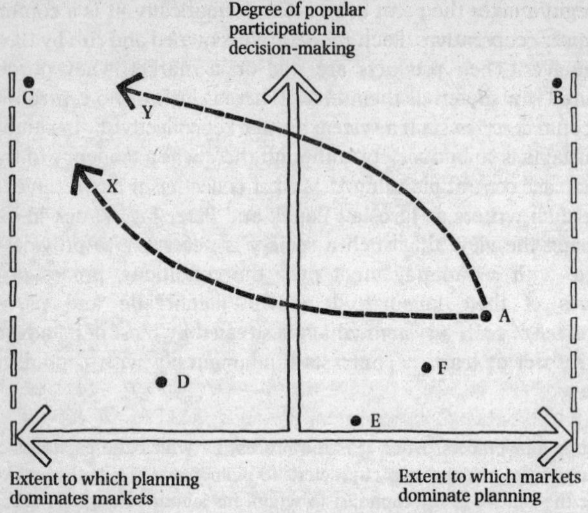

Here we have two dimensions: the points are arranged, not in a line, but on a plane. Point A, once again, would correspond to Western capitalism. Point B is the sort of market collectivism advocated by Vanek and others. Point C is the sort of 'socialism' traditionally advocated by the Left. Point D would represent a state collectivist society, such as the Soviet Union. E is fascism. F is corporatism.

According to the principle of impurity (see Chapters 6 and 7 above) points B and C are not feasible. It has been argued already that markets are necessary in any conceivable planned society, ruling out the 'extreme' option C. The Yugoslav experience confirms that a pure, Vanek-style, market collectivism is also not possible. Some degree of central planning is required. This rules out the 'extreme' option B. It should also be noted that hundred-per-cent popular participation in all decision-making is not possible, and such an 'extreme' position is above B and C.

The extent of common ownership is not made explicit in the diagram. As has been argued in Chapter 9, the precise relationship between popular participation and common ownership has not been firmly established in theory and practice, although high levels of participation are likely to correspond to cooperatives or other forms of common ownership. In addition, the dominance of the planning mechanism is likely to involve a high degree of public ownership, particularly by the state. Thus forms of common ownership are likely to be more prominent in the 'upper' and 'left' regions of the diagram. Some readers may object to the fact that common ownership is not made explicit. However, it should always be regarded as a means to an end, and not an end in itself. The primary ends are in fact popular participation in decision-making and social control of the economy through the planning process. The extent to which this primary goal of a democratic economy requires various forms of common ownership has to be determined in practice.

There are socialists of many varieties, advocating a number of outcomes: practically anywhere within the triangle formed by the points B, C and D. If a democratic economy is the chief aim, then we are obliged to consider an objective in the upper left hand side of the diagram. Other socialists veer towards point D, and still others advocate a position such as B. The objective here is closer to C.

The diagram can be useful in comparing routes as well as goals. It is implied in this book (see Chapters 9 and 13) that route Y is much more feasible and desirable than route X, which passes dangerously close to corporatist, fascist, and state collectivist social formations. In advocating an initial extension of public ownership while eschewing worker participation under capitalism, many socialists are arguing for route X. Such a stance is perhaps most common on the Left. In contrast, Y, the route advocated here, puts the initial emphasis on the democratization of the work process, the decentralization of planning, and the setting up of a large number of cooperative and participatory enterprises in preference to large-scale nationalization by the state. Greater overall planning and (perhaps) state ownership should come only after a higher degree of popular participation has been established. Then the momentum for even greater popular democracy may require greater state planning and ownership as a means to the democratic end, and such reforms may have a chance of obtaining the necessary majority support within the population as a whole.

It should be emphasized, however, that socialism must involve a reduction of market power. Markets are essential, but they should not be dominant, as they are under capitalism, rendering effective central planning and coordinated democracy impossible. Central planning is required especially in sectors such as energy, raw materials, transport, and heavy industry. For this reason a form of 'market collectivism', as proposed by Vanek and others, is not being advocated here.

A two-dimensional continuum can clearly distinguish between capitalism and a Yugoslav-type economy. It also has the advantage over a one-dimensional model in showing the difference between state collectivism and democratic socialism. Thus two dimensions are essential.

Politics is not simply between Left, Right and Centre, as popularly conceived. Nevertheless, even with the use of two dimensions, much is omitted from the model. In particular it cannot allow for any variation in the degree of inequality in the distribution of income or wealth. If there were a third dimension, some index of inequality would be a suitable candidate for it.

Markets under Socialism: Problems and Possibilities

The Left has been traditionally – and on the whole rightly – critical of market forms and the degrading role of money.[19] But such criticisms need to be evaluated in comparison with the feasible alternatives. There are two objections in particular which carry some weight. The first is that the market encourages acquisitive, self-seeking behaviour, and undermines commitment to broader social goals. The example of the United States comes to mind. However, it is arguable that the market alone does not achieve the egotistical and individualist culture that is found in that country: another contribution has been made by the 'Protestant ethic' and all that.[20] The contrast with the dynamic capitalism of Japan is illuminating. There the social culture is far less individualistic, with strong loyalty to corporate bodies such as the firm, the family and the imperial state.[21] Conversely, in the Soviet Union the banning of private enterprise has not abolished acquisitiveness and individualism. As Brus puts it:

> Having lived in the West for the last seven years, I must say that the spirit of acquisitiveness and general fetishization of 'things' among ordinary people seems to me weaker here than in the USSR and other Eastern European countries. It is simply untrue that only a market system generates these particular attitudes.[22]

Tony Benn and others fall into the error of a type of reductionism. The existence of capitalism is illegitimately and illogically reduced to the existence of market forms. The effect of this mistake is to belittle other important issues such as the existence or non-existence of authority relations within the enterprise; the existence of individual, joint-stock or cooperative forms of ownership; and in addition cultural and political factors. A holistic approach avoids this error by accepting the maxim that the system has to be understood not in its isolated parts, but as a whole.

The second important criticism of market forms is that they encourage and facilitate inequality in the distribution of income and wealth. By using the market it is possible for some people to get richer than others. These differences can be cumulative, as wealth means power, and power brings the means of accumulating more wealth. In response it has to be noted that large differentials of income are not absent from the Eastern Bloc. A recent study has shown that ratios of incomes per head after tax, comparing the top 5 per cent to the bottom 5 per cent, are very similar in Britain, Czechoslovakia, Denmark, Hungary, the Soviet Union, and Sweden. All these ratios lie between 3 : 1 and 6 :1.[23] In addition there is no reason to assume that large differences of income are inevitable with a market. After all, the extent of inequality varies a great deal between capitalist societies. In the United States, for example, taxes are not sufficiently progressive to avoid a ratio of nearly 13 : 1 between the richest and poorest 5 per cent (after tax).[24] In principle there is nothing to prevent an effective system of progressive taxation of income, coupled with a wealth tax, that would reduce differentials to considerably less than 3 : 1 – much less than the norm in the centrally planned economies. It would require a radical overhaul of the tax system and a great deal of courage and determination, but it is not beyond the bounds of possibility. The market does tend to generate inequality, but effective counteracting measures are possible, especially if the planning mechanism dominates the system as a whole.

A market mechanism has advantages and disadvantages. It seems appropriate to some areas of the economy but not to others. Before distinguishing them, we must outline some of the advantages. First, a market system seems to encourage flexibility and technical innovation. If, in contrast, the emphasis is entirely on plan-fulfilment, it is not easy to experiment with techniques of production, and the development of new products is a positive diversion from the task. Innovation is uncertain and potentially disruptive. It can endanger the production of the specified quota in the plan, and there is no guarantee that the overall planning authority will be able to evaluate the reasons for adopting the innovation and the public need for it, or to compensate for potential failure.

Another problem is quality variation. A plan necessarily sets its targets in terms of crude aggregates. Complete quality control is not possible because of the extensive amount of supervision involved. There is always a temptation in a planned system to reduce the quality of the product in an effort to reach the plan-target. The advantage of a market, in certain circumstances and in relation to certain types of product, is that some of the quality control can be left to the consumer, who chooses between competing types of product.

The Need for Planning

Where do markets fall down? It has been argued in Chapter 4 that markets can be insensitive to human needs that are obscured by ignorance or a lack of purchasing power. It is here that planning and non-market allocation must step in.

The Keynesian view that the market is an inappropriate and inefficient mechanism for determining the overall level of investment and output remains unrefuted. Left on its own, the market can lead to mass unemployment. Keynes argued that much investment needs to be taken over by the state and should not be entrusted to the stock market: 'When the capital development of a country becomes the by-product of the activities of a casino, the job is likely to be ill-done.'[25] However, Keynes had too much faith in the general efficiency of markets. He saw 'no reason to suppose that the existing system seriously misemploys the factors of production which are in use'.[26] Although he puts forward strong arguments for overall planning, he does not go far enough. Present circumstances should lead us to examine even more radical solutions.

Central planning can be superior to market regulation in sectors of the economy where long-term investment and decision-making are vital – for example in the use and management of the earth's natural and mineral resources. The market mechanism is not noted for its ability to consider the sort of environment that we may bequeath to our great-grandchildren. Its time-horizon is rarely as much as a decade. There is a strong environmentalist case for planning.[27]

Planning is required to determine the overall framework and priorities for production and consumption. In an original and useful article,[28] Michael Best argues that this overall framework is not achieved through market adjustment but through state intervention, and the political and other activities of large and powerful corporations. Furthermore, the market cannot easily make a 'choice' between, say, a planned public transport system and individual car ownership. This choice has to be made elsewhere. Best shows that in the United States, in the absence of government intervention to the contrary, the motor car, tyre and oil companies systematically bought up and dismantled rail and tram lines so as to create a market for the private car. The rail alternative was deliberately destroyed and removed from the competitive process, so that it was no longer possible for any 'individual preference' for public transport to express itself in market terms. From the individual point of view it became 'rational' to use the motor car. What was *socially* rational was a different matter. Best's article shows that the market cannot be relied upon to make big decisions such as the nature of the transport system. While some market provision and competition may have to remain, a considerable degree of overall planning is required for the system to work effectively.

As Keynes seemed to realize in his more radical moments, the unrestricted and unplanned market is not well suited to regulate the capital goods sector, even when full employment is reached. Capital equipment is structurally important to the economy as a whole. In an unplanned capitalist economy periodic fluctuations can be expected, but these fluctuations will be much greater in the sector producing capital goods. Firms will normally invest in new equipment only when there is no spare capacity in their plant. Thus the capital goods sector will be occupied only when the economy is working at full capacity; a reduction of as little as two per cent is enough to make the demand drop to zero. To a large extent, it is corrective planning and state intervention to solve this problem of demand instability in the capital goods sector that is responsible for the postwar economic success in France, West Germany and Japan.[29] Even the short-lived and limited National Plan of 1965–6 was beneficial in this respect, and two economists have regarded its abandonment as 'the decisive turning-point after which the structure of the United Kingdom economy deteriorated almost without interruption'.[30]

In some areas of the economy it is in practice impossible for the consumer to make a sufficiently informed and rational choice. The examples of the education and health services come to mind. I have no hesitation in saying that in these cases expert planners are in a better position than the individual to say what the individual needs. If we are sick, it is ridiculous to assume that the market is the best means of obtaining the best diagnosis. If we do not know the cause of our ills, how can we make an informed and rational choice between doctors? There is little incentive for a private health system to engage in preventive medicine; furthermore, some people may be too poor or too ill-educated to use such a system. In the case of health there is a strong case for the rationing of services and resources and for the health authorities themselves to assess needs. Here there is an argument for democracy, not markets. The public may not be expert in medical matters, but they should be able to elect the authorities and planners in charge. If they are entrusted with the right to elect governments, they should equally have the right to elect the local health committee, thus retaining choice over policy options within the health service without returning to the market.

A similar argument applies to education. A completely informed choice between educational institutions is not possible. If we knew the content of each course and curriculum we would not need the education in the first place. Instead of private, market relations in this sphere, the stress should be on a measure of democratic control of the governing body of the school or college, and on some choice between options within the curriculum. By their nature, in both education and health, the elements of choice are clouded by uncertainty. It is reasonable to rely on planning and guidance, as long as there is good reason to trust the experts concerned.

This does not mean that there is an easy or simple solution. In any situation where we are dependent on the judgement of a minority of experts there are dangers, and reasons for disquiet. But it is no less disquieting, in the spheres of education and health, to rely on the judgement of each and every individual. The solution must be to combine planning and state provision with both a measure of democratic control and an energetic programme of education and public discussion as to the nature, content and objectives of these vital services.

It has become established in Left thinking that the large monopolistic and multinational companies which dominate most modern capitalist economies are neither under democratic control nor operating according to the principles of a 'free' market. The case for substantial public ownership and democratic accountability has to be reiterated. As things stand, such large companies can evade government regulation and manipulate markets for their own ends. Both the New Right and the political parties of the Centre are silent as to this problem. There is an unanswered case for greater public accountability and democratic control in this area.[31] Consideration of the disproportionate power of the modern large corporation led Charles Lindblom, a mainstream liberal in the 1960s, to much more radical conclusions in the late seventies:

> The executive of the large corporation is, on many counts, the contemporary counterpart of the landed gentry of an earlier era, his voice amplified by the technology of mass communication ... It has been a curious feature of democratic thought that it has not faced up to the private corporation as a peculiar organization in an ostensible democracy ... They can ... insist that government meet their demands, even if these demands run counter to those of citizens ... The large corporation fits oddly into democratic theory and vision. Indeed it does not fit.[32]

It is impossible here to go through every sector of the economy and consider the case for planning. In some cases planning should involve complete state provision, without the use of a market mechanism. In other cases state provision should compete alongside a private sector. Competing municipal or cooperatively-owned enterprises may be more suitable elsewhere. In this section, however, a case has been made for overall planning, and public ownership of much of the economy. It is impossible to prescribe precise limits to planning and common ownership. But certain important conclusions can be drawn.

Conclusions

It should be clear from the argument in this chapter that markets are a necessary component of any planned economy which aims at devolving decision-making power to the region, the locality, the community, and the workplace. However, markets themselves are structured and moulded by the overall socio-economic framework. Markets under unplanned capitalism do not have the same character as markets in a socialist society where there is overall and polycentric planning. It is both desirable and necessary that a socialist society constructs a healthy symbiosis between planning and a subordinate market. The market, as John Eatwell puts it, is 'a good servant but a bad master'.[33]

Once again there is a strange parallel between the views of the New Right and some tendencies on the Left. Both seem to regard the market as a self-supporting mechanism, not only acting 'behind people's backs' but also functioning independently of institutions and social structures. With this view it is possible to see the market reaching social and economic results which are determinate and inevitable. It is also possible to attach an unambiguous moral sign to its operation. The difference between Left and Right, of course, is that in one case the sign is negative and in the other it is positive. In reality, however, the market is not determinate and independent: it takes up the character of the culture and social structure in which it operates. What both sides do not realize is that this structure can be changed without eliminating the market altogether.

The Hungarian economist Janos Kornai has used the following common but striking analogy to illustrate the necessary relationship between planning and markets in a socialist economy:

> In my opinion a modern economy – and especially a socialist economy – can dispense neither with planning nor with the market mechanism. What is needed is, however, not the 'happy mean' of the two, not their 'convex combination' with 50 per cent of market mechanism and 50 per cent of planning, both in half-developed, half-disintegrated form. Both should function in their fully developed form. In the human organism certain functions are controlled by the autonomous nervous system, others by the central nervous system. It would give rise to grave difficulties if the control of, let us say, breathing or the temperature of the body were to devolve on the central nervous system; this would absorb our mental capacities and it is by no means certain that control would be reliable. On the other hand, an activity of a higher order ... cannot be left to the autonomous nervous system. In

the economic organism it is primarily the market that will perform the role of the autonomous nervous system whereas planning performs that of the central nervous system. Neither can replace the other, and it must be endeavoured to keep both intact and in working order.[34]

As we have seen, many on the Left are hostile to the introduction of markets in a planned society, in contrast to the position of most Eastern Bloc dissidents and the Polish trade union movement Solidarity. 'From the very start, Solidarity has advocated far-reaching economic reforms ... a reduction of bureaucratic controls, the extension of the market mechanism, decentralization and substantive workers' participation in management.'[35] Some on the Left in the West have found this support for an enlarged market sufficient reason to dissociate themselves from Solidarity and the dissident movement elsewhere in the Eastern Bloc. Others maintain their support, regarding the positive policy towards markets as an aberration. In few cases has the full programme of Solidarity been fully understood and supported unconditionally. The extension of markets in Poland is not a regression towards capitalism. It is a necessary step towards an efficiently planned and democratic society.

At its first national congress, in September 1981, Solidarity approved a number of far-reaching economic reforms. In an attempt to break the grip of the state apparatus on the whole of Polish society, it was argued that the over-centralized economy had to be broken down. To this end Solidarity proposed decentralization, with a number of types of enterprise. There would be some privately owned firms, especially in agriculture, but common ownership would still prevail overall in the form of worker cooperatives, municipal enterprises, and state enterprises. Planning and coordination would remain. The introduction of democracy and political pluralism were seen as essential to the efficiency of the planned economy. Despite 'sympathy' in Washington and accusations from Moscow, Solidarity had no desire to move in the direction of capitalism. The proposed reforms would, in contrast, have represented the introduction of genuine socialism for the first time in any country. Since then, of course, Solidarity has been banned and the system of state collectivism remains intact. It would be tragic if the events of 1980–81 passed by without a full realization in the West of their significance.

It should be emphasized that what is being proposed in this chapter, and what is inscribed in the programme of Solidarity, is not a wishy-washy argument for a 'mixed economy' similar to that proposed by some social democratic thinkers.[36] The social democratic 'mixed economy' retains the dominance of capitalist relations. It involves about three-quarters of the economy being in private hands, and the absence of strong social coordination and planning. For a planned and democratic economy a greater proportion of industry would have to be publicly owned, in one form or another. Overall coordination would not be left to the market, although the market would play a vital role. Although the impurity principle applies to both capitalism and socialism it does not give us a *carte blanche* for any mixture between public and private forms; in a stable and viable system, one of them must prevail. Under capitalism, private ownership and the market are dominant; under socialism it is common ownership and the plan.

The key difference between the two is that capitalism involves a private and atomistic system of regulation, whereas under socialism overall regulation is social and in the public domain. It is not sufficient that this public domain is the central state. The public character of socialist regulation necessarily implies both decentralization and democracy.

Twelve

What is Wrong with Marxism?

Marxism, after drawing us to it as the moon draws the tides, after transforming all of our ideas, after liquidating the categories of our bourgeois thought, abruptly left us stranded . . . it had no longer anything to teach us, because it had come to a stop.

Jean-Paul Sartre, *Search For a Method*

Much of the analysis in this book uses Marxian categories. Indeed, in the use and elaboration of the concept of a socio-economic system a great debt is owed to Marx. No other tradition in political economy would enable us to go so far. Marx's great contribution was to develop a theoretical framework in which different socio-economic systems may be analysed. This provides an invaluable insight for the study of history and for social science as a whole, and puts Marx on the same footing as Sir Isaac Newton in physics, Charles Darwin in biology, and Sigmund Freud in psychology. It is the prevailing political prejudice of our times which has prevented universal acceptance of this fact. It will be a mark of maturity when Marx's achievement is recognized as being as immense as those of Newton, Darwin and Freud elsewhere.

On the other hand, there are in Marxian theory a number of greater or lesser flaws. In his *Considerations on Western Marxism*, Perry Anderson devotes two pages to a concise assessment of Marx's theoretical contribution, detecting flaws in three main areas. First, in his treatment of the capitalist state 'Marx never produced any coherent or comparative account of the political structures of bourgeois class power at all'.[1] Second, Anderson notes Marx's 'incomprehension of much of the nature of the later epoch through which he lived',[2] particularly the significance and strength of bourgeois nationalism. Third, the 'economic architecture of *Capital* itself, Marx's greatest achievement, is not immune to a number of possible doubts'.[3] In this regard Anderson mentions the labour theory of value,[4] the distinction between productive and unproductive labour,[5] the law of the tendency of the rate of profit to fall,[6] and the tenet of an ever-increasing class polarization between capitalists and workers. Anderson concludes: 'The very absence of any political theory proper in the late Marx may thus be logically related to a latent catastrophism in his economic theory, which rendered the development of the former redundant.'[7]

The reader familiar with my previous published work will not need to be informed of my agreement with Anderson. I do not feel the same way, however, about Leszek Kolakowski's recent monumental study.[8] Much of its critical impact is marred by an obvious impatience, pitted with exaggeration, and coloured by emotional hostility. This does not mean that it is without insight and a measure of truth. But it is dangerous to dismiss Marxism as 'religion' or 'fantasy' without a comparative assessment of the undemocratic and authoritarian ideology which some on the Right would desire to take its place. Another fault of Kolakowski's critique is that it pays disproportionate attention to the philosophical aspect of Marxism, to the detriment of a serious evaluation of Marx's positive contribution to history and social science.

However, there is a hint in Kolakowski's work of what in fact may be the central problem. He indicates that the concept of the proletariat has a central and crucial role in Marxian theory:

> In the class-consciousness of the proletariat, historical necessity coincides with freedom of action; the opposition between human will and the 'objective' course of events ceases to exist, the dilemma of utopianism and fatalism is resolved. The working class, and it alone, enjoys the privilege that its hopes and dreams are not condemned to beat against the wall of inexorable destiny; its will and initiative are themselves part of the necessary course of history.[9]

Kolakowski is not explicit on this point, but it would appear that it is in the Marxian relation between the concept of social class and the development of history that there is a potential weakness – a weakness also detected in a recent work by André Gorz. Although very critical of Marxism, Gorz does not have the same hang-ups as Kolakowski, and his interesting and challenging thesis deserves more attention here. He contends that the new technology has broken the power of the working class, depriving it of its Marxian 'historic' role:

> There is a crisis in marxist thinking because a crisis has developed within the labour movement. Over the past 20 years, the link between the development of the productive forces and the growth of class antagonism has been broken ... Capitalism has never been able to solve the problems it has generated. Yet this inability has not been fatal ... It has become able to accommodate its dysfunctions, even drawing renewed strength from this state of affairs. For the problems it has found to be insoluble are also intrinsically insoluble ... [The marxist] tradition is based

upon a number of interconnected assumptions *which will remain unverified in the future as they have been in the past.* They are:
1. The development of the productive forces will create the *material* base for the development of socialism.
2. The development of the forces of production will create the *social* preconditions for the establishment of socialism, in the form of a working class collectively capable of taking over and managing the forces of production whose development brought it into being.
Reality however is quite different.[10]

There are strong and weak points in this argument. The major part of the book is based on a central and unsubstantiated assumption that the problems and principal features of capitalism are the problems and principal features of industrialization. Furthermore, this industrial system is a huge machine-like entity, dominating present society, and reducing its members likewise to robots or machines. Thus workers' control or worker participation are impossible. There is no way in which democracy or self-management can establish itself within this rigid, hierarchical monolith.

The fatal weakness of this argument is that it assumes that it is possible for any industrial system to work as if it were a machine. As has been my thesis throughout, no hierarchical system of organization and control can be designed to cope with the variety of problems and events which are bound to crop up regularly over time. Although the industrial system has mechanistic features, it is not a machine. It has to grant some degree of autonomy and control to those that are doing the work, for complete supervision and control are not possible. Work is a purposeful activity, requiring some measure of self-determination and autonomy. This is a central contradiction within the capitalist industrial system: capitalist control of the labour process conflicts with limited but necessary worker autonomy in production.

Gorz's view of capitalist industry is very different. The picture is all negative. Hierarchy is all-powerful. Control from above is complete. The industrial system is an automaton which cannot be transformed. It has, therefore, to be ended. Gorz's own political evolution is relevant here. In the 1950s he was a supporter of the French Communist Party. The orthodox Communist believes that industry can be planned by a central committee, using hierarchy and control 'in the interests of working people'. The mistake is the same: society is conceived as a machine. The difference, however, between the Gorz of 1958 and the Gorz of 1980 is that the machine is now deemed *not* to be in the interests of the people. There is thus a link between Gorz's quasi-Stalinist position of the 1950s and his quasi-anarchist position today. In both cases the conflicts, contradictions, and necessary elements of autonomy within capitalist industry are belittled. The system is a monolith. The role of necessary impurities is ignored. I do not think that these errors are consistent with an adequate analysis of the socio-economic system. Gorz's work is purely at the level of 'sociology', lacking economics of both a theoretical and practical kind.

Gorz's argument has been dwelt upon in part to criticize his dismissal of Marxism, and in part to recognize an important strength in his book, for in its first chapter there is a powerful and valid critique of the theory of the proletariat which has serious consequences for Marxism as a whole. Gorz points out that Marxism assigns to the working class a historical role which 'is not based upon either empirical observation of class conflict or practical involvement in proletarian struggle'.[11] It is invested with a mission: it is the agency of revolution against capitalism, and its victory is the only true basis for the building of socialism. The working class is both the means and the end of the socialist movement.

As Gorz observes, this is a dogmatic and unfounded pronouncement. It is based on faith. A total picture of history is assumed, in its evolution from the 'primitive communism' of tribal society to the higher stage of communism itself. The working class is the universal agent in the transition to a classless society. It is endowed with a destiny and equipped with the force of (inevitable) historical development.

Classes and Systems in History

This combination of a total view of history with the identification of the key agency of social change is one of the reasons why Marxism is so persuasive and attractive a doctrine. This, however, does not mean that it is valid. Let us examine these notions of history and agency in more detail.

The working class is created by capitalism. According to Marx it is the agency of the transformation of capitalism into the next system: socialism. Similarly, before that, the bourgeoisie created under feudalism became the agency of the transformation of society from feudalism to capitalism. Thus each system creates a class which is antagonistic to it and which becomes the agency of social change, the means by which the system is overthrown, and finally the new ruling class which creates a new economic system or 'mode of production'. Each class has a historical function, a historical destiny, and a future form of society to create in its own image.

This type of association between the transformation of class relations and the replacement of one mode of production by another is not confined to the modern period. In Marxism there is a schema of historical development, whose relevant features may be summarized in the following form:

Mode of Production:	Slavery	Feudalism	Capitalism	Socialism
Ruling Class:	Slaveowners	Nobility	Bourgeoisie	Proletariat
Oppressed Classes:	Slaves and Poor	Serfs and Bourgeoisie ↗	Proletariat ↗	—
Form of Property:	Private (for Citizenry)	Feudal Tenure	Private Property	Common Ownership
(--> represents a 'social revolution')				

This schema is at the core of Marxism. It provides an analysis of the past and an indication of the path of progress in the future. It gives Marxism both a theory of social causality and a historical teleology. Within this schema the concept of class plays a central role, as Marx and Engels outlined in the *Manifesto of the Communist Party*.

A frequent line of criticism upon which we will not dilate is to question the supposed inevitability of this historical progression through modes of production. In any case many Marxists accept that the progression is not inevitable. This issue is indeed important, and grandiose claims of the 'inevitability of socialism' should be rebutted, but it is not the central problem. We shall approach this by first examining a few areas of persistent controversy.

A recurrent debate between Marxist and non-Marxist historians is over the role of class in the transition from feudalism to capitalism. Let us first take the example of England. It is clear that private ownership of the means of production, commodities, wage-labour, and capitalist relations in agriculture and commerce were well established by the beginning of the eighteenth century. Industrial capitalism, of course, developed later, but it does not seem unreasonable to conclude that in England in 1700 capitalism was the dominant mode of production. If this was so, according to the Marxian schema the bourgeoisie had replaced the nobility and become the ruling class.[12]

There are serious problems with this interpretation of history. It can be accepted that capitalism was the dominant mode of production at the time; but when the concept of social class is brought into the drama it does not fit the facts. There is no doubt that the aristocracy in England remained dominant in society and politics until the end of the nineteenth century. In short: the bourgeoisie did not 'rule' as a class for two centuries of capitalism's economic dominance. They indeed had great power and growing wealth, particularly after the Industrial Revolution. But it is a distortion of the facts to say that they were the ruling class. They did not dominate Parliament or the state. In fact they tried to emulate the aristocracy by investing a great deal of their new-found wealth in landed property.

Most Marxists point to the Revolution of the 1640s as the decisive event in the transition from feudalism to capitalism in Britain. This point is not contested here. This period was of momentous importance. A tremendous social and political rupture took place. Neither are we repeating the tired old debate between gradualism and revolution. All that misses the point. The anomaly in the orthodox Marxian position is that although the English Revolution was indeed a decisive event in the transition from feudalism to capitalism, it was not a war upon the nobility immediately followed by the ascendancy of the bourgeoisie. The English Revolution was a conflict between factions of the landed aristocracy, not a class war in the classic sense of the term. Its immediate result was a restructuring of state and society, but not a radical alteration in the disposition of class power. That did not occur until the 1800s.

Other anomalies can be found elsewhere. For example, in Japan capitalism was introduced in the late nineteenth century by the aristocracy. It was a revolution from above which did not alter the balance of class power according to the Marxian schema. The bourgeoisie did not lead, or immediately ascend into political and social dominance. In Tsarist Russia the character of the state did not reflect dominant capitalist relations in the economy. In few countries has there been a clear correspondence between the rise of capitalism and the political ascent of the bourgeoisie.

The retention of the Marxian historical schema in these circumstances has created enormous problems and protracted attempts to find a solution. Nowhere is this illustrated more dramatically than in relation to the theory of the state. According to orthodox Marxism the state has to be a class state. Thus we have a set of contorted explanations and theories. In the *Manifesto of the Communist Party*, the state under capitalism is regarded as a special 'committee' staffed by, and acting on behalf of, the bourgeoisie. When an examination of the historical personnel involved does not match this description, the state is called an 'instrument' of the capitalist class. Then further problems arise as to the analysis of the precise mechanisms connecting the bourgeoisie with its chosen 'instrument'. The debate on the capitalist state continues, without resolution. The problem that has to be solved is why the existence and dominance of the capitalist mode of production necessarily means that the bourgeoisie is a ruling class and necessarily means that there is a specifically bourgeois state. This problem is created by Marxism itself. In response, many Marxists simply beg the question and assert that the state is bourgeois, and the bourgeoisie is the ruling class, *because* capitalism is dominant. This is not convincing. In the absence of a solution to the problem it is necessary to abandon the Marxian historical schema.

The problems become even more obvious and serious in regard to the transition from a capitalist to a post-capitalist society. According to the Marxian schema, the working class should be the main agency in this transition. It should institute a 'dictatorship of the proletariat', thus constituting itself the ruling class. In the post-revolutionary transition period, according to Marxian orthodoxy, society is organized around a 'workers' state'. Let us assume that we may rightfully describe the Eastern Bloc countries as post-capitalist in character. The problem that orthodox Marxism has to face up to is this: In only one of these countries (i.e. Russia) did the working class play a major role in the transition from capitalism, and even here they were but a small minority of the population. Elsewhere the transformation was carried out by foreign invasion, or internally by revolutionary armies staffed by intellectuals and peasants. The industrial proletariat either did not exist in these revolutions, or it played a negligible role. For example, in China after the defeats of the urban risings in the 1920s the scene of operations moved to the countryside, where it remained until the victory of Mao's army in 1949. Albania and Yugoslavia were also transformed by an army acting with the support of the peasantry from a rural base. The remainder of Eastern Europe changed its character as a result of the armed imposition of Soviet power. The working class was not inert, but it did not play a decisive part. In the transition from capitalism to a post-capitalist society the working class has not been the leading actor.

To retain the orthodox Marxian schema in these circumstances it is necessary to regard the Eastern Bloc as a collection of 'workers' states'. Both orthodox Communists and Trotskyists have described these countries as being under a 'proletarian dictatorship'. However, not only did the working class play a minor role in the creation of these states, but also it is almost entirely excluded from political power. Orthodox Marxism presents us with an immense paradox. Within its terms the contradiction cannot be resolved.

Less orthodox Marxists offer us two ways out of the dilemma. One is to follow Max Shachtman and describe the Soviet Union and other Eastern Bloc countries as a new form of class society called 'bureaucratic collectivism' which has to be added to the historical schema as an alternative post-capitalist mode of production. Under 'bureaucratic collectivism' the bureaucracy is said to be a ruling class. In response, orthodox Marxists have argued that this 'class' has no means of passing on all its wealth and power to successive generations. In addition, bureaucracies are evident elsewhere, particularly in advanced capitalist societies. So are bureaucracies everywhere to be regarded as a 'new class'? This view was affirmed by James Burnham, who, in *The Managerial Revolution*, predicted a world-wide convergence to a bureaucratic and managerial society.[13] Thus, he thought, fascism and Communism were essentially similar. In response it has been pointed out that capitalist forms of property and organization have been very prominent under fascist regimes. To equate the Eastern Bloc with fascism seems to ignore a number of vital differences between two types of (unpalatable) social system. The 'bureaucratic collectivism' theory does not fit easily into a Marxist framework. It is no accident that it has not been popular among Marxists.

The second attempted escape route is to describe the Eastern Bloc countries as 'state capitalist'.[14] This involves erecting a definition of capitalism with public rather than private ownership, and with planning rather than market regulation. Clearly, such an approach involves a break from Marx's definitions in *Capital*. Furthermore, it is difficult then to make any clear distinction between capitalist and other non-socialist modes of production. All that is said is that they are not socialist because the working class is not in control. The idea that it is competition in the world economy which makes each individual nation capitalist, instead of internal competition between private firms, fares no better.[15] 'Competition' between East and West is very different in character from that between capitalist firms or nations. It does not involve substantial trade or market exchange. Furthermore, the theory of 'state capitalism' implies that an individual socialist government that is not immediately rescued by world revolution remains 'capitalist' in perpetuity. The theory thus transforms Marxism into a millenarian hope in an impossible scenario of simultaneous world revolution. In the meantime, 'capitalism' is everywhere.

History does not fit into the Marxist schema. Orthodox Marxists can go on endlessly transforming and 'developing' their theories but the anomalies will remain. It is like trying to explain the nature of the solar system with the astronomy of Ptolemy: it can be done, but only in a tortuous and excessively complicated fashion.

A central problem is the very notion of a 'ruling class' and the association of different modes of production with different 'ruling classes'. According to the Marxian schema, no fundamental change in the economic system is possible without the elevation of a new ruling class. It is assumed that there is a one-to-one relationship between economic systems and basic configurations of class power. It is these tenets that must be abandoned.

Towards a New Perspective

First, the very idea of a class 'ruling' should be challenged. At the very most it is a weak and misleading metaphor. It is possible to talk of a class being dominant in a society, but only by virtue of the dominance of a particular type of economic structure. To say that a class 'rules' is to say much more. It is to imply that it is somehow implanted into the apparatus of government. A class may have influence, even massive influence, over the state and government, but that is not the same thing. The state may even reflect the dominant structures of the economy in terms of its own function and internal organization, but that does not imply the existence of a ruling class.

Second, there is a more fundamental problem with the orthodox Marxist schema. Classes are themselves defined by reference to relations of property or possession. For example, the working class is defined as the class which lives by selling its labour-power as a commodity. The notions of sale and a commodity have to be defined in terms of property relations and the institution of a market. Other classes also have to be defined by reference to social relations and structures. In consequence, social classes are not independent and self-sufficient entities, struggling and clashing through historical time. Their very existence and definition depend on the nature of the socio-economic system which is the context of their action. Classes cannot be the primary objects of theoretical construction and historical analysis. They have to be defined after, and in relation to, social relations and economic systems.

In contrast, much Marxist writing, including the *Manifesto of the Communist Party*, treats social classes as the elemental building blocks of historical analysis. They struggle, they clash, they rise, they fall. As they do so the economic structure may change. But it is forgotten that classes can only have meaningful definition in a structural relation with other classes. The configuration of class power does not define the system: the system defines a set of possible configurations of class power.

To accept this point does not necessarily mean the adoption of a functionalist perspective. Instead of social classes we have systems, structures and social relations as the primary objects of analysis. This approach would be functionalist if it did not embody internal conflict and the possibility of fundamental structural change. There is nothing to stop the inclusion of a notion of internal conflict or contradiction. The traditional Marxist conflict between forces and relations of production may be retained, for example. There is also the conflict between different types of economic structure.

It also has to be emphasized that this new perspective does not involve the abandonment of the concept of social class, nor the potential role of classes as agents of social change. Let us take the transition from capitalism to socialism as an example. While this does not necessarily mean that the working class has to play a leading part in the process, in industrial capitalist countries this is indeed likely to be the case. Socialism is no longer defined as a system in which the working class is a ruling class. But the general emancipation which socialism brings will benefit, above all, the working class.

With this new perspective, the historical anomalies outlined above disappear. It is no longer strange, nor necessarily exceptional, that the basis of capitalism can be constructed by a section of the landed gentry (as in England) or by a large part of the aristocracy (as in Japan). We are not forced to define the countries of the Eastern Bloc as 'workers' states', or to search there in desperation for a new 'ruling class'. It is clear that the state collectivist formations emerged as the result of the actions of a number of groups and classes, without uniformity between the countries involved. They are described, primarily, in terms of their internal structures and relations. It is a secondary question as to whether the bureaucracy constitutes a new dominant class. Our attention is generally directed towards the internal structures of the system as a whole, including their legal, political and economic dimensions. It is the system as a whole which determines the relations of power between classes, not the historical origin of the system or a superimposed historical schema.

The notion of a 'ruling class' is abandoned. Along with it go such unacceptable phrases as the 'dictatorship of the proletariat' and the 'dictatorship of the bourgeoisie', both of which have been associated indiscriminately in Marxist writing with democratic and dictatorial regimes alike. Gone are the tortuous attempts to fit the complex realities of the modern state into a schema in which there is a 'ruling class'. Instead of a temptation to relapse into conspiracy theories and unwarranted conspiratorial formulations (e.g. 'the capitalist class decided . . .') we are led to examine more concretely the structures and relations of power, and the forces of social change.

Above all, however, it is not necessary to see all issues and ideologies as purely class based. Greater meaning is given to universal and supra-class categories. In some senses concepts such as 'peace' and 'justice' could be constructed in this way. In terms of this book the third example is obvious: we can sustain a supra-class concept of democracy. A distinction and division between 'proletarian' and 'bourgeois' democracy is therefore necessarily rejected. Democracy cannot separate itself entirely from the fate and fortune of social classes, but it becomes a 'populist' or universal notion nevertheless.[16]

Some Political Consequences

What has just been said is neither difficult nor entirely original. It is reasonable to ask why it has not been said clearly before. It is also reasonable to wonder why Marx's manuscript for the third volume of *Capital* breaks off at the very point where he begins to define and discuss the concept of social class. He never resumed the work, and on his death nearly twenty years later it was revised and published by Engels. It does not seem unreasonable to suggest that Marx had nagging doubts about his view of the world.

It should be pointed out that heresy lurks within the alternative perspective that has been outlined here. Perhaps that is one reason why it has not emerged before. Speculation aside, let us make things more clear. It has been asserted in this chapter that classes are not the primary objects of historical analysis: it is structures and systems that are primary. Thus a working class is defined in terms of its socio-economic integument. Clearly a worker in one country does not necessarily face the same set of institutions and social relations as a worker in another. In part, such structures are national in character. Consequently, it is not true to say that 'the working class has no nation'. Without a given nation there is no specific socio-economic structure, and it is impossible to sustain an independent notion of social class. Consequently, some working-class interests are entwined with the fate of 'the nation'. There is thus a place for a theory of nationalism which, as Anderson notes, Marxism has traditionally ignored.[17]

Most emphatically, however, this does not legitimate every chauvinist and imperialist policy. Just as there are supra-class interests and objectives *within* nations there are supra-national interests and objectives *between* nations. 'Peace', it could be said, is one of the latter. A recognition that classes cannot be disentangled from nations does not imply support for any and every form of nationalism. It does, however, mean a final break from unfounded notions of 'world revolution' which Marxism has been forced to harbour in its midst. Above all it means taking the nation seriously as a forceful and weighty institution in politics and economics.

A second important consequence of the argument in this chapter concerns the nature of socialism itself. The supra-class character of democracy has been noted already. In general it is necessary to detach socialism from the immediacy of the interests of a single class. Socialism is more than the emancipation of the working class: it is the emancipation and liberation of humanity as a whole. The struggle for socialism is therefore a question of creating a broad and powerful consensus for radical social change that will lead to the implementation of a socialist programme. The notion of democracy is necessarily central to the ideology of this consensus.

Marx and Markets

Just as socialism does not mean the exclusive victory of a single social class, it does not mean the imposition of a single form of (collective) social property. The impurity principle can be invoked here. Within Marxism there is a connection between the dogma of class rule and the idea that it is possible to form a social system on the basis of a single type of economic structure and a single type of collective property. The commitment of Marx and Engels to common ownership and collective organization was so extensive as to exclude the long-term survival of the market under socialism. Markets were not identified with capitalism *per se*, but they argued that they had to be phased out under socialism, in the process of transition to a communist society.

Recently, this standpoint has come under careful and critical analysis. In a thorough examination of Marx's works, Stanley Moore has shown that he failed to consider a socialist society where there was common ownership, but also decentralization and market regulation. Marx gives no clear and acceptable reason why the market should be entirely phased out under socialism.[18]

In addition, Moore identifies an apparent contradiction in Marx's writing. On the one hand, particularly in *The Poverty of Philosophy* and the *Contribution to the Critique of Political Economy*, Marx clearly argues that market exchange is necessary to reduce all different types of labour to their common equivalent: abstract labour. Accounting under socialism will be done using the measure of labour-time. Thus it would appear that the market would be necessary under socialism to establish this universal measure of concrete labour. But this contradicts Marx's moral critique of markets in the *Economic and Philosophic Manuscripts* and elsewhere. Moore shows that Marx's cavalier treatment of markets under socialism was challenged on a number of occasions during his lifetime. In each case Marx gave an inadequate and unreasoned response.

Conclusion

Marxism gives us an illuminating theory of socio-economic systems. Above all, Marx provided us with a majestic analysis of the capitalist system in *Capital*. This analysis, with all its flaws, has never been rivalled. Much of it needs to be retained. There is also, in Marxism, a conception of the working class as the agency of the transition to the socialist future.

A radical political economy indeed requires a theory of socio-economic systems. But it also requires a vision of the future, and the identification of the forces in present society which can help to lead to that future. For this the Marxian heritage is no longer adequate. History is not as simple or predetermined as is suggested in much Marxist writing.

Just as according to the impurity principle a pure economic structure cannot survive on its own, so there is no single or exclusive agency in the transition from one socio-economic system to another. The working class does not have a pre-ordained historical destiny. And the transition to socialism is not the sole prerogative of the working class. Other classes and groups can also be in the vanguard. All that we can say is that the working class is likely to play an important role because of its position in production. This position, as Gorz suggests, could be undermined by the growth of labour-saving technology. However, it is no time, as yet, to say farewell to the working class.

The most important characteristic of socialism is a full and extensive democracy. This does not arise from a single set of property relations or come about at the behest of a single social class. It results from complicated social struggle leading to a general social transformation. We can point to the elements of this process as they exist in present society. But we cannot presume that a single class is involved on the positive side of that struggle. Indeed, democracy is sometimes resisted by elements of the working class itself. No class, or group, or set of persons, has the 'destiny' to bring about the democratic socialist transformation. That 'destiny' is formed in the process of struggle, and it cannot be claimed in advance of success.

I would not go as far as Herbert Marcuse, who argues that students and intellectuals have replaced the working class as the agency of this transformation.[19] In a country such as Britain, where the trade union movement is highly organized, such working-class movements are likely to be very prominent in the leadership of the movement for democratic socialism. Neither would I accept the argument of Eric Hobsbawm that the working class has become significantly more divided and significantly less class conscious, and that its 'forward march' has halted in the last few years.[20] Divisions have always been prominent, 'class consciousness' has always been limited and sporadic, and we should not ignore the massive growth in trade unionism in the 1970s.[21] But Hobsbawm and Marcuse are right to question the pre-destined position of the working-class vanguard in the move towards socialism.

I would go further than these two writers by placing much more emphasis on the nature of the socialist objective itself. When it is realized that this objective is defined, fundamentally, in terms of *structures of power*, then it becomes more clear that there is no pre-ordained agency in the transformation. Without an adequate theory of socio-economic systems, and a detailed vision of the future, much discussion of the agency of transformation, and whether its march has halted or not, is irrelevant. The forces of change towards a socialist objective become clear only through a serious analysis of what future is both possible and desirable. As I have argued already in this work, Marxists and other socialists can no longer afford to take this objective for granted.

According to the conventional wisdom, Marx's most important contribution to modern thought was in the realm of history and sociology. He is more highly regarded as a political theorist than he is as an economist. If the arguments in this chapter are valid, then the conventional wisdom is the reverse of the truth. A number of key problems make Marx's contribution to our understanding of history less enduring. His view of class has serious flaws, giving grave cause for doubt about his 'sociological' vision. As a social scientist he lacks, above all, an adequate and comprehensive theory of politics. His enduring contribution is to economics, where, like no other thinker, he has helped us to understand the inner workings of the capitalist system.

Thirteen

What is to be Done?

The fate of democracy is bound with the socialist movement.

Rosa Luxemburg, *Reform or Revolution*

The slogan of the reformist approach to socialism was coined by Eduard Bernstein near the end of the last century. He wrote: 'The final goal, no matter what it is, is nothing; the movement is everything.'[1] In eulogizing piecemeal advance, he disregarded utopia – a silence about the future maintained by other, 'revolutionary' socialists who rejected his reformism. They too refused to speculate on the final goal, regarding it, in any case, as 'inevitable'.

But no movement, 'reformist' or 'revolutionary', can afford to dispense with utopia. A goal of some sort is necessary for any purposeful advance. The future, whatever it may be, is not inevitable.

In the preceding chapters an attempt has been made to develop a theoretical basis on which to formulate a desirable and possible goal of the foreseeable future. The existing body of economic knowledge about planning and markets has been utilized and scrutinized, to draw out some guidelines. Many questions remain unanswered, and the analysis is far from complete. But this book is about goals, not about piecemeal movements or isolated reforms.

In general, socialists talk of goals in ill defined terms. Socialism is equated with 'common ownership ... and the best obtainable system of popular administration and control of each industry or service'.[2] On the right of the socialist movement we find an even less specific commitment to 'more equality'. The orthodox Marxist may talk of socialism being about the dominance in political and economic power of the majority, the working class. This is a worthy objective. There is no dissent from it here. But it is hopelessly inadequate for a movement which aims to change the world.

It is vague values and aims such as these which are incapable of advancing the socialist movement. The sincere socialist who sees socialism as being mainly about nationalization finds that he or she is opposed by a reactionary tide of populism which is rejecting the authoritarianism and bureaucracy of the over-centralized state. The well-intentioned legislator for more equality finds that people have lost all faith in paternalistic reform, and comes up against an establishment which is abandoning the manipulated politics of consensus for an epoch of austerity. The orthodox Marxist finds strange bedfellows on the Left and the Right of the trade union movement: people who talk about more power, more money, more everything except responsibility. They find then that in failing to provide an alternative vision their best allies become those that are playing the market game of 'free collective bargaining'. In refusing to accept a measure of responsibility in the present, they play into the hands of those who claim a divine right to manage and control. Behind the three vague faces of modern socialism we have unwitting concessions to conservatism.

It is necessary to reject both the worker-centred fatalism of the orthodox Marxists, and the myopia of reformist socialism. The fudging, consensus politics which has predominated in the West has broken down. The future is in the hands of the radicals and visionaries.

Where Do We Go From Here?

Of course, a vision of the future is not everything. Marxists are right to point out that any successful radical movement must base itself on the conditions and forces of the present. Whatever future we desire, we have to discover the real forces for change in present society. What is necessary is an amalgam of an analysis of present conditions with a picture of a feasible future goal.

It has not been the purpose of this book to concentrate on the question of strategy for change. I have attempted that elsewhere.[3] But strategies and goals can never be completely divorced. Means and ends condition each other. An assessment of our present situation is therefore required.

The picture is not simple, but the main features are these. The background is the long and dynamic boom of Western capitalism, based on the postwar settlement of the 1940s and the international hegemony of the United States of America. With the breakdown of the world monetary system in 1971, the oil crisis of 1973, and the synchronized world recession of 1974, that boom has come to an end. The United States is no longer in a position of supreme dominance; it is rivalled in the capitalist world by West Germany, France and Japan.

We have entered a period of extreme political and economic instability. There is international tension and a growing arms race between East and

West. Competition and chaos in the world economy is leading to protectionism and a breakdown in world trade. Growing indebtedness in the Third World threatens to bring down the world financial system in one sudden, computer-assisted crash. The days of apparent certainty are gone forever.

This is the background to the current world recession. It does not, however, mean that the end of the capitalist system is inevitable in the next few years. We are faced with an international and structural crisis; and several outcomes are conceivable. A just and humane society of the future will not create itself automatically out of the fragments of the existing system.

In terms of economic structures, the breakdown of consensus and stability creates additional antagonisms between the dominant capitalist economic system and other structures or impurities. The most obvious is that between East and West, in the spiralling arms race and the ever more strident propaganda of the Cold War. But other conflicts are found *within* social formations. The New Right, for example, have declared war on non-capitalist elements within the capitalist economies of the West, not simply on the issue of public ownership versus markets, but also on those of democracy versus hierarchy, accountability versus authoritarianism, open government versus secrecy, decentralization versus centralization, equality versus inequality, and so on. What lies behind this conflict? It is the reaction of the dominant capitalist economic structure to the world recession, and to the past encroachment of impurities such as the welfare state. It is the response of an economic structure acting as if it were aware of the threat to its survival.

The political and economic offensive of the New Right should not be underestimated; but it is not all-powerful, and neither will it reach its objective of a purified private enterprise system. In a sense, the formulation of such an impossible aim is a sign of actual and potential weakness: an incapacity to sustain an enduring coalition in society for its ends, and to span the real interests of different groups.

In these circumstances it is an even weaker response for the Left to place a minus where the New Right puts a plus. In one case nationalization is the panacea, and the market is the substance of all ills. In the other, the state is the enemy and the market is the source of all virtue. Both standpoints are as naive as they are impossible, as loud and harsh as they are fundamentally unconvincing.

The New Right asks us to believe that the individual always knows best; that when there is chaos and discord, self-interest should prevail; that the solution of our problem is best entrusted to the institution of private property and the workings of the market; that only the egotism of the individual can be relied upon to bring about the best possible outcome. To propose nationalization as a panacea is to make an opposite and equal error: that the state can become the guardian of our interests; that all individual expression of need or desire has to be overruled for the good of the whole; that the state alone can become the representative of the people. In this war of dogma against dogma, nothing is assured but mutual attrition and eventual destruction. The pursuit of the pure attacks the essential elements of symbiosis within any socio-economic system. Neither side can achieve a triumph over the other on its own terms – the result is the breakdown of an overall framework in which a feasible solution can be constructed.

The situation is full of irony and contradiction. As the New Right pursues its goal of a purified capitalist system it creates mass unemployment, a collapse of social solidarity, and a smouldering urban rebellion – which in turn have led to the growth of the police and the army and the repressive arm of the state. An attempt is made to heal the fractures by militarist adventures such as the Falklands War, and an orchestrated appeal to the crudest form of nationalism. Thus the New Right achieves the very opposite of what it proclaims. Power is not distributed to the people; it is concentrated to an even greater degree in the hands of the most undemocratic and authoritarian institutions of the modern state.

To place all emphasis on nationalization in these circumstances is unhelpful. It ignores current realities as well as underlying theoretical problems. In two senses it plays into the hands of the New Right: by allowing them to define themselves as the inverse, and by preventing an effective critique from the Left of the serious dangers in an over-centralized system.

The politics of the modern Social Democrats offers few advantages. Essentially, they yearn for a return to consensus politics on the old basis, on the foundation of a postwar settlement which has broken down and cannot be reconstructed. They crave for stability in an essentially unstable world. But there is one thing they do not do: that is to look at the roots of the problems. Thus we have analyses which solve the difficulties created by large, undemocratic, multinational corporations by pretending they do not exist. We are asked to return to a reflated, reconstructed, full-employment capitalism, much as before. But history is never reversible, and the world in which all that was possible is long gone. Gramsci wrote from his prison: 'The crisis consists precisely in the fact that the old is dying and the new cannot be born; in this interregnum a great variety of morbid symptoms appear.'[4]

We are in an interregnum. The crisis is not to be resolved by wishing away the problems or harking back to a past era. It is necessary to create a radical alternative, and provide the progressive forces with a new sense of direction. Neither the worship of old prescriptions nor the incantation of that which we find most reassuring will necessarily serve us well.

The objective that we should seek is to maximize autonomy while retaining social coherence, to decentralize decision-making while retaining a measure of overall democratic control. It is a society in which both state and market exist, but are subordinate to democracy.

Democracy and Autonomy

Democracy grants power to the majority. A full democracy is unrealizable without removing concentrations of wealth and privilege from the hands of minorities which can effectively overrule this majority power. The difficulties that lie in the way of this radical transformation of society will be raised below. The point to be made here is that democracy is not viable if it moves towards the position where the majority becomes a monolith, and all dissent is stifled. To prosper, democracy must encourage what is in a sense its opposite, i.e. autonomy, or the self-rule of the minority. But autonomy will be constituted in such a way that it remains subservient to overall democratic control.

Democratic control and planning have to be retained in order to determine the character and development of the economic infrastructure, to encourage the evolution of a technology which minimizes damage to the environment, to reduce inequality in wealth and power, and to assure the overall coherence of the system. At the same time, democratic processes have to be guided and pressured to facilitate autonomy. The object should be to create communities with the maximum degree of self-sufficiency. Thus the objectives of overall planning and control should not be framed exclusively in terms of what is deemed most efficient for the majority. Progress is measured by the extent to which autonomy can develop within a framework of equality and democracy.

All this may sound rather abstract and far from the world as we find it. This is not so. The development of autonomy and democracy has to be based on the conditions of the present. The potential for such developments is unfolding before our eyes.

For example, modern mass production has brought the computer into millions of homes and offices. Jobs are being destroyed in the large factories. But there is the possibility that more rewarding and valuable work can be created, with the assistance of automation, in the growing information sector of the economy. Cheaper printing techniques and more efficient methods of distribution make possible an enormous explosion of creativity in literature and art. The general reduction in the hours required for routinized and arduous work liberates time and resources for education and leisure.

These issues are with us today. They are not simply for the millennium. We have to create a social movement that will ensure that the changes we are experiencing do not lead to mass unemployment and a police state. The slogan, once again, is democracy and autonomy. In this context, therefore, the demand for a 30 hour week is perhaps more important than that for the nationalization of all the banks; the erosion of civil liberties is of more concern than the loss of free collective bargaining; the humanization of life and work has priority over the pursuit of economic growth.

In the meantime, some attitudes have to be changed. While the small private business does not encourage the best of human characteristics, within limits it has to be tolerated, and no longer regarded as the cancer of the community. Measures of autonomy such as these, which do little overall harm, and give millions of people some sort of control over their lives, have positive as well as negative features. Traditionally, the Left has identified the private and market-based features of the small business as sufficient to condemn them in the future. Yet the real problem arises when private business defies the interest of the majority and conducts its internal affairs in a dictatorial fashion. Thus the emphasis should not be on getting rid of the small businesses and market relations, but on encouraging democratic and cooperative forms of enterprise on a small scale, in sectors of the economy where they are appropriate.

A move towards a democratic economy will come about only on the basis of formal or informal alliances between all sorts of interest groups in society. Perhaps the main impetus will come from the trade union movement in large-scale industry, in pressuring for greater worker participation in decision-making. But this cannot succeed on its own. The ideal of a democratic economy has to be prefigured in the community, the domestic sphere, and the small business as well. These elements have to be linked to a political movement which will help bring about structural reforms in the economy and the political system.

It is not a matter for legislative reform alone. Change cannot come about solely from above. A combination of parliamentary and extra-parliamentary action is required. Extra-parliamentary action may take the form of mass demonstrations and civil disobedience: in opposing nuclear arms, nuclear power, and other by-products of the authoritarian state, there should be little hesitation in using such methods. But much valuable extra-parliamentary action is out of the glare of the media. It consists of initiatives to set up worker cooperatives, to develop community child-care facilities, to extend worker participation, to campaign for alternative and socially useful work, and generally to involve people in collective projects to improve their life and work.

At the same time, the spontaneity of the people is not sufficient to bring about radical change in society as a whole. Leadership is necessary. Furthermore, capitalist structures block many routes to reform from below. What can be changed is limited. Legislative reform at the level of government as well as extended public ownership are necessary to assist this transformation.

Another important reason why action at governmental level is necessary is that parliamentary institutions play a role in legitimating social change. People regard parliament as the arena for the resolution of fundamental conflict and debate. Thus a movement for radical change has to win the battle at the electoral level as a necessary condition for achieving its objectives. But this condition is not itself sufficient for such radical change. It is a combination of parliamentary and extra-parliamentary action that is required.

The Transition to Socialism

A society based on the fullest extension of popular participation in power, where democracy predominates, and where there is no great inequality in income or wealth, must be a form of socialism. Such a society is incompatible with the concentration of ownership of the means of production in the hands of a small minority, as obtains at present in all Western societies. Thus in the transition to a democratic economy a threat to some vested interests is unavoidable. But that does not mean that we should not attempt to seek the smoothest possible transition. The orthodox Marxist account sees it as conceivably peaceful but more likely to be violent. This is largely because of the flawed and over-simplified picture of one class removing another from the position of power: the proletariat replaces the bourgeoisie as ruling class in a single revolutionary action. In this rapid and cataclysmic process, the 'ruling class' is bound to resist.

It may come to that. Who knows? But we cannot exclude the possibility that the dominance of the capitalist class will be eroded over time. This will not necessarily be a smooth or gradual process; it will probably involve a succession of political and social crises. But there is no reason to assume that the transition to socialism will be compacted in a single, revolutionary event. There is no single date for marking the beginning of the millennium.

The practical consequences of this should be clear. The process of building the future has already started, now. It is necessary for all of us to press for changes that will prefigure the democratic economy and form part of the overall process of transforming society. Socialism is not about waiting and hoping for a single event, but about using and developing social forces which can together constitute a real process of advance and social transformation.

The question is which forces and advances are to be given priority? The traditional socialist answer is to put the main emphasis on reform from the centre: particularly an extension of public ownership and taxation policies to reduce inequality. These matters are important, and they have to be tackled at some time. But it can be argued that extensions of democracy, participation, decentralization and autonomy should be pressed for first. To put the matter more strongly, the present terms of debate should be changed from nationalization versus markets and private enterprise, to the issue of how is democracy to be combined with autonomy. This creates the important possibility of a socialist consensus, which can gain wide popular support, and pose issues in terms which clear the way for the democratic economy.

This does not mean that the issue of public ownership is forgotten or avoided. The point is that it must be tackled when the necessity arises – that is, as an extension of the movement for a wider democracy. Thus the traditional socialist configuration of means and ends is reversed. Instead of democracy being a means to achieve the goal of greater public ownership, public ownership is a means when necessary to achieve greater democracy. It could take a variety of forms, and it should not be conceived of as old-style nationalization. In any case the pre-existence of a strong and pluralistic movement for democracy, participation and autonomy will help to prevent the emergence of state collectivist forms.

In times of crisis people look for leadership. We turn to governments for solutions. We await the outcome of elections. These things are important, but in placing too much emphasis on them we imply that change is based on the centres of power. The real loci of the changes that must come about are diffused in our culture, our consciousness, and above all our social practices. Reform from the centre should not distract us from the immediate tasks of extending participation and autonomy in our everyday lives. All substantial and enduring change comes not from others, but from ourselves.

Appendix A

On Socio-Economic Systems

The truth is the whole.

G. W. F. Hegel, *Phenomenology of Mind*

No comprehensive theory of socio-economic systems is presented in this work – that is a task requiring much greater analysis and study. However, it is necessary to deal with an important controversy surrounding Marx's conception of history and of socio-economic systems.

Over the years, many theorists have slowly moved away from the strict conception of history and systems presented by Marx, particularly in the famous Preface to his *Contribution to the Critique of Political Economy*. This shift is evident in the works of Georg Lukács, Antonio Gramsci, Louis Althusser and Lucio Colletti, among others.[1] In an important study, Gerald Cohen presents a defence of Marxian orthodoxy, and in particular the famous Preface, against the tradition of 'Western Marxism'.[2] On the whole, it appears that Cohen's interpretation of Marx at least is valid: the 'technological determinism' that many have been keen to renounce is firmly rooted in Marx's work. What is not valid, I would argue, is the theory itself, as presented by Cohen or Marx.

It will become evident that this dispute is highly relevant to the themes of this work. If Marx and Cohen are right, my attempt to combine the analysis of democracy with that of the economy is doomed from the start. Further important consequences will be outlined below.

Systems and History in the Thought of Karl Marx

Marx's theory of history and of socio-economic systems involves a three-fold division of society. First there are the 'material productive forces', consisting of the means of production, labour-power, and technical and scientific knowledge. Second there is 'the economic structure of society', consisting of the 'sum total of relations of production'.[3] These relations of production are social relations of possession or effective control; for example P is the slave of Q; R employs S; T possesses this factory. Third, upon the 'economic structure of society, the real basis' rises 'a legal and political superstructure' to which correspond 'definite forms of social consciousness'. This third level includes the state and, if they exist, democratic institutions.

Marx continues to summarize the alleged relationship between these three levels:

> At a certain stage of their development, the material productive forces in society come into conflict with the existing relations of production, or – what is but a legal expression of the same thing – with the property relations within which they have been at work hitherto. From forms of development of the productive forces these relations turn into their fetters. Then begins an epoch of social revolution. With the change of the economic foundation the entire immense superstructure is more or less rapidly transformed.[4]

The first concern here is to examine the notion of 'relation of production' in Marx's theory, and as defended by Cohen. This concept is indeed central, as it is the 'sum total' of such relations which is said to form the 'economic structure'. To be consistent with the Preface, and much of Marx's other writing, it is necessary to detach legal relations from such relations of production, for they belong to the 'superstructure', as is made explicit by Marx.

In contrast, 'relations of production' are independent of strict legal conceptions of ownership, obligation, etc. Relations of production are relations of effective power – of persons over persons, or persons over things. This effective power may be maintained by the use of force, of ideology, or of law. But that, Cohen points out, is irrelevant. The definition of production relations does not include, and it does not have to include, the means by which the power is wielded. Cohen writes:

> our definition of production relations does not stipulate how the powers they enfold are obtained or sustained. The answer to that question does involve force, but also ideology and the law. The programme says what production relations are, not what sustains them.[5]

The fundamental objection to Cohen's impressive attempt to defend Marx's theory is that it is impossible to say 'what production relations are' without reference to 'superstructural' factors such as ideology and law. Compare the position of a slave in Ancient Rome and a serf in feudal England. Neither the slave nor the serf has the 'effective power' to escape the domination of his master. He is tied to the estate or domain. The legal and 'superstructural' difference between the slave and the serf is that the slave is owned by his master, and is devoid of legal rights, whereas the serf does have some rights as well as strict and burdensome obligations to his lord.

Slavery concentrates legal rights in the hands of those who are not slaves. Feudalism embodies a complex social hierarchy, with important variations in rights and duties at every level. If, however, we ignore the legal 'superstructure' it is very difficult to distinguish between feudalism and slavery. Slave and serf alike are bound to their masters. Both are obliged to work on the land. Their pattern of labour may be identical. The duty to pay 'cornage' or rent-in-kind means that virtually the only difference between the serf and the slave is the proportion of output that he is compelled to render to his master. The right of the serf to sell a proportion of his product on the market is best regarded – as pointed out in Chapter 7 – as an impurity within the feudal system. Otherwise there is no major difference between the 'relations of production', and it is difficult or impossible to distinguish between the 'economic structures' of feudalism and slavery.

Let us move on to compare capitalism with other economic systems, using the definitions of Marx and Cohen. In terms of 'effective power' there is apparently a more important distinction between capitalism on the one hand, and feudalism and slavery on the other. Cohen distinguishes between the proletarian, i.e. the worker under capitalism, and the slave in the following terms: 'the proletarian has the power to withhold his labour power, while the slave does not'. He then puts forward a possible objection to the meaningfulness of this distinction, followed by a reply:

> Objection: The reason the slave is said to lack this power is that if he does not work he is likely to be killed, and he will certainly die. But a similar fate awaits the withholding proletarian, since he loses his means of subsistence. Therefore the proletarian is also unable to withhold his labour power. Therefore the description of the production relations of slaves and proletarians no longer contrast when they are purged of legal terms in accordance with our programme.
>
> Reply: It is relevant that the withholding slave is liable to be killed and the proletarian is not, but we shall not rely on this difference. We concede that the withholding proletarian dies. But note that he may be able to withhold his labour power from a given capitalist, including his current employer, without fear of death. The slave cannot withhold his labour power from his particular master and still live.
>
> The proletarian is constrained to offer his labour power not to any particular capitalist, but to some capitalist or other. If he wishes to survive, he must present himself on the labour market to the capitalist class, and he is forced to serve that class. This accords well with Marx's frequent statement that the proletarian is owned not by any given capitalist, but by the capitalist class as a whole. The matching non-legal statement of his position is true.[6]

Cohen then goes on to cite no less than eight cases where Marx refers to the worker as 'belonging to', or 'owned by', or even 'enslaved by', the capitalist class as a whole. In addition he often described the working class as wage-slaves. According to Marx (and Cohen), therefore, in at least one major respect the positions of the slave and the proletarian are identical. This is not a mere quibble about the use of language, which, in certain passages, is purely metaphorical. It is intended to make two points. The first is that the removal of the legal aspect from the definition of 'relations of production' does indeed blur a crucial distinction between wage-labour and slavery. The proletariat is seen as enslaved.

The second point is that the polemical impact of the (partial) application of the word 'slavery' to capitalist wage-labour is entirely removed by the existence of old-age pensions and of unemployment benefits under conditions of mass unemployment. The worker is not therefore 'forced' to work for *any* capitalist; these hand-outs are sufficient for survival. That these are mere pittances and not, on their own, a basis for emancipation is an objection to Marx's own justification for applying the word 'slavery' to capitalism, not to my counter-example. Those who argue that the 'enslavement' of the working class results from the fact that they are 'forced' to sell their labour to the capitalist class must admit that an instrument of liberation from this 'enslavement' is a weekly pittance at the front of a dole queue. One can develop a far more effective critique of capitalism first by noting its real difference from other socio-economic systems, and second by examining the nature of its exploitation and the structural mechanisms by which such exploitation is maintained.

Confusion of types of production relation can also arise concerning the institution of the family. At least until the last few decades of the nineteenth century, in most advanced capitalist countries married women were effectively 'bound' to their husbands. Divorce was difficult, if not impossible, for all but the very rich, and most women had little chance other than prostitution of an independent income. Yet were married women slaves to their husbands, and the unmarried slaves to the male sex as a whole? According to Marx's argument, they were. But it is no denial of the very real exploitation and subjugation of women, yesterday and today, to insist that their situation was, in important respects, different from slavery or serfdom.

A final example of this confusion of categories concerns the position of the worker in the Soviet Union. The adult male of pre-retirement age is even less able to escape the pressures to work in the USSR than his counterpart in the West. Furthermore, he has little or no choice of employer: he must, in almost every case, work for the state. He must therefore, according to Marx, be a slave. It is paradoxical that many right-wing thinkers would (for different reasons) agree with this conclusion, yet Marxist defenders of the Soviet Union would regard it as a 'dictatorship of the proletariat'.

If we take Marx literally, at least in Cohen's strict interpretation, we begin to see slavery everywhere: not only in Ancient Greece and Rome, but in the entire feudal epoch, within capitalism, in relation to the majority of the female sex, and in post-revolutionary Russia. The term is devalued and begins to lose all meaning. Likewise, the distinctions between different types of socio-economic system blur and begin to dissolve. And this, ironically, is the result of a theory which insists on the essential distinction between different types of human society, explicitly abandons the untenable universalism of orthodox economic science (which attempts to explain all forms of society in terms of a single set of categories, such as choice and scarcity[7]), and claims to discover the forces behind the revolutionary transformation of economic structures and the entire progress of human history. If slavery is everywhere, then there has been no major successful social revolution and little or no progress. History has stagnated for more than two millennia. This does not bode well for the possibility of radical progressive change in the next thousand years.

Redefining Production Relations

An alternative approach to that of Marx and Cohen, which is adopted by many other Marxist writers, is to accept that legal (and perhaps other) relations must be included in the description of production relations. For example, Perry Anderson asserts that 'pre-capitalist modes of production cannot be defined *except* via their political, legal and ideological structures',[8] and Lucio Colletti notes that under capitalism

> the relationship between labour-power and other means of production, i.e. capital, is inconceivable unless we already take into account the juridico-political forms which make the modern labourer a 'free' labourer, that is a labourer free to dispose of his own person, to enter into a *contract*. In other words, unless we already take into account that formal or legal 'equality' which Marx is *obliged* in fact to bring to our attention . . .[9]

In other words, both pre-capitalist social relations and the basic social relation between labour and capital cannot be separated from legal and political forms. This is not merely a question of semantics: the choice of definition for 'production relations' is not arbitrary, unless we are to descend into an extreme philosophical nominalism, which asserts that the definitions of words are entirely separate from their actual or potential usage.

The decisive argument for the inclusion of legal and other relations within the economic structure is that division of society into the 'economic' and the 'non-economic' encourages a view that the former can function with considerable autonomy from the latter. Any adequate analysis of the system must continuously cross and re-cross the threshold between the two spheres. A fruitful independent analysis of the workings of 'the economy' is impossible. A holistic approach is to be preferred.

In particular, ideas, conceptions, norms, conventions and expectations have a fundamental role. Labour, for example, is a purposeful activity: it does not take place only because the master has 'effective power' over the worker. Investment is governed, as Keynes insisted, by expectations of the future. The economy is not a machine, neither can it be adequately described in mechanistic terms.

There are two important additional points to make. The first concerns 'work relations' – i.e. formal or informal interaction between managers and workers, and workers and workers – which exist in all socio-economic systems where production is not carried out by isolated individuals. Examples are: P works in association with Q; R supervises the work of S. The slave estate, the feudal manor, and the capitalist firm all have an organizational structure and a set of work relations between people.

In an earlier article, Cohen placed work relations within the general category of 'production relations',[10] but by the time he came to write *Karl Marx's Theory of History* he no longer regarded them even as part of the 'productive forces': only *knowledge* of work relations is put into that class. Thus work relations are banished from the economic structure, because, allegedly, they are material rather than social in character.[11]

This characterization is dubious from beginning to end. Cohen's defence of his statement that work relations are not social is to point out that they are a 'material fact'. But this description, whatever it means, could by the same criterion be applied to the 'production relation' that P has 'effective power' over Q. Cohen is not able to invoke Marx in defence of his categorization. He is obliged to adopt it because if work relations were deemed part of 'production relations' and the 'economic structure', he would have to abandon a strict *technological* determinism. Characteristically for this book, he massages and manoeuvres definitions to render a theory more consistent, rather attempting to make the theory fit the facts.[12] But logical consistency, though necessary, is not everything. We should be alarmed by a categorization which regards work relations as asocial. Formal consistency is worthless if it is achieved without reference to the real world and the real object of analysis.

Do work relations have important effects on production in the real world? In Chapter 9 above it was demonstrated that the organization of work is a crucial element in determining the level of productivity, among other things. It should also be noted that Marx paid particular attention to work relations in *Capital*.

Cohen would reply that the dynamic potential of work relations is recognized by his inclusion of the *knowledge* of such relations among the 'productive forces'. This defence is not plausible. Within capitalist society it is not *knowledge* of the organization of work but the relations themselves that are crucial. Differences in work organization can have profound effects on economic performance. At the same time, it is unlikely that any one person knows the actual pattern of organization within the firm. The wall-chart in the office of the managing director gives information about the formal structure only, not the true state of affairs. Yet all the evidence indicates that informal structures are very important as a partial determinant of productive performance,[13] and that many of them are not known by the management, nor in their entirety by any single person.

A well-known illustration of the importance of informal structures is what happens when they are deliberately abandoned, as a sanction against management, in a 'work to rule'. Cohen's rather cavalier treatment of formal and informal knowledge at work amounts to an underestimation of the phenomena of uncertainty and partial ignorance. These are important in any economic system, and especially under capitalism. To undervalue them leads, once again, to a mechanistic view of the economy. A much more acceptable procedure is to regard work relations as social, as part of the set of production relations as well as of the economic structure. Knowledge of the advantages of certain types of work relations and organizational structures could be regarded as part of the 'productive forces', but it does not necessarily correspond with the reality; for example, in capitalism today, management theory is way in advance of the norm in practice.[14]

The treatment of work relations within a 'technological determinist' Marxism is linked to a second deficiency: the failure to give as much attention to the production of services as to the production of tangible goods. The prominence of the service sector in all advanced capitalist countries is well known. It is not, however, given due weight or recognition in the mechanistic versions of Marxist theory. Services are part of an output which is elusive and variable. In any real economy quality variation, in particular, creates uncertainty and problems of regulation and control. It does not fit into a mechanistic schema.

Conclusion

The main point of this appendix has been to show that social relations cannot be properly conceived without reference to legal and other elements within the socio-economic system. Consequently, the crude base–superstructure analogy of orthodox Marxism must be rejected, and along with it much of the thinking associated with the famous 1859 Preface. A socio-economic system produces and reproduces social relations, information, and ideas, as well as services and material goods. It is not a mechanistic entity: architectural or mechanistic analogies are therefore misleading.

A machine can be broken down into parts which can be examined in isolation. It is not possible to do this, in theoretical terms, with socio-economic systems. A given social relation is part of the whole system and it cannot be defined independently of key elements within that system. This does not mean, however, that we are left with an impenetrable mass of categories and relations. Some relations are more important than others. Some structures dominate others. It is still possible to examine the processes of causation and development within the system. It is still possible to single out certain types of social relation as being dominant, and characteristic of the system as a whole. In Marx's view it is *relations of production* (and here we should include work relations as well as property relations) which dominate each form of society. The relations of production are, in general, more significant than, for example, relations of kinship, or many elements of the political constitution. It is this notion of dominance that is the key, and it still survives after the removal of the base–superstructure analogy.

Why should we regard relations of production as dominant? Marx and Engels' defence of this principle in *The German Ideology* and other writings is still relevant. The conditions, processes and relations governing the reproduction of human social life are primary. They mould and govern all other social relations and phenomena because without the reproduction of human social life such phenomena would not exist. It is the production of the conditions of human social life, including necessities such as food, clothing and so on, that is prior to all other human activities and relations. In short, production is primary. This statement, however, should not be confused with the misleading notion that 'the economy' is primary or determining in 'society as a whole'. This usually involves a vulgar conception of 'the economy' divorced from legal and other social relations which this book has been at pains to demolish. The crucial importance of this point should be obvious. It has been consistently argued here that, under modern capitalism at least, democratic and other political structures should not be divorced from 'the economy', and it is in an attempt to ditch all mistaken and over-narrow definitions of the economy that such terms as the 'socio-economic structure' have been used instead.

Appendix B

Impurity, Dominance and the Modern State

It can be argued that very ancient philosophical, ethical and political arguments are now being conducted within a common Marxist vocabulary, and that incompatible positions (from terrorists to statist bureaucrats to determined libertarians) have got entangled in a common network of categories and terms.

E. P. Thompson, *Writing By Candlelight*

It is commonplace to note that, far from providing us with a systematic analysis of the state, Marx and Engels left little more than scattered remarks and sometimes inconsistent notes. The task of developing a coherent and substantial theory of the state has devolved upon later Marxists. Unfortunately, the very inconsistency and sparseness of this legacy has given rise to a large variety of interpretations, and still no systematic and complete analysis of the state. There is a veritable bazaar of theories, each offering its own degree of 'relative autonomy', each claiming its special virtues. We are offered varied 'problematics', a multitude of 'levels of abstraction'. Theoretical advances have been made, but there is more chaos than coherence.

An approach to the theory of the state is implied in this work, but it is not here codified or presented as a systematic whole. It is the purpose of this Appendix to bring together a few notes on this issue, both to clarify the implied conception of the state, and to help provide a basis for future theoretical work.

Let us first make it clear what is *not* implied. Lenin's theory of the state as an expression of class antagonisms and an instrument of class rule has been rightly criticized for reducing the state exclusively to (undefined) 'class' terms, and for laying undue emphasis on the relations of physical force between classes, to the neglect, for example, of ideology and institutions. Lenin's view, in *The State and Revolution* and elsewhere, is both 'instrumentalist' (in that the state is seen as an instrument of class rule) and 'class reductionist' (in that it is a phenomenon that is explained in purely class terms). These approaches are incompatible with the holistic and integrated analysis that has been used in this work, and the rejection of the idea that classes are the prime objects of social and economic analysis.

A view of the state that is prominent in the socialist movement but rarely theorized is the 'reformist' one in which government and parliamentary institutions are regarded as having supreme power within the state and society as a whole. According to this view, it is possible for a political party to ascend to the pinnacle of power by winning an election. It is then able to carry out substantial reforms 'at the stroke of a pen'. It also involves an instrumentalist conception of the state. The difference from Leninism is that the reformist regards any democratic state as a potential instrument, whereas Lenin argued that the capitalist state could not be so used, and had to be 'smashed'.

Another important difference between Leninism and reformism is that reformism considers the state to be above classes, and detached from dominant relations of production; its extension into the sphere of production must therefore be synonymous with the extension of socialism. This view of the state is shared by classic liberals: they too see clear boundaries between the market and the state. However, the value judgements are of reverse sign: reformists desire an extension of the state, classic liberals its confinement. Reformists are classic liberals with their morality turned on its head: the state rather than the market, the state rather than the individual. The theoretical basis, however, is similar.

The most prominent alternative to instrumentalism is the functionalism of writers such as Talcott Parsons.[1] Functionalism puts emphasis on the system as a whole. The state is seen as responding to developments within the economy and society, and as part of that total system. Absent, however, is a role for conscious, active human beings (as individuals, groups or social classes) helping to shape their own history, and purposefully creating new socio-economic structures. The idea of contradiction within each socio-economic system, preparing the ground for crises and socio-political ruptures, is played down.[2] In contrast, Marxism recognizes that society is an integrated whole, but accepts at the same time the importance of contradictions and class conflict. This approach, both holistic and positing 'crisis' or 'conflict', has been part of its traditional appeal and has helped to account for its endurance.

However, the developed alternative to functionalism often presented by Marxism is not entirely satisfactory. As shown in Appendix A, orthodox Marxism breaks from a holistic approach in some respects by imposing rigid divisions on the socio-economic system. In addition, much orthodox Marxist writing on economics is functionalist in nature, giving low importance for example to the economic effects of class struggle and to the expectations of individual capitalists. There is a picture of a capitalist system grinding out its inevitable historic destiny, rather than one which can (within limits) be continuously affected by the wills and actions of individuals and classes. The idea of economic crisis is there, of course, but as a mechanical result of the 'economic base' rather than being subject to ideology or class action.

Impurity and Dominance

We now turn to the consequences of the principle of impurity in this area. Underlying most of the Marxist literature on the state is an assumption that a pure economic structure would be capable of sustaining itself, without the interaction of different structures and relations. With this assumption one can pass straight on to a purified theoretical object: 'the capitalist state', 'the feudal state', and so on. Notably, recent and relatively sophisticated analyses pay negligible attention to (for example) the family and the domestic structure;[3] exclusive emphasis is laid on the role of the state in promoting the accumulation of capital. It is as if the family, domestic labour, the sexual division of labour, and the oppression of women did not exist.

With the impurity principle such errors are avoided. We are forced to pay attention to important impurities such as the domestic economic structure, and their role in the socio-economic system as a whole. Any theory of the state which does not cover such necessary impurities is inadequate. The modern state cannot be treated purely and simply as the objectification of capital.

The state, first of all, acts as a regulator, a connector, and an agent of cohesion, spanning the dominant economic structure and its adjoining impurities. For example, in modern capitalism connections with the domestic sphere are made through family law, housing policy, food subsidies, taxation structures, health and education programmes, and so on. Through such relations and activities the domestic economic structure is tied to the capitalist economy, and many of its functions are regulated.

The same connecting and regulating role of the state can be found in other social formations. For example, under feudalism there are developed markets, simple commodity production, and mercantile capital, all based on the town. The state connects the dominant, land-based feudal structure with the town by the legislative mechanism of the charter, which is required before a market and extra-feudal activities become established. In this way many towns were given permission to trade, and a measure of self-government, in the Middle Ages. In practice the town became a haven from feudal relations: 'Town air makes you free,' as it was said in Germany and elsewhere.

However, regulation is rarely systematic and perfect, and the cohesion of the system as a whole is never flawless. In general, the state connects, but it reproduces disconnection. Thus, for example, the modern state has to intervene in the domestic sphere and elsewhere by creating welfare facilities; otherwise the production of a fit, trained and healthy workforce is not guaranteed. In doing this, however, it has to abandon the dominant capitalist norms of profit and loss. The persistent controversy over the alleged 'burden' of the welfare state is symptomatic of conflict between different and partially discordant economic structures. Likewise, under feudalism, the conflict between the economic structures and relations based on the market and the towns on the one hand, and the landed nobility on the other, had repercussions at the level of the state, which could partially regulate the growth of markets and the urban centres, but could not remove the antagonism between the different types of economic structure.

As has been made clear, however, the state is not the only regulator; each economic structure has some internal methods of regulation of its own. Under capitalism the rate of profit plays an important role, but it has little influence in the domestic sphere: a household is not run according to a profit motive, even if it has to keep within a monetary budget. Thus there are many different types of regulator within the system as a whole. The state, in fact, is a supra-regulator: a regulator of the regulators to be found in each economic structure.

However, some sections of the state themselves constitute an economic structure, as illustrated in Chapter 7 with the economic role of the military in classical antiquity. The state as economic structure is evident, of course, in modern capitalism, for example with the nationalized industries. This role is extended to the limit in the state collectivist societies of the Eastern Bloc. Here there is an internal regulatory mechanism based on planning; but this arm does not constitute, but instead is regulated by, the state as a whole. In part, therefore, the state has to regulate itself. This, once again, can lead to conflict.

Let us now consider the international dimension: the relations between states. Although this has received more attention from theorists than the domestic structure, it has not been given sufficient general emphasis. Lenin, for example, saw the state largely as an expression of internal class conflict. If, instead, we focus on economic structures, it is conflicts between socio-economic systems that move into prominence. In fact, to a great extent the development and growth of the state were due to conflict and potential conflict between nations, rather than to internal class struggles. Consider the results of Michael Mann's investigation of the finances of the early modern English state:

> From an analysis of state finance, the functions of the state appear overwhelmingly military and overwhelmingly international rather than domestic. For over seven centuries, somewhere between 75 per cent and 90 per cent of its financial resources were almost continuously deployed in the acquisition and use of military force ... Even as late as 1815 its civil functions were negligible in financial terms.[4]

Historically, relations between nation states have been regulated by means of treaties or of military force. The twentieth century has seen the emergence of institutions of international regulation, and supranational blocs such as Comecon and the European Economic Community. The supra-national state is the next possibility, although it is unlikely to be realized in the near future.

Much theorizing about the state is preoccupied with its relationship with the dominant economic structure: for it is this which is held to determine its overall character. While national defence, wars, and so on, are often mentioned, little attention is given to international relations or structures. With the impurity principle, however, things can begin to change. Once it is recognized that no single economic structure can possibly determine the whole character of the state apparatus, the way will be open to admit other factors, including politico-economic and military relations between countries.

We now come to the principle of dominance, and its relation to the state. According to this principle, each (impure) economic system has a dominant economic structure. It is therefore still reasonable to suggest that the dominant economic structure might, in turn, dominate the state and give it a specific character. Thus, despite all the impurities, and despite the international aspect of the issue, it is still possible to talk of 'the capitalist state', 'the feudal state', etc. However, there are some important anomalies; for example, Perry Anderson notes that although pre-1917 Russia had a predominantly capitalist economic structure in its later years, the state machine was of a quite different character:

> there was a *dislocation* between the social formation and the State in the last years of Tsarism. The Russian *social formation* was a complex ensemble dominated by the capitalist mode of production, but the Russian *State* remained a feudal Absolutism. The disjunctive articulation between the two remains to be explained, and founded, theoretically.[5]

Other important, but less clear-cut and dramatic, counter-examples are found in nineteenth-century Britain, Japan after the Meiji Restoration of 1867, and Germany from 1871 to 1918. In each case economic relations were predominantly capitalist in character, yet the government and state apparatus were dominated by the old pre-capitalist aristocracy. Marxists often contend that all that is odd here is a contrast between the social class of the personnel within the state machine on the one hand, and the character of the social formation and the state machine itself on the other. However, if we do not point to personnel (and perhaps, for the sake of the argument, we should not), how do we know *what* determines the character of the state apparatus? There is a danger of relapse into the simplistic formula: the state apparatus is of type X because the social formation is dominated by an economic structure of type X. Then the aristocratic rulers of Victorian Britain, Meiji Japan, or Bismarck's Germany are regarded as surrogates for the capitalist class. It all slips into place and the contradiction disappears. But this is tautology masquerading as science: the harmony between state and dominant economic structure is proved only by definition.

The problem is one of working out what is meant by the 'character' of the state machine. It is not helpful simply to focus on the functions of the state. To say that the state assists and regulates the process of capital accumulation does not mean that the character of the state itself is completely determined or described: the Tsarist state in Russia played a considerable role in promoting the accumulation of capital, yet it was quite different in character from the capitalist states of the West.

This problem cannot be resolved here. We can only reiterate that the state cannot encapsulate all the characteristics of another economic structure. There is a danger, well exemplified by some analyses of 'the capitalist state', that the state is seen as the embodiment of capital. This view should be dismissed. The state has a conceptual as well as a real autonomy.

We need not necessarily go so far as to abandon the concepts of 'the capitalist state', 'the feudal state', and so on. By focusing on the state's relational role with different economic structures, as well as its functions as an institution, it may well be possible to sustain these theoretical categories, and give them a non-tautological meaning. But what *must* be included in any general theory is a recognition that the state is a *contradictory* entity, which does not entirely or unambiguously serve the dominant economic structure.

Furthermore, as a consequence of the impurity principle, the state always (in all socio-economic systems so far discussed) has a *supra-structural* (not 'superstructural') character because, as discussed above, it is a supra-regulator of economic structures. In this sense the state does have a measure of autonomy from the dominant economic structure: in this sense also it is above social classes.

Since the proposition that the state is above social classes is often attributed to liberal and reformist thinkers, it is necessary to clarify what is, and what is not, being asserted here. To say that the state, in a sense, is above social classes is not by any means to say that it is detached from them. Contrary to the liberal and reformist view, it is recognized here that the state penetrates civil society just as civil society penetrates the state. Second, neither is an instrumentalist view of the state implied. Again contrary to the liberal and reformist view, it is held here that the state is both a set of social relations, and a complex expression of diversity and contradiction within society; it is not simply a 'thing' to be used at will by a group or social class. Third, it is not implied that the state is neutral: it can in fact incorporate and express dominance, and will be disposed towards one economic structure rather than another. In asserting that the state is above social classes, the liberals and reformists conclude that the state is detached from the economic system: it is the opposite, holistic approach which is being emphasized here.

Democracy and the State

The most important point, as far as this work is concerned, is that democratic structures (where they exist) are generally part of the supra-regulatory apparatus of the state. It is this which enables them to span different socio-economic systems through history. For example, in England, Parliament has survived and evolved from the days of Simon de Montfort in the thirteenth century. It arose during the civil war of 1264–5 under a classic feudal regime. It persisted during the feudal decline and the rise of absolutism in the fifteenth and sixteenth centuries. It played a crucial role in the English Revolution of the 1640s and eventually became a relatively stable part of the constitution after the Glorious Revolution of 1688. By the nineteenth century it was the powerful legislative assembly of a capitalist social formation. The very continuity of the English Parliament for over seven hundred years, albeit with significant breaks, shows that it cannot be written off as a 'feudal' or a 'capitalist' institution. Although it takes on the hue of the dominant economic structure of the epoch, it is never its prisoner. In fact, Parliament has played a crucial role in the periods of transition from one socio-economic system to another. It has governed in years of crisis and disruption as well as during long decades of stability. Consequently, the

Leninist division into 'bourgeois' and 'proletarian' democracy has to be rejected. Parliamentary democracy is likely to survive the transition from a capitalist to a post-capitalist democratic society, even if Parliament itself is transformed, and supplemented by many other democratic institutions, in the process.

It is important, however, to avoid a mechanistic picture. From the fact that the state is supra-structural it does not follow that it is a *thing*, detached and suspended 'above' society as a whole. This would lead to a mistaken and instrumentalist view, in which, for example, democratic institutions orchestrate history from on high. The sense in which the state is above other elements is the structural priority of its regulatory functions.

This does not mean that isolated democratic elements within the state apparatus are sufficient to constitute a democracy. It is possible for democracy (typically of the parliamentary variety) to perform an important regulatory function without becoming dominant in the socio-economic system. A truly democratic state is one which reflects the presence of democratic structures and practices throughout society. It is a system which is socialized rather than privatized. As Marx pointed out in his early writings, an elected assembly will not represent general, social interests if society is dominated by egoism, private property, and interpersonal strife.[6] The character of the state is determined by the system as a whole: by its dominant structure, in part by its impurities, and by its relations with other states.

In giving priority to the holistic approach, the inherent conflict within a social formation should not be disregarded. There are a number of types of antagonistic relationship within most socio-economic systems: between one social class and another; between the various economic structures and impurities; and between (if they exist) hierarchic authority and democracy, both of which can have either a stabilizing or a destabilizing function.

Thus, while the state is, in part, both an expression of the dominant interests and structures within society, and a feature of dominance itself, such dominance is never total or immovable. The conflict within the state, and its *partial* supersession of class interests, creates the space for potential instability. It is insights such as this which make Gramsci's writings on the subject so poignant and relevant today:

> It is true that the State is seen as the organ of one particular group, destined to create favourable conditions for the latter's maximum expansion. But the development and expansion of the particular group are conceived of, and presented, as being the motor force of a universal expansion, of the development of all the

'national' energies. In other words the dominant group is coordinated concretely with the general interests of the subordinate groups, and the life of the State is conceived of as a continuous process of formation and superseding of unstable equilibria.[7]

Notes

2 Is Democracy Really Necessary?

1. V. I. Lenin, 'The Immediate Tasks of the Soviet Government', in *Selected Works*, vol. 2, Lawrence and Wishart, 1967, p. 672.
2. F. A. Hayek, *The Constitution of Liberty*, Routledge and Kegan Paul, 1960, p. 106.
3. K. Marx and F. Engels, 'Manifesto of the Communist Party', reprinted in the Pelican Marx Library, Political Writings vol. 1, *The Revolution of 1848*, edited and introduced by D. Fernbach, Penguin, 1973, p. 86.
4. F. Claudin, *Eurocommunism and Socialism*, NLB, 1978, pp. 79–80.
5. L. Trotsky, *The Revolution Betrayed*, Merit, 1965, p. 248.
6. The idea that collective ownership means socialism is also rejected by those who describe the Eastern Bloc countries as 'state capitalist'. The rejection of the socialist label is valid, but its replacement by 'capitalism' is not, for it stretches the definition of that system to absurd limits. For these countries it is necessary to find an alternative label: neither 'socialism' nor 'workers' state' nor 'state capitalism' are acceptable. See Chapters 7 and 12.
7. This metaphor appears in the much quoted Preface to the *Contribution to the Critique of Political Economy* by Karl Marx (Lawrence and Wishart, 1971, p. 20). Lucio Colletti asserts that the distinction between 'structure' or 'base' and 'superstructure' 'rarely occurs in Marx and is little more than a metaphor for him; in later Marxism it has acquired an inordinate importance' (*From Rousseau to Lenin*, NLB, 1972, p. 65n). For a further discussion of this issue see Appendix A.
8. See F. A. Hayek, *The Constitution of Liberty*, Routledge and Kegan Paul, 1960; Milton Friedman, with the assistance of Rose D. Friedman, *Capitalism and Freedom*, University of Chicago Press, 1962; Milton Friedman and Rose Friedman, *Free to Choose*, Penguin, 1980. For useful discussions of this literature see A. Gamble, 'The Free Economy and the Strong State', *Socialist Register 1979*; C. Mouffe, 'Democracy and the New Right', *Politics and Power 4*, Routledge and Kegan Paul, 1981.
9. So far as this author is aware, Marx himself never made a distinction between 'bourgeois' and 'proletarian' democracy, writing only of 'democracy'. However, Engels does make such a distinction, later followed and systematized by Lenin and Trotsky.

10. See, for example, M. Friedman, *Capitalism and Freedom*, ch. 1; and F. A. Hayek, *The Road to Serfdom*, Routledge and Kegan Paul, 1944.
11. I. Gilmour, *Inside Right*, Hutchinson, 1977, p. 211.
12. E. Powell, *Freedom and Reality*, Batsford. 1969, p. 33.
13. J. K. Galbraith, *The New Industrial State*, Penguin, 1969, and see also his *The Affluent Society*, Penguin, 1970, chs. 9–11. Other notable contributions include P. Baran, *The Political Economy of Growth*, Penguin, 1973, pp. 19–28; P. Baran and P. M. Sweezy, *Monopoly Capitalism*, Penguin, 1968, ch. 5; P. Donaldson, *Economics of the Real World*, Penguin, 1973, ch. 12.
14. M. Friedman, 'The Line We Dare Not Cross', *Encounter*, November 1976.
15. The key work is P. Sraffa, *Production of Commodities by Means of Commodities*, Cambridge University Press, 1960. For relevant commentaries see G. Harcourt, *Some Cambridge Controversies in the Theory of Capital*, Cambridge University Press, 1972; E. K. Hunt and J. G. Schwartz (eds.), *A Critique of Economic Theory*, Penguin, 1972.
16. See V. I. Lenin, *The State and Revolution*, Lawrence and Wishart, 1967; L. Trotsky, *The Revolution Betrayed*, Merit, 1965; E. Mandel, *On Bureaucracy*, IMG, no date; W. Brus, *Socialist Ownership and Political Systems*, Routledge and Kegan Paul, 1975. The classic study of bureaucracy in R. Michels, *Political Parties*, Free Press, 1949, was inspired by contact with the socialist movement.
17. For a useful summary of the 'Great Debate' on planning (involving the Webbs, G. D. H. Cole, L. von Mises, F. A. Hayek, O. Mosley and others) see T. Smith, *The Politics of the Corporate Economy*, Martin Robertson, 1979, chs. 1–4.
18. For an excellent short account of different interpretations and justifications for democracy see C. B. Macpherson, *The Life and Times of Liberal Democracy*, Oxford University Press, 1977. For an extended discussion of participatory democracy see C. G. Benello and D. Roussopoulos (eds.), *The Case for Participatory Democracy*, Viking, 1971. Another useful volume is C. Pateman, *Participation and Democratic Theory*, Cambridge University Press, 1970.
19. Note Bernard Crick's classic defence of pluralism: *In Defence of Politics*, Penguin, 1st edn, 1962, new edn, 1982. In the light of recent developments (see in particular Chapter 4 below on the 'economics of politics' brigade) Crick should have added a new chapter: 'A Defence of Politics Against the Orthodox Economist'.

3 Capitalism and Freedom

1. M. Friedman, *Capitalism and Freedom*, University of Chicago Press, 1962, pp. 14–15.
2. A. Smith, *The Wealth of Nations*, Penguin edition, with an introduction by A. Skinner, 1970, p. 169.
3. C. B. Macpherson, *Democratic Theory: Essays in Retrieval*, Oxford University Press, 1973, p. 146. See also my *Capitalism, Value and Exploitation*, Martin Robertson, 1982, pp. 52–3, 209.
4. H. Steiner, 'Liberty and Equality', *Political Studies*, December 1981.

5. See, for example, A. B. Atkinson, *Unequal Shares*, Penguin, 1972, and A. B. Atkinson (ed.), *Wealth, Income and Inequality*, Penguin, 1973.
6. K. Marx, *Capital*, vol. 1, Penguin in association with New Left Review, 1976, p. 280.
7. For an important model based on this assumption see H. A. Simon, 'A Formal Model of the Employment Relationship', *Econometrica*, July 1951.
8. See my *Capitalism, Value and Exploitation*, pp. 191–6, 204–11.
9. C. Lindblom, *Politics and Markets*, Basic Books, 1977, p. 47.
10. For discussions of this issue from different points of view, see, for example, N. Abercrombie, S. Hill and B. S. Turner, *The Dominant Ideology Thesis*, Allen and Unwin, 1980: J. Habermas, *Legitimation Crisis*, Heinemann, 1976; and R. Miliband, *The State in Capitalist Society*, Quartet, 1973.
11. K. Marx, op. cit., vol. 1, p. 899.
12. S. Lukes, *Power: A Radical View*, Macmillan, 1974, p. 23.
13. J. Westergaard and H. Resler, *Class in a Capitalist Society*, Penguin, 1976, pp. 142–4. See also A. Giddens, *New Rules of Sociological Method*, Hutchinson, 1976, pp. 81–6.
14. A. Marshall, *Principles of Economics*, 8th edn, Macmillan, 1920, p. 89.
15. L. von Mises, *Human Action: A Treatise on Economics*, William Hodge, 1949, p. 164.
16. For much of this discussion of preferences and choice I am indebted to Ian Steedman. See his 'Economic Theory and Intrinsically Non-Autonomous Preferences and Beliefs', *Quaderni Fondazione Feltrinelli*, no. 7/8, 1980. See also Herbert Gintis, 'Consumer Behaviour and the Concept of Sovereignty: Explanations of Social Decay', *American Economic Review*, papers and proceedings, 1972, and his 'A Radical Analysis of Welfare Economics and Individual Development', *Quarterly Journal of Economics*, November 1972.

4 Markets Versus Democracy

1. M. Crozier, S. P. Huntington, and J. Watanuki, *The Crisis of Democracy: A Report on the Governability of Democracies to the Trilateral Commission*, New York University Press, 1975.
2. Lord Hailsham, *The Dilemma of Democracy*, Collins, 1978, p. 36.
3. S. Brittan, *The Economic Consequences of Democracy*, Temple Smith, 1977, pp. 248–62.
4. J. Schumpeter, *Capitalism, Socialism and Democracy*, 4th edn, Allen and Unwin, 1952. For a critical discussion of the 'competing elites' theory of democracy see C. B. Macpherson, *The Life and Times of Liberal Democracy*, Oxford University Press, 1977, pp. 77–92.
5. See Chapter 2, above.
6. C. K. Rowley, 'Liberalism and Collective Choice', *National Westminster Bank Quarterly Review*, May 1979.
7. W. A. Niskanen, *Bureaucracy and Representative Government*, Aldine-Atherton,

New York, 1971; W. A. Niskanen, *Bureaucracy: Servant or Master?*, Hobart Paperback, Institute of Economic Affairs, 1973.

8. W. A. Niskanen, 'Review of "Corruption: A Study in Political Economy" by Susan Rose-Ackerman', *Journal of Economic Literature*, June 1979.
9. In his seminal work *Anarchy, State and Utopia* (Blackwell, 1974) Robert Nozick gives a spectacular restatement of the view that it is unjust for even the majority to redistribute income from the rich to the poor. Note the critique of Nozick *et al.* by H. Steiner, 'Liberty and Equality', *Political Studies*, December 1981. See also A. Sen, 'The Profit Motive', *Lloyds Bank Review*, January 1983, and his classic article 'Rational Fools', *Philosophy and Public Affairs*, Winter 1976–7 (reprinted in F. Hahn and M. Hollis (eds.), *Philosophy and Economic Theory*, Oxford University Press, 1979).
10. A. Downs, *An Economic Theory of Democracy*, Harper, 1957.
11. For neoclassical articles in the form 'The Economics of X', where X is a member of a seemingly unbounded set of social topics, see past issues of the Chicago School's *Journal of Political Economy*.
12. Edmund Burke, *Reflections on the Revolution in France*, first published 1790 (Penguin edn 1968).
13. Notable works include J. M. Buchanan and G. Tullock, *The Calculus of Consent*, University of Michigan Press, 1962; J. M. Buchanan, *The Limits of Liberty*, University of Chicago Press, 1975; G. Tullock, *The Vote Motive*, Hobart Paperback, Institute of Economic Affairs, 1976; J. M. Buchanan and R. E. Wagner, *Democracy in Deficit*, Academic Press, 1977; J. M. Buchanan, R. E. Wagner and J. Burton, *The Consequences of Mr Keynes*, Hobart Paperback, Institute of Economic Affairs, 1978.
14. J. M. Buchanan, *The Limits of Liberty*, p. 161.
15. ibid., p. 35.
16. K. Arrow, *Social Choice and Individual Values*, Wiley, 1951.
17. A. Sen, 'A Possibility Theorem on Majority Decisions', *Econometrica*, April 1966.
18. J. Tomlinson, 'The "Economics of Politics" and Public Expenditure: A Critique', *Economy and Society*, November 1981.
19. N. Kaldor, 'Monetarism and UK Monetary Policy', *Cambridge Journal of Economics*, December 1980; reprinted in N. Kaldor, *The Scourge of Monetarism*, Oxford University Press, 1982.
20. B. M. Barry, *Sociologists, Economists and Democracy*, Collier-Macmillan, 1970, p. 23. For other criticisms of the 'economics of politics' approach see C. B. Macpherson, *Democratic Theory: Essays in Retrieval*, Oxford University Press, 1973, esp. pp. 185–94; and J. F. J. Toye, 'Economic Theories of Politics and Public Finance', *British Journal of Political Science*, vol. 6, pt. 4, 1976. For an eloquent formalization of the principle that voting involves 'duty' and other non-selfish considerations see H. Margolis, *Selfishness, Altruism and Rationality*, Cambridge University Press, 1982.
21. D. E. Moggridge, *Keynes*, Fontana, 1976, pp. 37–8.
22. See J. M. Buchanan, R. E. Wagner and J. Burton, op. cit., pp. 48–9.

23. See P. Addison, *The Road to 1945*, Quartet, 1977.
24. See R. H. Coase, 'The Problem of Social Cost', *Journal of Law and Economics*, vol. 3, 1960, pp. 1–44; H. Demsetz, 'Toward a Theory of Property Rights', *American Economic Review (Proceedings)*, May 1967; and S. C. Littlechild, *The Fallacy of the Mixed Economy*, Hobart Paperback, Institute of Economic Affairs, 1978, pp. 62–6.
25. E. K. Hunt and H. J. Sherman, *Economics: An Introduction to Traditional and Radical Views*, 2nd edn, Harper and Row, 1975, p. 207.
26. Source: M. Ahluwalia, 'Inequality, Poverty and Development', *Journal of Development Economics*, December 1976. Ahluwalia gives data for sixty countries in all. According to his figures for the five countries he mentions which do not have a dominant market system of allocation (namely Bulgaria, Poland, Hungary, Czechoslovakia and East Germany) inequality of income is slightly less severe in the Eastern Bloc. (An average of 33 per cent of income for the richest 20 per cent, and 10 per cent of income for the poorest 20 per cent.)
27. For recent work in the tradition of Keynes see the *Journal of Post Keynesian Economics*. For other notable defences of Keynes's economics see F. Blackaby, 'The Keynesian Position Today', *British Review of Economic Issues*, no. 7, November 1980; and A. P. Thirlwall, 'Keynesian Employment Theory is Not Defunct', *Three Banks Review*, September 1981.
28. First introduced into economics by J. von Neumann and O. Morgenstern, *Theory of Games and Economic Behaviour*, Princeton University Press, 1944. However, as G. L. S. Shackle shows in his *Epistemics and Economics* (Cambridge University Press, 1972), game theory does not provide an entirely adequate model of economic reality.
29. See F. Hahn, 'General Equilibrium Theory', in D. Bell and I. Kristol (eds.), *The Crisis in Economic Theory*, Basic Books, 1980, esp. p. 130.
30. F. A. Hayek, 'The Use of Knowledge in Society', *American Economic Review*, vol. 35, 1945, pp. 519–30; reprinted in H. Townsend (ed.), *Price Theory*, Penguin, 1971.
31. N. Weiner, *Cybernetics*, M.I.T. Press, 1965, pp. 158–9.

5 The Leninist Rebuttal

1. *Writings of Leon Trotsky* (1933–34), Pathfinder, 1972, p. 40. See also W. Reisner (ed.), *Documents of the Fourth International: The Formative Years* (1933–40), Pathfinder, 1973, pp. 16, 23, 62, 130.
2. *The Second Congress of the Communist International*, vol. 2, New Park Publications, 1977, p. 51. (See also J. Degras (ed.), *The Communist International*, vol. 1, Frank Cass, 1971, pp. 151–2, for a slightly different and incomplete translation.)
3. ibid., pp. 52–3 (Degras, op cit., pp. 152–3).
4. ibid., pp. 53–4 (Degras, op. cit., pp. 153).
5. For a majestic historical analysis of Communism see F. Claudin, *The Communist Movement, From Comintern to Cominform*, Penguin, 1975. For a study

of the British Communist Party see my *Socialism and Parliamentary Democracy*, Spokesman, 1977, ch. 4.

6. For a statement of Eurocommunist ideas see S. Carrillo, *'Eurocommunism' and the State*, Lawrence and Wishart, 1977. For different assessments see E. Mandel, *From Stalinism to Eurocommunism*, NLB, 1978 and F. Claudin, *Eurocommunism and Socialism*, NLB, 1978.
7. B. Moore Jr, *Social Origins of Dictatorship and Democracy*, Allen Lane The Penguin Press, 1967, p. xii.
8. G. Therborn, 'The Rule of Capital and the Rise of Democracy', *New Left Review*, no. 103, May–June 1977.
9. See J. Liddington and J. Norris, *One Hand Tied Behind Us: The Rise of the Women's Suffrage Movement*, Virago, 1978.
10. See, for example, D. Guerin, *Fascism and Big Business*, Pathfinder, 1973; J. F. Petras and M. M. Morley, *How Allende Fell*, Spokesman, 1974.
11. C. B. Macpherson, *The Life and Times of Liberal Democracy*, Oxford University Press, 1977, pp. 108–14. See also R. Luxemburg, 'The Russian Revolution', in M.-A. Waters (ed.), *Rosa Luxemburg Speaks*, Pathfinder, 1970, p. 391.
12. For a discussion of the process of legitimation under capitalism see R. Miliband, *The State in Capitalist Society*, Weidenfeld and Nicolson, 1969, chs. 7–8.
13. For the relevant electoral statistics and an analysis of them see my *Labour at the Crossroads*, Martin Robertson, 1981, ch. 4.
14. See P. Hain (ed.), *Policing the Police*, 2 vols., John Calder, 1979 and 1980.
15. K. Marx and F. Engels, *Selected Correspondence*, Lawrence and Wishart, n. d., p. 318.
16. Quoted in K. Marx, *The Revolutions of 1848*, Political Writings – Volume 1, Pelican Marx Library in association with New Left Review, edited and introduced by D. Fernbach, 1973, p. 66.
17. K. Marx, 'Speech on the Hague Congress', in *The First International and After*, Political Writings – Volume 3, Pelican Marx Library, in association with New Left Review, edited and introduced by D. Fernbach, 1974, p. 324.
18. V. I. Lenin, 'The State and Revolution', in *Selected Works*, vol. 2, Lawrence and Wishart,N 1967, p. 294.
19. K. Marx and F. Engels, op cit., p. 86.
20. See Hal Draper, *Karl Marx's Theory of Revolution*, 2 vols., MR Press, 1977.
21. V. I. Lenin, 'The Proletarian Revolution and The Renegade Kautsky', in *Selected Works*, vol. 3, Lawrence and Wishart, 1967, p. 49.
22. V. I. Lenin, op. cit. (Note 18), p. 335.
23. M. Friedman, *Capitalism and Freedom*, University of Chicago Press, 1962, pp. 7–8.
24. ibid., p. 15.
25. An important example of this Leninist variant is the political tendencies which emphasize, to the exclusion of other factors, the lack of workers' control of production in both East and West. Any industrial society which lacks this feature is regarded as 'capitalist'.
26. For a stimulating discussion of this concept see L. Colletti, *From Rousseau to*

Lenin, NLB, 1972. For its application to the study of history see P. Anderson, *Passages from Antiquity to Feudalism*, NLB, 1974. and *Lineages of the Absolutist State*, NLB, 1974. See also R. Rowthorn, *Capitalism, Conflict and Inflation*, Lawrence and Wishart, 1980, ch. 1.

6 Capitalism and Markets

1. K. Marx, *Capital*, vol. 1, Pelican in association with New Left Review, 1976, pp. 291–2.
2. For two important contributions in this area see S. Himmelweit and S. Mohun, 'Domestic Labour and Capital', *Cambridge Journal of Economics*, March 1977, and J. Humphries, 'Class Struggle and the Persistence of the Working Class Family', ibid., September 1977.
3. K. Marx, 'Economic and Philosophical Manuscripts (1844)', in *Early Writings*. introduced by L. Colletti, Pelican Marx Library, 1975, p. 365.
4. R. H. Coase, 'The Nature of the Firm', *Economica*, November 1937.
5. K. Marx, op. cit. (Note 1), p. 132.
6. S. Aaronovitch and M. Sawyer, 'The Concentration of British Manufacturing', *Lloyd's Bank Review*, October 1974.
7. R. J. Barnet and R. E. Mueler, *Global Reach*, Cape, 1975, p. 230.
8. G. Locksley and T. Ward, 'Concentration in Manufacturing in the EEC', *Cambridge Journal of Economics*, March 1979.
9. See, for example, *Hearings Before the U.S. Subcommittee on Anti-Trust and Monopoly 1964–67*, Washington, 1967. For a good introductory discussion of the topic see S. Aaronovitch, 'The Firm and Concentration', in F. Green and P. Nore (eds.), *Economics: An Anti-Text*, Macmillan, 1977.
10. See J. A. Clifton, 'Competition and the Evolution of the Capitalist Mode of Production', *Cambridge Journal of Economics*, June 1977.
11. For discussions of this topic see D. M. Lamberton (ed.), *Economics of Information and Knowledge*, Penguin, 1971, and B. J. Loasby, *Choice, Complexity and Ignorance*, Cambridge University Press, 1976.
12. F. Machlup, *The Production and Distribution of Knowledge*, Princeton University Press, 1962.
13. See, for example, F. A. Hayek, 'The Use of Knowledge in Society', *American Economic Review*, vol. 35, 1945, pp. 519–30, reprinted in H. Townsend (ed.) *Price Theory*, Penguin, 1971.
14. K. E. Boulding, *The Economy of Love and Fear*, Wadsworth, 1973.
15. A. T. Peacock and J. Wiseman, *The Growth of Public Expenditure in the United Kingdom*, Allen and Unwin, 1967. For a discussion of this topic see A. J. Taylor, *Laissez-Faire and State Intervention in Nineteenth Century Britain*, Macmillan, 1972.
16. K. Polanyi, *The Great Transformation*, Beacon, 1957, pp. 140–41.
17. A. Gramsci, *Selections from the Prison Notebooks*, edited and translated by Q. Hoare and G. Nowell Smith, Lawrence and Wishart, 1971, pp. 159–60.
18. Unrealistically, F. A. Hayek argues for an end to state regulation and produc-

tion of money in his book *The Denationalisation of Money*. Hobart Paperback, Institute of Economic Affairs, 2nd edn, 1979. This contradicts the view of money as a necessary social cohesive force as put forward by, for example, G. Simmel, *The Philosophy of Money*, Routledge and Kegan Paul, 1977; J. M. Keynes, *The General Theory of Employment, Interest and Money*, Macmillan, 1936; and K. Marx, *Grundrisse*, Pelican Marx Library, 1973.

19. S. Hymer, 'The Internationalization of Capital', in W. J. Samuels (ed.), *The Economy as a System of Power*. vol. 2, 'Corporate Power', Transaction Books, 1979.
20. See, for example, D. Horowitz, *From Yalta to Vietnam*, Penguin, 1967.
21. See, for example, J. Eatwell, *Whatever Happened to Britain?*, BBC Publications, 1982.
22. D. Friedman, *The Machinery of Freedom*, Harper and Row, 1973.
23. M. Rothbard, *Man, Economy and State*, Van Nostrand, 1962, p. 884.
24. S. Brittan, 'Hayek, the New Right, and the Crisis of Social Democracy', *Encounter*, January 1980, p. 35.
25. K. Marx, *Capital*, Pelican Marx Library, 1976, pp. 408–9.
26. ibid., pp. 381n–382n.
27. ibid., p. 382n.
28. K. Polanyi, op. cit., p. 141.
29. Quoted in K. Marx, op. cit. (Note 25), p. 415n.
30. K. Marx, loc. cit.
31. ibid.
32. K. Polyani, op. cit., p. 147.
33. For discussions of the Western European experience of planning see F. Oulès, *Economic Planning and Democracy*, Penguin, 1966, and A. Shonfield, *Modern Capitalism*, Oxford University Press, 1965.
34. See T. Ozawa, *Japan's Technological Challenge to the West, 1950–1974*, M.I.T. Press, 1974.
35. See J. Eatwell, op. cit.
36. See R. L. Heilbroner, *Between Capitalism and Socialism*, Vintage, 1970, ch. 1.
37. R. C. O. Matthews, *The Trade Cycle*, Cambridge University Press, 1959, esp. ch. 10.
38. R. Luxemburg, 'The Accumulation of Capital – An Anti-Critique', in K. Tarbuck (ed.), *Imperialism and the Accumulation of Capital*, Allen Lane The Penguin Press, 1972, pp. 59–60. See also R. Luxemburg, *The Accumulation of Capital*, Routledge and Kegan Paul, 1951.
39. N. Bukharin, 'Imperialism and the Accumulation of Capital', in K. Tarbuck (ed.), op. cit.
40. J. Robinson, 'Introduction' to R. Luxemburg, op. cit.
41. R. Luxemburg, op. cit., p. 122. Three of the figures are calculated incorrectly, thus giving a false impression of 'erratic' development in this economic system.
42. See my *Trotsky and Fatalistic Marxism*, Spokesman, 1975.
43. M. Prior and D. Purdy, *Out of the Ghetto*, Spokesman, 1979.

44. See my review of *Out of the Ghetto* in *Labour Leader*, November 1979, and the review by Diane Elson in *Capital and Class*, no. 9, Autumn 1979.
45. See E. Laclau, *Politics and Ideology in Marxist Theory*, NLB, 1977.
46. For a useful survey of Marxist theories of the state see R. Jessop, *The Capitalist State*, Martin Robertson, 1982. See also Appendix B, below.
47. It should be noted that similar conclusions are suggested by J. K. Galbraith in, for example, *The New Industrial State*, Penguin, 1969, and by Alan Fox in his *Beyond Contract*, Faber and Faber, 1974. Galbraith's analysis is somewhat impressionistic but that of Fox is based on a more sturdy theory of the necessity of trust in any contract.

7 Economic Pluralism

1. See, for example, K. Marx, *Pre-Capitalist Economic Formations*, translated by J. Cohen, edited with an introduction by E. J. Hobsbawm, Lawrence and Wishart, 1964: B. Hindess and P. Q. Hirst, *Pre-Capitalist Modes of Production*, Routledge and Kegan Paul, 1975; and P. Anderson, *Passages from Antiquity to Feudalism*, NLB, 1974.
2. P. Anderson, op. cit., p. 23n.
3. ibid., p. 76.
4. See M. Bloch, *Feudal Society*, Routledge and Kegan Paul, 1962, pp. 163–76.
5. ibid., pp. 130–31.
6. See, for example, M. Prestwich, *The Three Edwards: War and State in England, 1272–1377*, Weidenfeld and Nicolson, 1980, pp. 193–5.
7. For a more detailed discussion of the economic dynamism of the feudal system see P. Anderson, op. cit., pp. 182–90.
8. D. M. Nuti, 'Socialism on Earth', *Cambridge Journal of Economics*, December 1981, p. 391. See also G. Silver and G. Tarpinian, 'Marxism and Socialism: A Reply to Paul Sweezy and Ernest Mandel', *Review of Radical Political Economics*, Winter 1981.
9. E. Mandel, 'The Class Nature of the Soviet Union', *Review of Radical Political Economics*, Spring 1982, p. 61.
10. L. Trotsky, *The Revolution Betrayed*, Merit, 1965.
11. M. Shachtman, *The Bureaucratic Revolution*, Donald Press, 1962.
12. T. Cliff, *Stalinist Russia: A Marxist Analysis*, Michael Kidron, 1955.
13. The 'state collectivist' label is also used by J. Fantham and M. Machover, *The Century of the Unexpected*, Big Flame, 1979.
14. A. Nove, 'The Soviet Economy: Problems and Prospects', *New Left Review*, no. 119, January–February 1980.
15. ibid., p. 7.
16. See, for example, M. Dobb, *Soviet Economic Development Since 1917*, Routledge and Kegan Paul, 1966; A. Nove, *An Economic History of the USSR*, Penguin, 1982.
17. Quoted in M. Ellman, *Socialist Planning*, Cambridge University Press, 1979, p. 45.

18. A. Nove, op. cit. (Note 14), p. 6.
19. See, for example, P. G. Hare, 'Economic Reform in Hungary: Problems and Prospects', *Cambridge Journal of Economics*, December 1977.
20. A. Nove, *The Soviet Economy*, Allen and Unwin, 1961, p. 202.
21. See K. Marx, *Early Writings*, Penguin, 1975, p. 236, and many other examples from Marxist writings.
22. E. Mandel, *Marxist Economic Theory*, vol. 2, Merlin, 1968, p. 568.
23. See, for example, P. Anderson, *Lineages of the Absolutist State*, NLB, 1974; R. Hilton *et al.*, *The Transition from Feudalism to Capitalism*, NLB, 1976. More abstract studies include L. Althusser and Étienne Balibar, *Reading Capital*, NLB, 1970; and N. Poulantzas, *Political Power and Social Classes*, NLB and Sheed and Ward, 1973.
24. K. Marx, *Grundrisse*, Pelican Marx Library in association with New Left Review, translated by M. Nicolaus, 1973, pp. 106–7.
25. W. R. Ashby, *Design for a Brain*, Wiley, 1952, and *An Introduction to Cybernetics*, Methuen, 1964.
26. J. Tinbergen, *On the Theory of Economic Policy*, North-Holland, 1952.
27. S. Beer, *Cybernetics and Management*, Science Editions, 1964; *Decision and Control*, Wiley, 1966; *The Heart of Enterprise*, Wiley, 1979; *Brain of the Firm*, Wiley, 1981. See also the work of J. D. McEwan, 'The Cybernetics of Self-Organizing Systems', in C. G. Benello and D. Roussopoulos (eds.), *The Case for Participatory Democracy*, Viking Compass, 1971, and O. Lange, *Wholes and Parts: A General Theory of Systems Behaviour*, Pergamon, 1963.
28. R. Espejo and N. Howard, 'What is Requisite Variety? A Re-Examination of the Foundation of Beer's Method', University of Aston Management Centre, Working Paper no. 242, September 1982.
29. For introductory readings on cybernetics and systems theory see F. E. Emery (ed.), *Systems Thinking*, 2 vols., Penguin, 1981.

8 Capitalism and Democracy

1. See H. N. Brailsford, *The Levellers and the English Revolution*, edited by C. Hill, Spokesman Books, 1976, for a full account of Leveller politics.
2. S. Bowles and H. Gintis, 'The Invisible Fist: Have Capitalism and Democracy Reached a Parting of the Ways?', *American Economic Association, Papers and Proceedings*, May 1978.
3. Barrington Moore, Jr, *Social Origins of Dictatorship and Democracy*, Allen Lane The Penguin Press, 1967, p. xii.
4. C. Lindblom, *Politics and Markets*, Basic Books, 1977, pp. 161–4. Note that Lindblom takes a far more radical and socialist position in this book than he does in his earlier writings.
5. Barrington Moore, op. cit., chs. 1, 2, 5, 7 and 8.
6. Göran Therborn, 'The Rule of Capital and the Rise of Democracy', *New Left Review*, no. 103, May–June 1977.
7. S. Bowles and H. Gintis, op. cit. See also S. Bowles, 'The Post-Keynesian Capital-

Labor Stalemate', *Socialist Review*, no. 65, September–October 1982; and S. Bowles and H. Gintis, 'The Crisis of Liberal Democratic Capitalism: The Case of the United States', *Politics and Society*, vol. 11, no. 1, 1982.

8. S. Bowles and H. Gintis, 'The Invisible Fist', op. cit., p. 361.
9. L. C. Thurow, *The Zero-Sum Society*, Penguin, 1982, p. 6.
10. I. Gough, *The Political Economy of the Welfare State*, Macmillan, 1979, pp. 151–2.
11. A. Glyn and R. Sutcliffe, *British Capitalism, Workers and the Profits Squeeze*, Penguin, 1972.
12. R. Bacon and W. Eltis, *Britain's Economic Problem: Too Few Producers*, Macmillan, 1976.
13. See ch. 10 below.
14. See, for example, S. J. Prais, *Productivity and Industrial Structure*, Cambridge University Press, 1981.
15. For a discussion of the question of variable productivity, including the 'X-inefficiency' theory of Harvey Leibenstein, see my 'Theoretical and Policy Implications of Variable Productivity', *Cambridge Journal of Economics*, September 1982.
16. Figures from A. Gorz, *Farewell to the Working Class*, Pluto, 1982.
17. See J. L. Simon, *The Ultimate Resource*, Martin Robertson, 1981.
18. S. Gomulka, 'Britain's Slow Industrial Growth – Increasing Inefficiency Versus Low Rate of Technical Change', in W. Beckerman (ed.), *Slow Growth in Britain*, Oxford University Press, 1979, p. 180.
19. See my *Labour at the Crossroads*, Martin Robertson, 1981, pp. 152–7.
20. See J. Habermas, *Legitimation Crisis*, Heinemann, 1976.
21. This argument is presented convincingly in J. Eatwell, *Whatever Happened to Britain?*, BBC Publications, 1982.
22. See, for example, R. G. D. Allen, *Mathematical Economics*, Macmillan, 1959.
23. C. Lindblom, op. cit., pt 5.
24. See S. Holland, *The Socialist Challenge*, Quartet, 1975.
25. For discussions of corporatism see, for example, L. Panitch, 'The Development of Corporatism in Liberal Democracies', *Comparative Political Studies*, April 1977; T. Smith, *The Politics of the Corporate Economy*, Martin Robertson, 1979; P. C. Schmitter and G. Lehmbruch (eds.), *Trends Towards Corporatist Intermediation*, Sage, 1979.

9 Economic Arguments for a Participatory Democracy

1. A. C. Pigou (ed.), *Memorials of Alfred Marshall*, Macmillan, 1935, p. 114.
2. J. S. Mill, *Principles of Political Economy*, vol. 2, 7th edn, Longmans, 1871, p. 352.
3. P. Jay, 'A Co-operative Economy', in A. Clayre (ed.), *The Political Economy of Co-operation and Participation: A Third Sector*, Oxford University Press, 1980.
4. See K. Skalicky, 'The Catholic Church and Workers' Participation', in J. Vanek (ed.), *Self Management: Economic Liberation of Man*, Penguin, 1975, and Pope

John Paul II, *Laborem Exercens* (encyclical letter on human work), Catholic Truth Society, 1981, esp. pp. 49–55.

5. See, for example, the collection of readings in K. Coates and T. Topham (eds.), *Workers' Control*, Panther, 1970.
6. J. Bellers, *Proposals for Raising a Colledge of Industry*, 1695, reprinted with an introduction by K. Coates, IWC Pamphlet no. 68, n. d.
7. See G. D. Garson, 'Recent Developments in Workers' Participation in Europe', in J. Vanek, op. cit.
8. See K. Coates and T. Topham, *The New Unionism*, 2nd ed., Penguin, 1981.
9. See my *Labour at the Crossroads*, Martin Robertson, 1981, for a discussion of *Labour's Programme 1973* and relevant extracts.
10. TUC–Labour Party Liaison Committee, *Economic Planning and Industrial Democracy*, The Labour Party, 1982.
11. ibid., p. 5.
12. J. G. Espinosa and A. S. Zimbalist, *Economic Democracy: Workers' Participation in Chilean Industry 1970–1973*, updated student edition, Academic Press, 1981, pp. 2–3.
13. F. W. Taylor, *Principles of Scientific Management*, Harper, 1911.
14. See the collection of readings in V. H. Vroom and E. L. Deci (eds.), *Management and Motivation*, Penguin, 1970.
15. See A. S. Tannenbaum, 'The Group in Organizations', in V. H. Vroom and E. L. Deci, op. cit., and M. Burawoy, *Manufacturing Consent*, University of Chicago Press, 1979.
16. A. Lane, 'Industrial Strategy and Trade Union Politics', *Politics and Power*, no. 3, 1981, p. 291.
17. H. Braverman, *Labor and Monopoly Capital*, MR Press, 1974.
18. R. Edwards, *Contested Terrain*, Heinemann, 1979, esp. p. viii.
19. A. L. Friedman, *Industry and Labour*, Macmillan, 1977.
20. For viewpoints on this issue see S. Wood (ed.), *Work, Deskilling and the Labour Process*, Hutchinson, 1982.
21. This example is cited, with discussion and evaluation of the experiment, in P. Blumberg, *Industrial Democracy: The Sociology of Participation*, Constable, 1968, pp. 96–9.
22. See my 'Worker Participation and Macroeconomic Efficiency', *Journal of Post Keynesian Economics*, Winter 1982–3, for a discussion of this point.
23. Quoted in D. Jenkins, *Job Power: Blue and White Collar Democracy*, Doubleday, 1973, pp. 314–15.
24. H. de Man, *Joy in Work*, Allen and Unwin, 1929, p. 202.
25. S. A. Marglin, 'What Do Bosses Do?' *Review of Radical Political Economics*, part I, Summer 1974, Part II, Spring 1975.
26. For example, Arthur Scargill has stated: 'workers' control means in effect the castration of the trade union movement, means in effect a total collaboration as far as the working class is concerned, and certainly in practice, will result in compromise with society as it exists'. The reply of Audrey Wise is apposite: 'every breath a worker draws is a compromise with capitalism ... every time

you are going to work you are collaborating with the system'. See A. Scargill, A. Wise and M. Cooley, *A Debate in Workers' Control*, IWC Pamphlet no. 64, 1978, pp. 4, 9.

27. P. Blumberg, op. cit., p. 123.
28. C. Pateman, *Participation and Democratic Theory*, Cambridge University Press, 1970.
29. See, for example, C. Argyris, 'Personality and Organisation Theory Revisited', *Administrative Science Quarterly*, June 1973; M. Carnoy and H. Levin, 'Workers' Triumph: The Meriden Experiment', *Working Papers for a New Society*, Winter, 1976; J. Gooding, *The Job Revolution*, Macmillan, 1976; S. Gouldner, *Patterns of Industrial Bureaucracy: A Case Study of Modern Factory Administration*, Free Press, 1964; D. Jenkins, op. cit.; S. Melman, *Dynamic Factors in Industrial Productivity*, Wiley, 1956; R. Oakeshott, 'Mondragon: Spain's Oasis of Democracy', in J. Vanek, op. cit.; D. Zwerdling, 'Managing Workers', *Working Papers for a New Society*, Fall, 1974. See also the other studies cited below.
30. J. G. Espinosa and A. S. Zimbalist, op. cit., p. 161.
31. K. V. Berman, 'The United States of America: A Co-operative Model for Worker Management', in F. H. Stephen (ed.), *The Performance of Labour-Managed Firms*, Macmillan, 1982, p. 83.
32. The examples in this paragraph are taken from M. Bosquet, *Capitalism in Crisis and Everyday Life*, Harvester, 1977, pp. 98–9.
33. J. Cable and F. FitzRoy, 'Co-operation and Productivity: Some Evidence from West German Experience', in A. Clayre, op. cit.
34. Central Statistical Office, *Economic Trends*, HMSO, October 1982.
35. B. Chiplin and J. Coyne, 'Property Rights, Industrial Democracy and the Bullock Report', in B. Chiplin, J. Coyne, *et al.*, *Can Workers Manage?* Institute of Economic Affairs, 1977, p. 25.
36. A. A. Berle and G. C. Means, *The Modern Corporation and Private Property*, Harcourt, Brace and World, 1932.
37. Cooperative Development Agency figures. The same growth has been observed elsewhere. See, for example, E. Batstone, 'France', in F. H. Stephen (ed.), op. cit.
38. See D. C. Jones, 'British Producer Co-operatives', in K. Coates (ed.), op. cit. For evidence of the 'superior survival ability' of cooperatives in France see E. Batstone in F. H. Stephen, op. cit.
39. J. A. C. Brown, *The Social Psychology of Industry*, Penguin, 1954, pp. 14–17. See also M. Argyle, *The Social Psychology of Work*, Penguin, 1972, and D. S. Pugh (ed.), *Organization Theory*, Penguin, 1971, for further critiques of Taylorist and pro-hierarchy views.
40. E. Mandel, 'Self-Management – Dangers and Possibilities', *International*, vol. 2, no. 4, Winter/Spring 1975.
41. J. T. Addison and A. H. Barnett, 'The Impact of Unions on Productivity', *British Journal of Industrial Relations*, July 1982.
42. J. Tomlinson, *The Unequal Struggle? British Socialism and the Capitalist Enterprise*, Methuen, 1982, pp. 34–5. For a recent non-neoclassical analysis

of the firm see S. Moss, *An Economic Theory of Business Strategy*, Martin Robertson, 1981.

43. J. M. Ball and N. K. Skeach, 'Inter-Plant Comparisons of Productivity and Earnings', *Employment Gazette*, October 1980.
44. See, for example, G. Strauss and E. Rosenstein, 'Workers' Participation: A Critical View', *Industrial Relations*, vol. 9, pp. 197–214, reprinted in M. Gilbert (ed.), *The Modern Business Enterprise*, Penguin, 1972; T. Clarke, 'Industrial Democracy: The Institutionalized Suppression of Industrial Conflict?', in T. Clarke and L. Clements (eds.), *Trade Unions Under Capitalism*, Fontana, 1977; H. Ramsay, 'Cycles of Control: Worker Participation in Sociological and Historical Perspective', *Sociology*, September 1977; T. Nichols (ed.), *Capital and Labour*, Fontana, 1980, pp. 275–9, 381–94.
45. See, for example, R. L. Freeman and J. L. Medoff, 'The Two Faces of Unionism', *The Public Interest*, Fall 1979.
46. 'Distribution and Concentration of Industrial Stoppages in Great Britain', *Employment Gazette*, November 1976.
47. See L. Panitch, *Social Democracy and Industrial Militancy*, Cambridge University Press, 1976.
48. H. Ramsay, op. cit.
49. Note in particular the work and publications of the Institute for Workers' Control (Nottingham).
50. See G. D. Garson, op. cit.; K. Coates and T. Topham, op. cit.; and M. Sloman, *Socialising Public Ownership*, Macmillan, 1978. For a defence of the Bullock Report see P. Hirst, 'On Struggle in the Enterprise', in M. Prior (ed.), *The Popular and the Political: Essays on Socialism in the 1980s*, Routledge and Kegan Paul, 1981.
51. M. Barrat Brown, K. Coates and T. Topham, 'Workers' Control versus "Revolutionary" Theory', *Socialist Register* 1975, in reply to R. Hyman, 'Workers' Control and Revolutionary Theory', *Socialist Register* 1974.
52. G. Orwell, *The Road to Wigan Pier*, Penguin, 1962, p. 138.
53. C. Pateman, op. cit., p. 53.
54. A. Maslow, *Motivation and Personality*, Harper and Row, 1970.
55. For an argument along these lines see B. Horvat, 'Searching for a Strategy of Transition', *Economic Analysis and Workers' Management*, vol. 14, no. 3 (1980), pp. 311–24.
56. M. A. Lutz and K. Lux, *The Challenge of Humanistic Economics*, Benjamin Cummings, 1979.
57. See E. F. Schumacher, *Small is Beautiful*, Blond and Briggs, 1973; and M. A. Lutz and K. Lux, op. cit., ch. 14.
58. J. G. Espinosa and A. S. Zimbalist, op. cit., p. 21.
59. ibid., p. 24.
60. H. Wainwright and D. Elliot, *The Lucas Plan: A New Trade Unionism in the Making?*, Allison and Busby, 1982, p. 264.
61. For a relevant discussion see R. Green and A. Wilson, 'Economic Planning and Workers' Control', *Socialist Register* 1982.

62. See E. Batstone, 'Industrial Democracy and Workers' Representation at Board Level', in *Industrial Democracy – European Experience*, Her Majesty's Stationery Office, 1977.
63. See the apposite pamphlet by Jo Freeman, *The Tyranny of Structurelessness*, USA, 1970, reprinted in *Berkeley Journal of Sociology*, 1970, and subsequently by various political groups.
64. For a discussion of the application of economic democracy to all levels of the economy see M. Carnoy and D. Shearer, *Economic Democracy*, Sharpe, 1980. For participation in the community see P. Hain, *Neighbourhood Participation*, Temple Smith, 1980.
65. M. Warner, 'Work Democracy: Towards a Three-Dimensional Approach', *Journal of Industrial Relations*, June 1982.

10 Political Pluralism and Economic Planning

1. J. S. Mill's brilliant argument for the expression of free opinion, first published in 1859, has the fallibility of all judgement as its central assumption. The force of this argument is sufficiently great to undermine Mill's own attachment to a limited 'representative' democracy, and to support a radical extension of democracy throughout industry and society. Mill's politics, Janus-like, has radical and conservative faces.
2. F. H. Knight, *Risk, Uncertainty and Profit*, Macmillan, 1937.
3. J. M. Keynes, 'The General Theory of Employment', *Quarterly Journal of Economics*, February 1937, reprinted in R. W. Clower (ed.), *Monetary Theory*, Penguin, 1969.
4. See B. J. Loasby, *Choice, Complexity and Ignorance*, Cambridge University Press, 1976; and M. Ellman, *Socialist Planning*, Cambridge University Press, 1979, pp. 66–73.
5. V. I. Lenin, *The State and Revolution*, reprinted in *Selected Works*, vol. 2, Lawrence and Wishart, 1967, p. 344.
6. H. Baisch, 'A Critique of Labour Values for Planning', *World Development*, vol. 7, 1979.
7. See R. Rowthorn, *Capitalism, Conflict and Inflation*, Lawrence and Wishart, 1980, ch. 1; and G. Hodgson, *Capitalism, Value and Exploitation*, pt. 4, Martin Robertson, 1982.
8. This is essentially the view of Marx in *Capital*, especially ch. 7 of the first volume. See my 'Marx Without the Labor Theory of Value', *Review of Radical Political Economics*, Summer 1982, and my 'Theoretical and Policy Implications of Variable Productivity', *Cambridge Journal of Economics*, September 1982.
9. K. Popper, *The Poverty of Historicism*, 2nd edn, Routledge and Kegan Paul, 1960, esp. pp. v–vii.
10. See M. Lippi, *Value and Naturalism in Marx*, NLB, 1980.
11. N. Georgescu-Roegen, 'The Mechanistic Dogma in Economics', *British Review of Economic Issues*, no. 2, May 1978, pp. 7–8. See also his *The Entropy Law and the Economic Process*, Harvard University Press, 1971.

12. J. Kornai *Anti-Equilibrium*, North-Holland, 1972; B. J. Loasby, op. cit.; J. Robinson, *Economic Heresies*, Macmillan, 1971; G. L. S. Shackle, *Epistemics and Economics*, Cambridge University Press, 1972.
13. G. Eliot, *Felix Holt, The Radical*, Penguin, 1972, p. 383.
14. L. Trotsky, *The Challenge of the Left Opposition* (1923–25), Pathfinder, 1975, p. 161.
15. See my *Trotsky and Fatalistic Marxism*, Spokesman, 1975. For other relevant and related criticisms see the essay by Sheila Rowbotham in S. Rowbotham *et al.*, *Beyond the Fragments*, Merlin, 1980.
16. W. Brus, *Socialist Ownership and Political Systems*, Routledge and Kegan Paul 1975.
17. Quoted in S. Starski, *Class Struggle in Classless Poland*, South End Press, 1982, p. 155.

11 Socialism, Decentralization and Markets

1. See, for example, F. Engels, *Socialism: Utopian and Scientific*. in K. Marx and F. Engels, *Selected Works*, vol. 2, Lawrence and Wishart, 1962. Marx's rare remarks on a future society are analysed in B. Ollman, 'Marx's Vision of Communism', *Critique*, no. 8, Summer 1977.
2. J. Tomlinson, *The Unequal Struggle? British Socialism and the Capitalist Enterprise*, Methuen, 1982, pp. 66–7.
3. Example taken from M. Lavigne, *The Socialist Economies of the Soviet Union and Europe*, Martin Robertson, 1974, p. 220.
4. F. A. Hayek. 'The Use of Knowledge in Society', *American Economic Review*, vol. 35, 1945, pp. 519–30; reprinted in H. Townsend (ed.), *Price Theory*, Penguin, 1971. See also F. A. Hayek (ed.), *Collectivist Economic Planning*, Routledge and Kegan Paul, 1935, esp. p. 210 and the included article by L. von Mises. The Austrian position is expertly summarized in K. I. Vaughn, 'Economic Calculation Under Socialism: The Austrian Contribution', *Economic Inquiry*, October 1980.
5. For a discussion of an attempt to decentralize control of local council services in Walsall see R. Shield, 'Power to the People?', *Chartist*, no. 91, June–August 1982. See also P. Hain, *Neighbourhood Participation*, Temple Smith, 1980.
6. See K. Coates (ed.), *The Right to Useful Work*, Spokesman, 1978; H. Wainwright and D. Elliot, *The Lucas Plan: A New Trade Unionism in the Making?*, Allison and Busby, 1982; Coventry, Liverpool, Newcastle and North Tyneside Trades Councils, *State Intervention in Industry*, Spokesman, 1982.
7. R. Bahro, *The Alternative in Eastern Europe*, translated by D. Fernbach, NLB, 1978, p. 439.
8. H. Wainwright and D. Elliot, op. cit., p. 254.
9. S. Bodington, *Computers and Socialism*, Spokesman, 1973, p. 165.
10. See R. Espejo, 'Cybernetic Praxis in Government: The Management of Industry in Chile 1970–1973', *Cybernetics and Systems*, vol. 11, 1980, pp. 325–38. See also S. Beer, *Brain of the Firm*, 2nd edn, Wiley, 1981.

11. P. M. Sweezy and C. Bettelheim, *On the Transition to Socialism*, Modern Reader, 1971, p. 29.
12. I have heard Tony Benn define socialism in this way at at least three public meetings, each time using the National Health Service as an example.
13. T. Benn, *Arguments for Democracy*, Penguin, 1982 p. 217.
14. T. Benn, *Arguments for Socialism*, Penguin, 1980, p. 160. Note that Benn's co-thinker Stuart Holland does not entirely dismiss markets in the same way. See S. Holland, *The Socialist Challenge*, Quartet, 1975, pp. 164–7.
15. K. Marx, *Capital*, vol. 3, Penguin, 1981, pp. 275–6.
16. See D. D. Milenkovitch, 'The Case of Yugoslavia', *American Economic Review*, Papers and Proceedings, February 1977.
17. J. Vanek, *The General Theory of Labor-Managed Market Economies*, Cornell University Press, 1970; J. Vanek, *The Participatory Economy: An Evolutionary Hypothesis and a Strategy for Development*, Cornell University Press, 1971; P. Jay, 'A Co-operative Economy', in A. Clayre (ed.), *The Political Economy of Co-operation and Participation: A Third Sector*, Oxford University Press, 1980.
18. K. Marx, *Capital*, vol. 1, Penguin, 1976, pp. 291–2. An example of how loyal Marxists can forget Marx is Hillel Ticktin's contribution to a debate on 'Is Market Socialism Possible or Necessary?', *Critique*, no. 14, 1981, where on two occasions (pp. 20, 35) he explicitly identifies the introduction of the market as logically the same thing as the introduction of capitalism. Robert Brenner makes the same elementary error, damning much of his analysis in the process, when he writes: 'the "predominance of exchange value" is nothing less than the predominance of free wage-labour, where labour power is a commodity'. See his 'Origins of Capitalist Development: A Critique of Neo-Smithian Marxism', *New Left Review*, no. 104, July–August 1977, p. 51.
19. See Marx's classic statement in his 'Economic and Philosophic Manuscripts' of 1844, in K. Marx, *Early Writings*, Penguin, 1975, pp. 345–79.
20. M. Weber, *The Protestant Ethic and the Spirit of Capitalism*, Allen and Unwin, 1952.
21. M. Morishima, *Why Has Japan 'Succeeded'? Western Technology and Japanese Ethos*, Cambridge University Press, 1982.
22. W. Brus, 'Is Market Socialism Possible or Necessary?' *Critique*, no. 14, 1981, p. 34.
23. P. Wiles, *Distribution of Income: East and West*, North Holland, 1974, pp. 48 and xiv.
24. ibid.
25. J. M. Keynes, *The General Theory of Employment, Interest and Money*, Macmillan, 1936, p. 159.
26. ibid., p. 379.
27. See, for example, K. W. Kapp, *The Social Costs of Business Enterprise*, Spokesman, 1978; H. Rothman, *Murderous Providence: A Study of Pollution in Industrial Societies*, Hart-Davis, 1972; G. Foley, *The Energy Question*, Penguin, 1976; and K. Coates (ed.), *Socialism and the Environment*, Spokesman, 1972.

28. M. Best, 'The Political Economy of Socially Irrational Products', *Cambridge Journal of Economics*, March 1982, p. 54.
29. See J. Eatwell, *Whatever Happened to Britain?*, BBC Publications, 1982, esp. ch. 7.
30. R. Bacon and W. Eltis, *Britain's Economic Problem: Too Few Producers*, Macmillan, 1976, p. 51. See also my *Labour at the Crossroads*, Martin Robertson, 1981, pp. 69–82, 209, for a discussion of the background to the National Plan.
31. An important analysis of the multinational has been provided by S. Holland in *The Socialist Challenge*, Quartet, 1975. Some of this analysis is seriously flawed (see J. Tomlinson, op. cit., pp. 99–121, and my *Labour at the Crossroads*, pp. 149–52). However, this does not undermine the case for democratic control of the large corporation.
32. C. Lindblom, *Politics and Markets*, Basic Books, 1977, p. 356.
33. J. Eatwell, op. cit., ch. 8.
34. J. Kornai, 'Mathematical Programming as a Tool of Socialist Economic Planning', in A. Nove and D. M. Nuti (eds.), *Socialist Economics*, Penguin, 1972, p. 486.
35. J. Wilczynski, 'The Domestic and International Significance of Independent Trade Unionism "Solidarity"', *Economics and Industrial Democracy*, May 1982.
36. Notably, in Britain, C. A. R. Crosland, *The Future of Socialism*, Jonathan Cape, 1956; S. Williams, *Politics is for People*, Penguin, 1981; D. Owen, *Face the Future*, Oxford University Press, 1981.

12 What is Wrong with Marxism?

1. P. Anderson, *Considerations on Western Marxism*, NLB, 1976, p. 114.
2. ibid.
3. ibid., p. 115.
4. See, for example, I. Steedman, *Marx After Sraffa*, NLB, 1977, and my *Capitalism, Value and Exploitation*, Martin Robertson, 1982.
5. See C. Driver, *Productive and Unproductive Labour: Uses and Limitations of the Concept*, Thames Papers in Political Economy, Thames Polytechnic, 1980.
6. See my 'The Theory of the Falling Rate of Profit', *New Left Review*, no. 84, March–April 1974; and, more recently, P. Van Parijs, 'The Falling-Rate-of-Profit Theory of Crisis: A Rational Reconstruction by Way of an Obituary', *The Review of Radical Political Economics*, Spring 1980.
7. Anderson, op. cit., p. 116. See also my *Trotsky and Fatalistic Marxism*, Spokesman, 1975.
8. L. Kolakowski, *Main Currents of Marxism*, translated by P. S. Falla, 3 vols., Oxford University Press, 1978.
9. ibid., vol. 1, p. 304.
10. A. Gorz, *Farewell to the Working Class*, Pluto, 1982, p. 14.
11. ibid., p. 16.
12. For a much-criticized attempt to fit real history into this Marxian schema

see C. Hill, *The English Revolution 1640*, Lawrence and Wishart, 1940. Hill is insistent in this work that the revolution of 1640 made the bourgeoisie a 'ruling class'. In his later works on the subject this insistence is absent, as he has moved away from a strict Marxian analysis.

13. J. Burnham, *The Managerial Revolution*, Penguin, 1945. See also M. Shachtman, *The Bureaucratic Revolution*, Donald Press, 1962.
14. T. Cliff, *Stalinist Russia: A Marxist Analysis*, Michael Kidron, 1955.
15. ibid., and N. Harris, *Of Bread and Guns*, Penguin, 1983.
16. See E. Laclau, *Politics and Ideology in Marxist Theory*, NLB, 1977.
17. See Tom Nairn's impressive treatment of this issue in 'The Modern Janus', *New Left Review*, no. 94, November–December, 1975.
18. S. Moore, *Marx on the Choice Between Socialism and Communism*, Harvard University Press, 1980.
19. H. Marcuse, *An Essay on Liberation*, Penguin, 1969.
20. E. Hobsbawm *et al.*, *The Forward March of Labour Halted?*, Verso-NLB, 1981.
21. For a discussion of this see my *Labour at the Crossroads*, Martin Robertson, 1981, pp. 64–137.

13 What is to be Done?

1. E. Bernstein, *Evolutionary Socialism*, Schocken Books, 1961.
2. Quotation from clause four, section four, of the Constitution of the British Labour Party.
3. See my *Socialism and Parliamentary Democracy*, Spokesman, 1977; *Socialist Economic Strategy*, ILP Square One, 1979; and *Labour at the Crossroads*, Martin Robertson, 1981.
4. A. Gramsci, *Selections from the Prison Notebooks*, Lawrence and Wishart, 1971, p. 276.

Appendix A: On Socio-Economic Systems

1. G. Lukács, *History and Class Consciousness*, Merlin, 1971; A. Gramsci, *Selections from the Prison Notebooks*, Lawrence and Wishart, 1971; L. Althusser, *For Marx*, Allen Lane The Penguin Press, 1969; L. Althusser and E. Balibar, *Reading Capital*, NLB, 1970; L. Colletti, *From Rousseau to Lenin*, NLB, 1972.
2. G. A. Cohen, *Karl Marx's Theory of History: A Defence*, Oxford University Press, 1978.
3. Quotations are from Marx's Preface to his *Contribution to the Critique of Political Philosophy* of which there is an excellent translation of the appropriate passage in Cohen, op. cit., pp. vii–viii. See also Cohen's ch. 2.
4. ibid., p. vii, and ch. 3.
5. ibid., p. 223.
6. ibid., pp. 222–3.
7. See my *Capitalism, Value and Exploitation*, Martin Robertson, 1982, pp. 26–31

for a critique of this 'universalist' approach in orthodox economic theory. See also L. Colletti, op. cit., esp. pp. 3–10.

8. P. Anderson, *Lineages of the Absolutist State*, NLB, 1974, p. 404.
9. Colletti, op. cit., p. 18.
10. G. A. Cohen, 'On Some Criticisms of Historical Materialism', *Proceedings of the Aristotelian Society*, Supplementary Volume, 1970.
11. G. A. Cohen, op. cit. (Note 2), pp. 35n, 111–14.
12. As a whole, Cohen's book is less a defence of Marx's Preface than an attempt to render it logically consistent by clarifying meanings and definitions. On several key issues Cohen does not even try to show that the 'technological determinist' explanation is valid: he merely indicates what such an explanation would take as its explanatory terms. (See esp. p. 248.) There is not much real history in this book: it is a defence of pure theory by means of pure theory alone.
13. See, for example, M. Burawoy, *Manufacturing Consent*, University of Chicago Press, 1979; R. Dore, *British Factory – Japanese Factory*, Allen and Unwin, 1973.
14. See V. H. Vroom and E. L. Deci (eds.), *Management and Motivation*, Penguin, 1970.

Appendix B: Impurity, Dominance and the Modern State

1. T. Parsons, *The Structure of Social Action*, 2 vols., McGraw-Hill, 1937.
2. See I. Gough, 'State Expenditure in Advanced Capitalism', *New Left Review*, no. 92, July–August 1975, pp. 55–7; and his *The Political Economy of the Welfare State*, Macmillan, 1979, pp. 7–9, 56, for a critique of functionalism in this context. For a more general critique of functionalism, but one which must be accepted with qualification, see A. Giddens, *A Contemporary Critique of Historical Materialism*, Macmillan, 1982. See also the symposium on Marxism and functionalism in *Theory and Society*, July 1982.
3. This charge applies to R. Jessop, *The Capitalist State*, Martin Robertson, 1982; R. Miliband, *The State in Capitalist Society*, Quartet, 1973; N. Poulantzas, *State, Power, Socialism*, NLB, 1978; and many other works. It does not, however, apply to I. Gough, op. cit., and A. Gramsci, *Selections from the Prison Notebooks*, Lawrence and Wishart, 1971.
4. M. Mann, 'State and Society, 1130–1815: An Analysis of English State Finances', in M. Zeitlin (ed.), *Political Power and Social Theory*, Jai Press, 1980.
5. P. Anderson, *Lineages of the Absolutist State*, NLB, 1974, p. 355.
6. See K. Marx, 'Contribution to the Critique of Hegel's Philosophy of Law', in K. Marx and F. Engels, *Collected Works*, vol. 3, Lawrence and Wishart, 1975, pp. 122–3.
7. A. Gramsci, op. cit., p. 182.

Index

Index

Index

Index

Index

MORE ABOUT PENGUINS, PELICANS AND PUFFINS

For further information about books available from Penguins please write to Dept EP, Penguin Books Ltd, Harmondsworth, Middlesex UB7 ODA.

In the U.S.A.: For a complete list of books available from Penguins in the United States write to Dept DG, Penguin Books, 299 Murray Hill Parkway, East Rutherford, New Jersey 07073.

In Canada: For a complete list of books available from Penguins in Canada write to Penguin Books Canada Ltd, 2801 John Street, Markham, Ontario L3R 1B4.

In Australia: For a complete list of books available from Penguins in Australia write to the Marketing Department, Penguin Books Australia Ltd, P.O. Box 257, Ringwood, Victoria 3134.

In New Zealand: For a complete list of books available from Penguins in New Zealand write to the Marketing Department, Penguin Books (N.Z.) Ltd, P.O. Box 4019, Auckland 10.

In India: For a complete list of books available from Penguins in India write to Penguin Overseas Ltd, 706 Eros Apartments, 56 Nehru Place, New Delhi 110019.

Published by Penguins

CORRUPTION AND MISCONDUCT IN BRITISH PARTY POLITICS

Alan Doig

The big corruption scandals that hit the headlines – the Poulson affair, the Operation Countryman investigation – are merely the tip of the iceberg.

So Alan Doig argues in this thought-provoking survey, focusing on recent cases and trials. How and why are some local government officials/MPs/civil servants/police officers susceptible to malpractice? Why do the powers that be persist in treating each case as an isolated incident? Why are the procedures and legislation still so patently inadequate? These are just some of the crucial questions raised in this stimulating – and disturbing – analysis of corruption in public life in Britain today.

Know Your Rights: the Questions and the Answers

WOMEN'S RIGHTS IN THE WORKPLACE

Tess Gill and Larry Whitty

Women and training * Working part-time * Maternity rights * Women and new technology * Paid work at home * Women and employment law * Crèches and child-care at work.

Whether you're employed in an office, a factory or a school, *Women's Rights in the Workplace* is designed to arm you with the information – and the expertise and confidence – to get a better deal at work. Containing full, up-to-date information on women's jobs, pay and conditions, it is the essential handbook for all working women

YOUR SOCIAL SECURITY

Fran Bennett

School-leavers and social security * Benefit and one-parent families * Retirement pensions * Family income supplement.

In practical question and answer format, here at last is a handbook to guide you through the maze of social security benefit regulations. Whether you are out of work, a single parent, retired, disabled or simply grossly underpaid, this book will give you the essential information to help you claim your rights from the State.

Other volumes in this new Penguin series Know Your Rights: The Questions and the Answers *cover marital rights and the rights of ethnic minorities.*

What is to be done about . . . ?

These short and simple books, published in connection with the Socialist Society, will deal with the central social and political issues of the day. They will set out the arguments, provide information and answer important questions, offering a political agenda for the eighties.

WHAT IS TO BE DONE ABOUT THE FAMILY?

Lynne Segal

The protective nuclear family seems to be breaking down: the divorce rate is high, children are alienated from parents, the old are neglected. Here the authors explain and argue exactly *why* it is crucial for the future of society that the issues surrounding the family become subject to political analysis and action.

WHAT IS TO BE DONE ABOUT LAW AND ORDER?

J. Young and J. Lee

What is *meant* by law and order? Whose law and what order? This timely study examines all the issues, discussing the concept of a 'breakdown of society', the present threat to our liberty, and what is to be done about the increasingly confrontational nature of forces within society in the British Isles.

Other books in this series will discuss the environment, health care, higher education, NATO, and violence against women.

Published in Pelicans

INSIDE THE INNER CITY

Paul Harrison

The early eighties have seen the breakdown of Western economies, the erosion of welfare states and the disappearance of social consensus. Nowhere have these processes cut more deeply than in the inner city, where industrial decline, low incomes, high unemployment and housing decay are fuelling crime and racial tension to create our most daunting social problem.

Combining interviews and eye-witness accounts with his own penetrating analysis, Paul Harrison provides a grim portrait of the human costs of recession and monetarism. From dying factories to social security offices, from single mothers to street thieves, it offers a unique insight into the stark realities of deprivation and social conflict in Britain today.

INSIDE THE THIRD WORLD

Paul Harrison

The Third World is increasingly in the news. Superpower confrontations and north–south negotiations have joined the old stories of famines, wars, coups and revolutions. This book fills in the background to those events.

It provides a comprehensive guide to the major problems behind mass poverty and political instability: from climate and colonialism, through land hunger, exploding cities and unemployment, to over-population, hunger, disease and illiteracy, placing them all in the context of national and international inequalities.

The wealth of facts and analysis are brought home in first hand, often harrowing accounts of the realities of life for poor people and poor communtities in Asia, Africa and Latin America. It is the tragic story of three-quarters of humanity.